FOUNDATIONS
OF MORAL EDUCATION

FOUNDATIONS
OF MORAL EDUCATION

An Annotated Bibliography

Compiled by
JAMES S. LEMING

GREENWOOD PRESS
Westport, Connecticut • London, England

Library of Congress Cataloging in Publication Data

Leming, James S., 1941-
 Foundations of moral education.

 Includes indexes.
 1. Ethics—Study and teaching—Bibliography.
 2. Moral development—Bibliography. I. Title.
 Z5873.L45 1983 [BJ66]   016.17'07   83-12834
 ISBN 0-313-24165-1 (lib. bdg.)

Library of Congress Catalog Card Number 83-12834
ISBN: 0-313-24165-1

First published in 1983

Greenwood Press
A division of Congressional Information Service, Inc.
88 Post Road West, Westport, Connecticut 06881

Printed in the United States of America

10 9 8 7 6 5 4 3 2 1

Contents

Acknowledgments

This work could not have been completed without assistance from many sources. The completion of the task was greatly expedited due to the excellent holdings of Morris Library on the campus of Southern Illinois University at Carbondale. Thanks also go to the Department of Curriculum, Instruction, and Media and the College of Education for their encouragement and support. Finally, my appreciation goes to Joan, Jimmy, and Jessica Leming for their good-natured tolerance of my benign neglect and work-induced neuroses during the preparation of this manuscript.

Introduction

In the late 1960s and early 1970s a traditional purpose of schooling was accorded renewed attention by contemporary educators. This rediscovered dimension of schooling has variously been called moral or values education. The focus on values or morality is not a new area of interest for those charged with the instruction of youth. Both Plato and Aristotle assigned central importance to questions regarding the nature of virtue and whether it could be taught. Ways of developing in youth the knowledge, sensitivity, dispositions, and habits necessary for social life have been a central focus of all people at all times. The reason for the recent resurgence of interest in moral education is not clear; however, it is highly probable that during times of rapid social change and social fragmentation people become increasingly sensitive to the need for the moral education of youth. It was not mere chance that following the turbulent social upheavals of the decade of the 1960s, the Journal of Moral Education made its appearance in 1971.

Because of the nature of the enterprise of moral education, the exact parameters of the field are not clear. In the opening line of one of the early significant works on moral education John Wilson observes, "'Moral Education' is a name for nothing clear."[1] The attempt to compile a reasonably comprehensive bibliography on the subject convinces one of the wisdom of Wilson's comment. The difficulty of defining the field is due in large part to the broad range of issues that must be considered to reach a fully informed understanding of the field. For example, for anyone attempting to undertake the moral instruction of youth the following questions would be relevant: How does one know what the good is?; What are the major influences on the values of youth?; What place does rationality play in man's behavior?; If one knows what the good is, will he act accordingly?; Is morality fundamentally personal or social?; What are the proper goals for the enterprise of moral education? Additionally there exists an important cluster of questions that center around more practical concerns: What instructional strategies should I use?; What materials are available?; How do I handle the community reaction?; How do we evaluate our programs?; and so on.

The enterprise of moral education can be conceptionalized as consisting of three major areas. In the initial issue of the Journal of Moral Education, the editors outlined three areas of inquiry that the journal was designed to promote: (1) sustained and reasoned reflection on the nature of morality, what it means to be a moral person, and on the purposes of moral education; (2) empirical studies of how children and adolescents actually acquire their values and controls, the way character evolves, and how they respond to moral challenges; and (3) the deliberate and planned practice of moral education: the contribution and evaluation of moral education programs.

This volume will cover the first two areas only. The focus of this volume, therefore, can properly be called the "foundations of moral education." That is, this volume will list references on those topics upon which any defensible approach to moral education must ultimately rest. The two major foundations of any examined approach to moral education are an adequate conceptualization of the nature of morality and what it means to be a moral person and an adequate psychological view of how morality is acquired and of the dynamics of moral conduct. These two broad areas of inquiry--philosophic and psychological--comprise the major content of this volume. This volume is not a guide to the literature on the practice of moral education. For that, the reader is referred to a complementary work: James S. Leming, Contemporary Approaches to Moral Education (New York: Garland, 1983).

The time frame of the present bibliography corresponds to that of the resurgence of interest in the topic of moral education--the mid-1960s through 1981. The amount of discourse concerning moral education produced during this time period has been immense. In 1966 two works appeared that signaled the beginning of this surge of interest. Raths, Harmin, and Simon published their highly influential book on values clarification, Values and Teaching,[2] and Lawrence Kohlberg in the School Review wrote the first article in which he discusses moral education.[3] Values clarification and the cognitive developmental approach to moral education remain the most coherent, well-developed, and popular approaches to moral education. During the 1970s two journals focusing exclusively on moral education began publication: the Journal of Moral Education (1971) and Moral Education Forum (1976). Since 1977 the Moral Education Forum has published an extensive annual bibliography on works related to moral education compiled by Don Cochrane. This bibliography indicates that annually since 1977 an average of twenty-five books, six special issues of journals and over two hundred articles have appeared on the subject of moral education. Another index to the extent of interest in moral education is the amount of research completed in graduate schools around the country. According to Dissertation Abstracts International, from three to fifteen doctoral dissertations on moral education and related topics were completed each year between 1964 and 1971. From 1972 on, the number of dissertations increased gradually from twenty per year in 1972 to eighty-two in 1979. Since 1979 the numbers have dropped off only slightly.

Content and Organization of the Bibliography

The bibliography was compiled through the following resources: the reference sections of the most salient works in the field, Dissertation Abstracts International, Current Index to Journals in Education (1969-

1981), Education Index (1965-1969), the ERIC document system, and other
bibliographies on the topic. While it is not limited to post-1965
sources, it is most exhaustive of the literature during this period.

The first major division of the bibliography, "Reflections on the
Domain of Moral Education," consists of citations that are predominately
philosophical in nature and concerned with clarifying and defining the
general purposes of moral education. Also included are four problematic
areas in the study of moral education and critiques of the enterprise
of moral education. The "proper goals" section (items 1-150) contains
general discussions about the purposes of moral education. These discussions do not center on a single approach, but rather, constitute
philosophical analyses that attempt to clarify the proper goals for the
enterprise of moral education. The "ethical theory" section (items 151-
272) presents representative sources on ethical theory or moral philosophy. The purpose of this section is to provide the reader with a background to the more influential thinking regarding the nature of moral
judgments. The section on "moral character" (items 273-329) presents a
variety of views on the nature of the moral person. This section is of
importance as any approach to moral education must have an "end in view"
--the morally educated person. The "indoctrination" section (items 330-
381) contains sources that argue the point of whether neutrality is possible or desirable in moral education and whether indoctrination is ever
justifiable. The "religion" section (items 382-446) contains sources
exploring the relationships between religion and morality. A central
topic dealt with in these references is whether morality and religion
can exist independent of each other. The final section, "critiques"
(items 447-478), presents a collection of references that question the
desirability of moral education.

The second major heading of the bibliography, "Moralization: The
Learning of Morality," contains references drawn largely from the behavioral sciences. Knowledge concerning the dynamics of the moral development of members of society is essential for one interested in developing
and evaluating approaches to moral education. The first section, "general accounts" (items 479-545), contains sources that take a generic or
pluralistic view of moral development. The next three sections, the
"psychoanalytic" (items 546-565), the "social learning" (items 566-587),
and the "cognitive developmental" (items 588-678), present sources on the
three dominant theories of moralization. The cognitive developmental
section contains both the work of Piaget and Kohlberg. Because the
cognitive development theory has been the dominant psychological influence on moral education in the 1970s, a separate subsection on empirical
tests of cognitive developmental theory is included (items 679-854).
Critiques of cognitive developmental theory follow the empirical tests
sections (items 855-945). These critiques focus on analyses of the
cognitive-developmental theory and not on the educational applications
of the theory. The cognitive developmental sections do not contain
citations in which discussions of educational issues constitute the
major focus. Such references may be found in the Contemporary Approaches volume mentioned above. The next section, "dimensions of the

moralization process," contains sources on the contributions to the moral development of youth of the family (items 946-976), the school (items 977-1094), and the society (items 1095-1125). In the section on the family, the focus is on the relationship of childrearing practices to moral development. In the schooling section, the influence of the "hidden curriculum" and the values embedded in textbooks are the major focus. The society subsection looks at general social factors, especially the influence of television, on moral development. The section on "psychology of moral behavior" (items 1126-1302) presents references on the antecedent determinants and situational influences on moral behavior. Such topics as altruism, prosocial behavior, and bystander intervention are included here. Clearly psychological information on why people behave morally, or immorally, is of crucial importance in the planning of moral education.

The first two sections of this bibliography cannot claim to be comprehensive. Ethical theory and the psychology of moral development are broad areas of human inquiry and are themselves subjects for separate bibliographies. The items in these first two sections were selected on the basis of the extent to which they are related to the major issues in moral education. Also considered important was the extent to which significant authors writing on the topic of moral education have considered these sources important in their deliberations.

The next heading in the bibliography, "Additional Topics," consists of four foundational areas not easily subsumed under the above two major headings. The "sociological perspectives" section (items 1303-1344) focuses on sociological analyses of the moral life. The majority of these references analyze the relationship between the nature of society, moral norms, and the place of the individual within this matrix. The "historical perspectives" section (items 1346-1428) presents references on the history of moral education, that is, how moral instruction has been carried out in Western society. The third section, "cross-cultural perspectives" (items 1429-1476), contains reports on how the practice of moral education is conceived of outside of North America and England. The "political perspectives" section (items 1477-1490) contains references that analyze the relationships among politics, citizenship, and moral development and instruction.

The volume concludes with a section containing the major collections of readings on the topic of moral education (items 1492-1532). These collections include many of the significant, more practical writings in the field. Collections of readings cited earlier in the volume are cited again in this location preceded by asterisks and without annotations to provide the reader with a single list of available collections of readings. Author and subject indexes complete the work.

A Guide to Using the Bibliography

This bibliography is designed to be used in one of two ways. First, through the author and subject indexes, the user will be able to identify items and authors of interest. Because this method is sometimes

time-consuming, the body of the bibliography is organized into significant topical sections. This allows the user to peruse related items of
interest within a set number of pages. This second method may constitute
the most efficient use of the bibliography; however, there are two obvious limitations to exclusive use of the bibliography in this manner.
First, the topic of the reader's interest may not be represented with the
degree of precision required by the topical headings. These headings
are general headings and subsume broad but related collections of references. Secondly, seldom if ever is an article or book adequately defined
by a single descriptor. Entries are placed under a heading in the body
of the bibliography based on the primary thrust of the item. In this
bibliography items are only entered once in the main body. The dual
focus of many items is reflected only in the subject index where items
are listed multiply by major descriptors. Therefore, the reader is urged
not to assume that the items collected under the topical headings are
the only items in the bibliography dealing with that topic. There may
well be a substantial number of additional related items in which the
topic of interest is not the major focus. The use of the subject index,
therefore, is called for to exhaust the included items related to the
reader's interest.

     The only abbreviations used in this bibliography follow the listing
of the individual items. "NR" is used to indicate that the listed item
was not reviewed by the author. Some items were included even though
not reviewed because of the significance of the author or the topic.
Occasionally, some items that were reviewed did not receive an annotation because it was judged that an annotation would add little to the
information already in the title.

     In order to allow the reader easily to access the abstracts of
doctoral dissertations, each dissertation is followed by the volume
number and page number in Dissertation Abstracts International (for
example, 34/06, p. 2318). Unless indicated by a "B" following the
volume number, one should refer to the humanities and social sciences
volumes of DAI. Otherwise, the abstract is to be found in the sciences
and engineering volumes.

     Entries available through ERIC microfiche document system are
followed by the access number of that item within the ERIC system (for
example, ED 101 063).

     Unpublished materials are not included in this bibliography as
accessibility of materials was held to be of great importance. The
author's own experiences in attempting to obtain unpublished materials
suggest that the reader of this bibliography should be spared the same
frustrations. Also, it has been my experience that very few significant ideas or research studies remain unpublished for long. The major
exception to this rule is the inclusion of the papers in the forthcoming
volumes by Lawrence Kohlberg, The Psychology of Moral Development (item
625) and Education and Moral Development (item 1505). In the introduction to the first volume of this three-volume series (item 624),
Kohlberg lists, with annotations, the contents of the two forthcoming

volumes. Since this three-volume series represents the culmination of
twenty years of work by one of the major figures in the field, it was
considered important to list these items prior to publication. This
was done with some apprehension, however, for within the literature on
moral education one observes a frequently cited book, L. Kohlberg and
E. Turiel, Eds. <u>Recent Research in Moral Development</u>, New York: Holt,
Rinehart and Winston (1973), which although never published, has been
cited repeatedly in the literature. How this phantom volume came to be a
part of the literature on moral education constitutes a fascinating
problem in the sociology of knowledge. I am trusting that history will
not repeat itself and that the contents of the last two volumes of this
series will appear as promised. The reader is urged, however, to compare
the listing in this bibliography against the actual contents of these
volumes when they appear.

Conclusion

Whatever the reasons, the recent resurgence of interest in moral
education is an educational movement of significant social interest and
importance. The purpose of this bibliography is to present, in an
organized and annotated manner, the important thinking and research that
underpinned the moral education movement of the 1960s and 1970s.

As the scope and breadth of this bibliography will attest, one of
the reasons why moral education is a "name for nothing clear" is that
moral education in a way is a name for a central task of all people in
all times. In this sense, there is no dimension of the study of the
human experience that does not shed light on mankind's efforts to bring
successive generations into the moral life of society. Although this
volume is extensive, the discovery of important sources at the last
minute convinces me that other sources may have been overlooked. I
would appreciate hearing from anyone using this bibliography concerning
any ommissions that fall within the inclusion criteria used.

Notes

1. John Wilson, Norman Williams, and Barry Sugarman, Introduction to Moral Education (Baltimore: Penguin Books, 1967), 11.

2. Louis E. Raths, Merrill Harmin, and Sidney B. Simon, Values and Teaching (Columbus, Ohio: Charles E. Merrill, 1966).

3. Lawrence Kohlberg, "Moral Education in the Schools: A Developmental View," School Review 74 (1966): 1-30.

THE BIBLIOGRAPHY

Reflections on the Domain of Moral Education

The Proper Goals of Moral Education

1. Abrell, R.L., and D.K. Archer. "Education's Search for the Ethical." Educational Leadership, 33 (1976): 377-380.

   Presents a general argument for the inclusion of the study of ethics in the schools. The goals of such a study would be to develop ethical literacy, to expose children to the works or great thinkers on ethical questions, and to provide moral motivation and inspiration.

2. Andrews, J.N. "Social Education and Respect for Others." Journal of Moral Education, 5 (1976): 139-143.

   Critiques the view that "respect for others" follows logically from the proper conceptualization of "person," along with the view that educators should therefore be involved in the purely cognitive task of helping children acquire the proper concept of a "person." Argues that the major tenets of this view cannot be supported.

3. Archambault, Reginald D. "Criteria for Success in Moral Instruction." Moral Education (item 171), pp. 159-169.

   Relating moral understanding to moral conduct implies a broader and more comprehensive notion of the school. The transition from moral knowledge to action is not automatic: the school must be concerned with both. Also in Harvard Education Review, 33 (1963): 472-483.

4. Arnstine, D.G. "Some Problems of Teaching Values." Educational Theory, 11 (1961): 158-167.

   Argues that although most values are learned by enculturation, there are ways of teaching them deliberately, e.g., by threatening, explaining, demonstrating, shaming. Concludes that values cannot be taught directly, but evaluation can be.

5. Aron, Israela. "Moral Philosophy and Moral Education II. The
    Formalist Tradition and the Deweyan Alternative." School
    Review, 85 (1977): 513-534.

    Continues her critique of Kohlberg (begun with item 857) by
    examining the reasons why a purely formalist approach to
    morality is so limited. Dewey's perspective on practical
    deliberation is offered as a solution to many of the problems of
    formalism. Concludes by arguing for an eclectic approach to
    moral education.

6. Attfield, D.G. "Preparation for Life." Journal of Moral
    Education, 2 (1973): 233-242.

    Argues that the utilitarian or instrumental view of education
    as preparation for life assumes far more than can ever be known
    about the future. Instead the person truly prepared for life is
    the educated person.

7. Axtelle, George E. "An Experimentalist View of Moral
    Education." Educational Theory, 16 (1966): 34-43.

    Presents a Deweyan interpretation of the purposes and
    processes of moral education. At the center of this
    interpretation is the growth of self through reaching out to
    embrace ever more comprehensive social objects. Authority is
    within human experience, and moral judgment is similar in kind
    to empirical judgment.

8. Baier, Kurt. "Ethical Pluralism and Moral Education," Moral
    Education: Interdisciplinary Approaches (item 1492), pp.
    93-112.

    Outlines four aims for a program of moral education
    (inculcating good will; understanding the nature and purpose of
    morality; inducing acceptance of the moral order; and
    establishing criteria of soundness of a moral order). Opposing
    moral viewpoints (pluralism) should be treated as competing
    moral hypotheses, but the burden of proof is on them, not on the
    existing system, which must be respected as it provides the
    basis for social life.

9. Baier, Kurt. "Moral Autonomy as an Aim of Moral Education."
    New Essays in the Philosophy of Education (item 219), pp.
    96-114.

    Argues that as a goal for moral education the ideal of
    "universal individual autonomy" is an absurdity. Instead Baier
    offers three interpretations of moral autonomy (moral self
    mastery, independence of moral judgment, and moral self-
    determination) which can provide a basis for construing the
    goals of moral education.

10. Bandman, Bertram. "The Teaching of Moral Beliefs." Education and Ethics. Edited by William G. Blackstone and George L. Newsome. Athens: University of Georgia Press, 1969.

    Argues that there is a difference between right and wrong in moral beliefs. Beliefs are used to make claims; claims are open to appraisal; appraising claims presupposes a system of rules for recognition, adjudication, and enforcement. The legal language of claims therefore provides an instructive example for understanding and teaching moral beliefs.

11. Beck, Clive. "A Philosophical View of Values and Value Education." Values and Moral Development (item 1501), pp. 13-36.

    Beck argues that "value" is a more appropriate word than "moral" to describe the field. He analyzes concepts implied in the word "value" and then defends his reflective utilitarian approach. He presents an overview of several approaches to values education and concludes with a controversial note on the relation between values and religion.

12. Bell, Gordon H. "Imagining and Moral Education." Journal of Moral Education, 8 (1979): 99-109.

    Relations between what it is to imagine and what it is to become educated are explored. The implications of this relationship for moral education are presented.

13. Belok, Michael, et al. Approaches to Values in Education. Dubuque, IA: William C. Brown, 1966.

    Written as a textbook on educational foundations this volume contains chapters on the sources of contemporary values, moral and spiritual values in the schools, and the nature of character formation.

14. Benedict-Gill, Diane. "Goodwill and Respect: A Fundamental Moral Theory and Its Application in Public Moral Education." Ph.D. dissertation, University of Washington, 1980. 41/05, p. 2001.

    Argues that the fundamental moral principles of goodwill and respect possess a sufficiently universal moral character to provide a defensible basis for public moral education. Shows how these principles can be used to resolve controversy over the nature of moral education.

15. Benedict-Gill, Diane. "A Subject Matter Description of Moral
    Education." Educational Theory, 25 (1975): 103-115.

    Analyzes moral education from the perspectives of subject
    matter (vehicle) and action components (goals). Argues that
    subject matter ought to meet the requirements or necessary
    conditions of one's goal. Presents a list of action components
    for principled action. This analysis is offered to assist
    educators in determining their goals in relation to the subject
    matter used and in predicting the result of a given type of
    subject matter.

16. Benjamin, Martin. "Moral Knowledge and Moral Education."
    Growing Up with Philosophy (item 1507), pp. 311-326.

    Argues that there is sufficient likeness between the pursuits
    of scientific and moral understanding to establish the
    objectivity of moral knowledge. Such an analogy between science
    and ethics provides the teacher with a flexible and suitable
    model for moral education.

17. Beversluis, Eric. "Moral Education and Being Moral."
    Educational Theory, 24 (1974): 297-306.

    A theory of moral education must contain three elements: a
    developed and defended ethical theory, an account of what it is
    to be moral, and an explanation of how we can get youth to be
    moral.

18. Bhattachanga, N.C. "Moral Education: Some Philosophical
    Observations." Journal of Educational Thought, 11 (1977):
    112-118.

    Argues that "education" itself has a moral connotation and
    that there are many theoretical problems that must be resolved
    before "moral" can be added to "education." Also discusses the
    practical difficulties likely to be encountered in attempting to
    teach this subject in a morally confused and pluralistic
    society.

19. Blackham, H.J. "The Curriculum in Moral Education." Progress
    and Problems in Moral Education (item 1530), pp. 48-59.

    Argues against Wilson that it is not enough to teach a logical
    moral methodology, we must also teach the rationale for the
    context of those decisions: social morality. Moral behavior
    cannot be learned solely in educational contexts. Social action
    activities outside of the school are required to teach social
    responsibility.

20. Broudy, Harry S. Building a Philosophy of Education. Englewood
    Cliffs, NJ: Prentice-Hall, 1961.

    In chapters 2, 6, and 10 Broudy discusses the necessity of
    determining what values are most important in education,
    differing value theories and their implications for education,
    and the origin of moral values and the role of the school in
    moral education.

21. Brown, H.C. "The Dilemma of the Present-Day Moralist."
    American Scholar, 9 (1940): 164-174.

    Asks whether the teaching of ethics should deal with the good
    life in the real world or in the world as it should be. Relates
    this discussion to the ethical views of Plato, Aristotle,
    Bentham, and Mill.

22. Bruneau, Sandra R. "Peters on Moral Education." Ed.D.
    dissertation, University of British Columbia, 1979. 40/11, p.
    5653.

    Explores the reason why Peters' ideas on moral education have
    not been translated into curriculum. Explicates in a condensed
    manner Peters' ideals on morality and education and makes
    suggestions for moral educators and researchers.

23. Butts, R. Freeman. "The Public School as Moral Authority." The
    School's Role as Moral Authority. Washington, D.C.:
    Association for Supervision and Curriculum Development, 1977,
    pp. 5-29.

    In contrast to pluralistic emphases in contemporary education,
    which Butts feels do not develop a sense of civic community,
    schools should teach the common civic values of justice,
    freedom, and equality.

24. Callahan, Daniel. "The Rebirth of Ethics." National Forum, 2
    (1978): 9-12.

    Discusses the evaluation of the Hastings Center Report (item
    1493) and its focus on ethics. Discusses his views on the goals
    of ethics instruction, how ethical instruction should take
    place, and who should teach ethics. The question of the
    competence of instructors is raised.

25. Caplan, Arthur L. "'Ethics' and 'Values' in Education: Are the
    Concepts Distinct and Does It Make a Difference?" Educational
    Theory, 29 (1979): 245-253.

Claims that there are major differences between those who wish to teach ethics and those who wish to teach values. "Values" signifies a commitment to both eclecticism and practicality and its advocates have little use for philosophical insights. Different interpretations of the relationship between the two terms are presented.

26. Carbone, Peter F. "Reflections on Moral Education." Teachers College Record, 71 (1970): 598-606.

Argues that we ought to conceive of moral education as including two phases: inducing the child to accept the values, attitudes, and standards of behavior that prevail in the social environment, and then advancing the child beyond this level--that is, developing reflective moral agents, people capable of furnishing a reasoned justification for the principles that guide their behavior.

27. Chazan, Barry I. "An Analysis of the Moral Situation in the Context of Moral Education." Ed.D. dissertation, Columbia University, 1968. 30/01, p. 201.

States that existing analyses of moral education have construed the moral situation too narrowly. Urges a broader view involving moral principles moral choice, moral behavior, moral reasoning, the moral individual, and the moral context.

28. Clayton, A. Stafford. "Education and Some Moves Toward a Value Methodology." Educational Theory, 19 (1969): 198-210.

Argues that values pervade and undergird the educational process. Discusses the competencies necessary to making value judgments and the general role of value judgments in human affairs.

29. Cochrane, Don. "Prolegomena to Moral Education" The Domain of Moral Education (item 30), pp. 73-88.

Presents a broad overview of the entire area of moral education. Makes a distinction between moral education and values socialization. Presents a chart of components of moral reasoning with respect for persons as the absolute, though formal, first principle of morality. Concludes with a scheme for moral development with education, training, and psychological components. Also in Theory into Practice, 14 (1975): 236-246.

30. Cochrane, Donald B.; Cornel M. Hamm; and Anastasios C. Kazepides, eds. The Domain of Moral Education. New York: The Paulist Press, 1979.

A series of philosophical essays designed to clarify the parameters of the moral domain and examine the nature and importance of its constitutive elements. Contains sections on the limits of moral education, the nature of moral education, form and content in moral education, and a review of the developmental perspective.

31. Coles, Robert. "What about Moral Sensibility?" Today's Education, 66 (September/October 1977): 40-44.

Recounts the story of a ten year old youth who wanted to spend time with and help migrant workers. He was considered sick and received psychiatric help. Coles argues that what is needed in this society is more of moral anguish, not less. Teachers should cultivate youths' moral feelings, not discourage them.

32. Cordero, Ronald A. "Ethical Theory and the Teaching of Values." Educational Forum, 40 (1976): 205-209.

Examines the implications of existential and noncognitivist ethical theory for the teaching of morality. If ethical statements cannot be held as either true or false, then the teacher should avoid the use of value terms in discussing value questions. The educator should be teaching about things valued or disvalued.

33. Craig, Robert P. "Some Thoughts on Moral Growth." Journal of Thought, 13 (1978): 21-27.

Spells out the moral issues and practical difficulties inherent in the enterprise of moral education. The questions of moral neutrality, what it means to be moral, indoctrination and hidden curriculum are addressed. Kohlberg's and Simon's positions on these issues are critically analyzed.

34. Crittenden, Brian. Form and Content in Moral Education. Toronto: Ontario Institute for Studies in Education, 1972.

Questions whether one can hold to a morality based purely on formalistic criteria. Argues that content is an inescapable component in any moral perspective. Argues that the study of literature should be a major component of moral education, for in the study of literature the entire context of moral beliefs, attitudes, feelings, dispositions, and abilities can be fostered.

35. Crittenden, Brian S., ed. "Method and Substance in Moral Education," Moral Education: Interdisciplinary Approaches (item 1492), 328-354.

Baier, Scriven, Gauthier, Kohlberg, et al. discuss problems concerning the proper method of inculcation of precepts and attitudes and the problem of pluralism-which principles to teach.

36. Daly, Charles E. "The Epistemology and Ethical Theory of Erich Fromm as the Basis for a Theory of Moral Education," Ph.D. dissertation, New York University, 1977. 38/12, p. 7389.

Traces the historical evaluation of moral education in this century and indicates how the epistemological and ethical theory of Erich Fromm might help to solve some of the obvious problems of the current movement.

37. Degenhardt, M.A.B. "Learning from the Imaginary." Journal of Moral Education, 8 (1979): 92-98.

Argues that it is a mistake to base educational practice on the assumption that children can advance their moral understanding by exploring imaginary worlds of others. Instead, imagination, properly used, can contribute to expanding moral possibilities and to understanding others.

38. Delattre, Edwin J. "The Straightjacket and the Vacuum in Moral Education." The Humanist, 38 (November/December 1978): 19-21.

Asks "How can we avoid confining students in the straightjacket of absolutist doctrinaire teaching without thrusting them into the moral vacuum of idiosyncrasy and relativism?" Argues that the solution lies not in teaching morality isolated from other disciplines, but in treating decision making as a central part of life, recognizing the differences between what is morally problematic and what is morally important and to teaching children that reasonable people can disagree about matters of moral complexity but not about whether evidence deserves consideration or that persons deserve respect.

39. Dewey, John. Democracy and Education. New York: Macmillan, 1963.

Argues that morals shouldn't be taught as a separate subject, but rather should permeate the school. Democratic values will be transmitted only through the democratic organization of the school. Dewey objects to moralizing. Morals are embedded in the social fabric of life and that is where they are learned.

40. Dewey, John. Moral Principles in Education. New York: Philosophical Library, 1959.

Argues that traditional conceptions of moral education are narrow, formal, and pathological. Moral education should be the development in the child of moral ideals, not necessarily ideals about morality. The best moral education is participation in social life. Morality is not a separate branch of knowledge it is the knowledge; we have, placed in relation to moral purposes.

41. Dewey, John. "The Need for a Philosophy of Education." Developmental Counseling and Teaching (item 1498), pp. 2-9.

In this article, which first appeared in 1934, Dewey states that education is a process of development. The importance of interests, environment, and goals is stressed throughout. The concept of development is used to critique traditional education and to suggest new directions for educational practice.

42. Diller, Ann. "Teaching Moral Rules: A Preliminary Analysis." Philosophy of Education 1975: Proceedings of the Thirty First Annual Meeting of the Philosophy of Education Society. San Jose, CA: Philosophy of Education Society, San Jose State University, 1975, pp. 233-242.

Argues that it is not central to the acquisition of a moral rule to be able to formulate the moral rule, but it is central to know, in a given situation, the moral significance of such aspects of the situation that the rule establishes as morally relevant. Contends that it is not necessary to teach moral principles but it is necessary to help young children to become conscious of what is morally important in a situation.

43. Dixon, K. "Moral Philosophy and Moral Education." Philosophy of Education and the Curriculum. Edited by K. Dixon. London: Pergamon Press, 1972, pp. 135-163.

Argues that there can be no "philosophically-grounded" final basis for moral education since moral argument is just that-argument. Beliefs cannot be guaranteed; they are always open to challenge. Concludes that moral education must be based on pluralistic and relativistic notions; this is seen as much preferable to a program based on the transmission of "established values."

44. Dixon, Keith. "On Teaching Moral Procedures." British Journal of Educational Studies, 16 (1968): 17-29.

Argues that although moral proceduralism acts as a useful and necessary check on the excesses of the moral traditionalist, the teaching of a totally validated set of moral propositions or procedures is not possible.

45. Duncan, A.R.C. "Escapes from Moral Thinking." The Domain of Moral Education (item 30), pp. 7-16.

Presents various ways that people think erroneously about
moral questions, thereby avoiding real moral thinking
altogether. Moral education is differentiated from other forms
of education that are often confused with or related to moral
education.

46. Ericson, Edward L. "The Aims of Moral Education." The
     Humanist, 32 (November/December 1972): 6-7.

     Argues that we need to develop a disciplined "value analysis"
     of the ways we live and the values--including low and false
     values--that contemporary society seems to impose. We must
     determine what we need to abandon if we are to realize deeper
     values and more humanizing goals.

47. Frankena, William K. "Toward a Philosophy of Moral Education."
     Moral Education (item 171), pp. 148-158.

     The responsibility of morally educating youth is twofold: (1)
     passing on a knowledge of "good and evil" or "knowing how" to
     act, and (2) ensuring that children's conduct will conform to
     this knowledge. Frankena's claim is that the two processes are
     interrelated and may be implemented concurrently. Also in
     Harvard Educational Review, 28 (1958): 300-313.

48. Freeman, Helen. "Egoism, Community and Rational Moral
     Education." Educational Philosophy and Theory, 9 (October
     1977): 1-18.

     Argues that since many children find egoism to be rational a
     rational moral education is of dubious efficacy. It is
     concluded that since egoism and life in community are
     incompatible, efforts at moral education should stress social
     and political life.

49. Goodrich, Rachel. "Moral Education: A Thomist Contribution."
     British Journal of Educational Studies, 14 (1966): 165-172.

     Thomist morality is ultimately dependent on religion, yet
     there is a common core of rational morality which can be taught
     in the public school.

50. Greene, Maxine. "John Dewey and Moral Education." Contemporary
     Education, 48 (Fall 1976): 17-22.

     A brief but detailed analysis of contemporary moral education
     from a Deweyan perspective. Concludes that Dewey has yet to be
     heard.

51. Greene, Maxine. "Toward the Concrete: An Approach to Moral
     Choosing." Moral Education Forum, 5 (Summer 1980): 2-12.

Argues that the contemporary focus on moral principles, rational discourse, and the nature of good reasons has diverted attention away from the question of what makes people feel moral obligation in concrete situations. Because of the complexity of moral situations, generalizations concerning one's moral obligations become almost inconceivable. What remains crucial is the taking of responsibility to alter situations in the light of some notion of something better, something that ought to be.

52. Gustafson, James M. "Education for Moral Responsibility," Moral Education: Five Lectures (item 1524), pp. 11-27.

The salient aspects of persons who act morally are enumerated. These include unconscious motivation beliefs and convictions, traits, affect, motives and intentions, and moral judgments. Three possible approaches to moral education are outlined: instruction in making moral decisions, study of moral themes in literature and the arts, and action projects. The paper concludes with an analysis of the relationship between religion and moral education.

53. Hague, William J. "Positive Disintegration and Moral Education." Journal of Moral Education. 5 (1976): 231-240.

Dabrowski's theory of positive disintegration is discussed and its implications for moral education presented. The theory holds that lower-level disintegration must take place before integration on higher levels can occur.

54. Hall, Robert T. "Moral Education Today: Progress, Prospects, and Problems of a Field Come of Age." The Humanist, 38 (November/December 1978): 8-13.

Presents a general analysis of educational objectives in the moral domain, centered around psychological, philosophical, and sociological objectives. Makes a plea for a more comprehensive and coordinated view of the field. Concludes by criticizing a "hard line" approach to moral education that holds that there are fixed cultural values that ought to be transmitted to all youth and argues instead for an open approach to moral education.

55. Hamm, C. "Can Moral Judgment Be Taught?" Journal of Educational Thought, 8 (1974): 73-86.

The process of judgment is distinguished from the belief state arrived at as a product of the process. To the extent that it is possible to instruct others in the rules and principles governing judgment, it is possible and desirable to instruct others in moral judgment.

56. Hamm, C. "The Study of Ethics as Moral Education." Journal of
    Educational Thought, 12 (1978): 115-130.

    The advisability of teaching ethics to children and youth is
    examined, using the main proponents of contemporary moral
    philosophy. The major question explored is whether such study
    might lead to practical consequences. Concludes that such study
    would illustrate the relationship between moral theory and moral
    decision making.

57. Hamm, Cornel M., and L.B. Daniels. "Moral Education in Relation
    to Values Education," The Domain of Moral Education (item 30),
    pp. 17-34.

    The authors draw a distinction between two conceptions of
    value: moral value and non-moral value. The argue that the
    content, procedures, and justification for non-moral values
    education are radically different from the content, procedures,
    and justification for moral education.

58. Hare, R.M. "Adolescents into Adults." Moral Education (item
    171), 116-124.

    In dealing with the concept of indoctrination Hare develops a
    conception of moral education aimed at preparing students for
    autonomous moral decision making. He recognizes that the child
    must be trained in action until the time when he is able to
    think about moral issues. There is a point when a child passes
    from moral adolescence into moral adulthood-this rite de passage
    must be the ultimate and central concern of the moral educator.

59. Hare, R.M. "Platonism in Moral Education: Two Varieties." The
    Monist, 58 (1974): 568-580.

    Argues that is we may give two sorts of answers to Socrates'
    question about what moral goodness is: a descriptionist answer
    that focuses on the nature of moral goodness, or a pre-
    scriptivist answer that focuses on the form of moral goodness.
    Hare argues that moral education consists most essentially in
    learning a language-the universal prescriptive language.

60. Hare, R.M. "Value Education in a Pluralist Society."
    Proceedings of the Philosophy of Education Society of Great
    Britain, 10 (1976): 7-23.

    Argues that neutrality is not entirely preferable in
    education, that facts and values are not always distinct, and
    that a teacher should, as an equal, give his/her substantive
    opinion and reasons for choices. The teacher should set an
    example of the strenuous desire to find answers. Also in
    Growing Up with Philosophy (item 1507), pp. 376-391.

61. Harris, Alan. Thinking About Education. London: Heinemann
     Educational Books, 1970.

     In a brief introduction to the philosophy of education Harris
     devotes considerable attention to such topics as justifications
     for value judgments, mores and morality, sex education, and
     religious education. Wilson's components of being morally
     educated (item 324) receive considerable attention.

62. Harrison, J. "A Note on What 'Value' or Moral Education Is."
     Journal of Educational Thought, 9 (1975): 127-128.

     Argues that we must not forget that moral education is not a
     subject, but rather represents a concern to engage human beings
     persistently in an orientation of self toward the goals of good,
     right, justice, and caring.

63. Heben, Germaine F. "Value Development: A Model." Ph.D.
     dissertation, Case Western Reserve University, 1975. 36/07,
     p. 4221.

     Research into the formation of fully mature value systems
     finds that values are intrinsic, universal, developmental and
     subordinate to full development. Curricular suggestions are
     proposed.

64. Hill, Brian. "Education for Rational Morality or Moral
     Rationality." Educational Theory, 22 (1972): 286-292.

     Attempts to assess current schools of thought regarding moral
     education. Expresses the concern that the positivists and the
     pluralists will win the day and the movement will lapse into
     laissez-faire neutrality. Argues that the subjective side of
     commitment must be given equal weight with the objective
     criteria of morality.

65. Hill, Brian V. "Toward a Conception of Morality and a Theory of
     Moral Education." Ph.D. dissertation, University of Illinois,
     1973. 34/01, p. 67.

     Analyzes four paradigms of moral education: Social Relativism,
     Formalism, Personalism, and Naturalism. Finds all lacking and
     urges a Personalistic Naturalism as the most appropriate
     normative base for a theory of moral education.

66. Hirst, Paul H. Moral Education in a Secular Society. London:
     University of London Press, 1974.

Argues that a rational and autonomous morality based on principles of fairness, truth telling, consideration of interests, freedom, and respect for persons should be the basis of moral education. Discusses the relationship between moral and religious education and sees them as distinct enterprises. Argues that there are substantive moral rules that must be taught.

67. Hoffman, John F. "Moral Navigation: From Puzzle to Purpose." Teachers College Record, 75 (1974): 501-505.

Argues that there is a great need for clarity in moral education as to its purposes. Considers that a focus on the methods of moral decision making offers the most hope. Makes suggestions for improving teacher education relative to moral education.

68. Hoffman, John F. "A Philosophical Analysis of the Concept of Responsibility as a Methodological Approach for Moral Education." Ph.D. dissertation, State University of New York at Buffalo, 1973. 34/06, p. 2919.

Argues that before moral education programs are developed, there must be an analysis of what it means to be morally educated. From an analysis of the concept of moral responsibility Hoffman concludes that moral education should focus on inquiry and student discovery.

69. Hollins, T.H.B., ed. Aims in Education: The Philosophic Approach. Manchester, England: Manchester University Press, 1964.

A collection of six papers on moral education covering such topics as indoctrination, mental health, and Neo-Thomism.

70. Hollins, T.H.B. "The Problem of Values and John Dewey." Aims in Education (item 69), pp. 91-108.

Briefly reviews Dewey's central points on values and education: values are not fixed, children make meaning through problem solving and critical appraisal, the best knowledge is practical, school must be a form of community life, etc. Disagrees with Dewey and holds that there is a hierarchy of values.

71. Holmes, Mark. "Moral Education-What Can Schools Do?" Interchange, 7 (1976): 1-10.

After critically reviewing the major approaches to moral education, the author urges that educators come out of the closet, confess that schools do teach morals and values, determine what those values are, check to see if those are the values desired by all the significant constitutents of the schools, and, finally, reorganize school structure and curriculum to teach those values.

72. Houston, Barbara E. "The Paradox of Moral Education: An Attempted Resolution." Ph.D. dissertation, The University of Western Ontario, 1977. 38/09, p. 5524.

Addresses the question of how one educates morally while avoiding indoctrination regarding either method or content. The perspectives of Hare, Kohlberg, and Perry are analyzed, with modifications of Hare's and Kohlberg's theories seen as pointing the way to the resolution of the paradox.

73. Hyland, John T. "Moral Reasoning and Moral Education." Journal of Moral Education, 6 (1977): 75-80.

Takes the position, following Beardsmore (item 160), that although educators cannot be uncommitted on fundamental moral issues, they can, nevertheless, ensure that rational procedures are followed.

74. Jones, Hardy E. "The Rationale of Moral Education." The Monist, 58 (1974): 659-673.

Attempts to develop a rationale for providing moral education. Jones rejects rationales that posit reasons extrinsic to the child and insists that a moral education is intrinsically desirable because persons are valuable and a moral education enhances those characteristics which make them valuable.

75. Kachaturoff, Grace. "Teaching Values in the Public Schools." Social Studies, 64 (1973): 222-226.

Contrasts the idealist, realist, and pragmatist approaches to values. Concludes that if values are to be personally meaningful, the students must choose them themselves. The teacher's role in this process is to let students be themselves and choose their own values.

76. Kirschenbaum, Howard. "New Goals for Moral Education." The Humanist, 38 (November/December 1978): 17-19.

Suggests a framework of eight goals for an integrative moral education. The framework contains a mixture of three types of goals: five sets of skills, two sets of attitudes, and one set of concepts. Argues that these are goals all moral educators can agree upon.

77. Klein, J. Theodore. "Cultural Pluralism and Moral Education."
    The Monist, 58 (1974): 683-693.

    Argues that cultural pluralism is the model for the ideal
    democratic society. Implicit in a culturally pluralistic
    society are the moral values which should be taught as a part of
    moral education: freedom of choice, equality, participation,
    respect for differences, and cooperation.

78. Kristol, Irving. "Moral and Ethical Development in a Democratic
    Society." Moral Development--ETS (item 3174), pp. 3-14.

    Calls for a restoration of moral authority within our major
    social institutions. Argues that the absence of obligation
    means a diminution of humanity, and that moral deprivation
    results when no obligations are imposed.

79. Kurtz, Paul. "Why Moral Education?" The Humanist, 32
    (November/December 1972): 5.

    Argues that moral education is essential and raises the
    question whether we can find a middle ground between repressive
    morality and complete permissiveness.

80. Lambert, Garth R. "A Study of Aristotle's Concepts of Moral and
    Intellectual Education in the Context of Modern Educational
    Theory." Ph.D. dissertation, University of Toronto, 1975.
    37/10, p. 6553.

    Analyzes Aristotle's theory of moral education and compares
    his presuppositions with those commonly taught in schools of
    education; e.g., the ideas of Dewey, Kohlberg, Raths, Peters,
    and Wilson.

81. Lawson, David. The Teaching of Values. Montreal: McGill, 1970.

    Traces the shift in 19th- and 20th-century thought from
    ethical idealism as an approach to morality to a social
    psychological interpretation. The significance of this shift is
    that moral judgments and phenomena have come to be seen as
    rooted in experienced facts rather than as existing only as
    ideals. To demonstrate this shift, the ideals of Felix Adler,
    John Dewey, Harry Stack Sullivan, and Erich Fromm are presented
    in separate chapters. The implication of this shift for the
    teaching of values is discussed.

82. Lerner, Max. Values in Education. Bloomington, IN: Phi Delta
    Kappa Foundation, 1976. ED 128 285.

Reviews the centrality of value questions in educational planning and concludes that the goal of education should be to learn how to establish an education for the whole person in his/her lifetime.

83. Litke, Robert. "Who Is to Say What Should Be Taught in Values Education." Reflections on Values Education (item 1510), pp. 89-110.

Takes a broad view of who should be involved in determining the content and method for values education. Says that everyone should be involved: students, teachers, parents, community, society at large, etc. The classroom teacher, however, must make the final decision. The only way for a teacher to decide safely on the content of values education is from his/her own theory or philosophy of values education. A model and strategy for formulating such a theory is presented.

84. Livingstone, John R. "An Evaluation of the Moral and Value Schemas Proposed by Jean Piaget, Lawrence Kohlberg and Brian Hall." Ph.D. dissertation, St. Louis University, 1977. 39/03, p. 1441.

Evaluates the theories of Piaget, Kohlberg, and Hall and suggests that there are two moralities that are not addressed by the authors.

85. Livingstone, R.W. "Plato and the Moral Training of Character." Educational Forum, 25 (1958): 5-13.

Presents Plato's view on the role that music, physical education, the arts, and abstract studies play in character development.

86. Lorber, Neil M. "Conformity versus Nonconformity to Social Ethics: The Challenge to Educators." The Monist, 58 (1974): 674-682.

Argues that it is unnecessary for society to overtly or covertly impose its knowledge, values, behavioral preferences, etc., upon each new generation. Society's responsibilities in social and ethical education can be fulfilled simply by apprising youth of the consequences that his behavioral options will likely create for him.

87. Loukes, H. "Responsibility and Irresponsibility in Adolescents." Moral Education in a Changing Society (item 1515), pp. 138-156.

The essential virtue of the adolescent is compassion. Moral responsibility cannot be expected without it. Moral education should be based on personal and firsthand encounters, otherwise it will be mechanistic and without motivating power.

88. McClellan, J. "Two Questions about the Teaching of Moral Values," Educational Theory, 11 (1961): 1-14.

    A logical-linguistic analysis of moral truth vs. truth in science, and associated teaching problems. What is the relation between teaching moral truth and training in moral behavior? This is the central issue to be resolved in moral education.

89. MacIntyre, A.C. "Against Utilitarianism," Aims in Education (item 69), pp. 1-23.

    Presents an analysis of the ills of our society, which are perceived as being due to an inability to discover ends and to a tendency for individuals to be treated instrumentally--as utilitarian to some vague conception of the general welfare. The only help for the situation is for children to develop rational critical inquiry and thereby to weaken prevailing social values. The value of activity for its own sake must be stressed.

90. McNaughton, Anthony H. "Can Moral Behavior Be Taught Through Cognitive Means?--Yes." Social Education, 41 (1977): 328-331.

    Argues that reasoning about moral actions can lead to greater moral understanding, which is necessary to the improvement of moral behavior.

91. Mathis, B. Claude. "To Train or to Educate: A Moral Decision." Morality Examined (item 1528), pp. 199-217.

    The decision to train or to educate is a moral one. Training is seen as manipulating the learner to bring him to some goal. Education is leading the learner in the direction of the development of a personal maturity. In order to be satisfied in their role, teachers must teach from an ethical perspective consistent with the learner's development and the curriculum.

92. Miller, Ronald W. "Why Choose? A Conversation about Moral Education." Concord, MA: National Humanities Faculty, 1975. ED 125 988.

    Reports the results of a wide-ranging discussion between a college professor of religion and a high school social studies teacher. The need to address both means and ends in the process of values education is a central point of the discussion.

93. Molnar, Alex. "Modes of Values Thinking in Curriculum." Paper
     presented at the annual meeting of the Association for
     Supervision and Curriculum Development, Minneapolis, 1973. ED
     077 131.

     Argues that it is important to clarify one's unit of interest
     before entering into a dialogue concerning values in curriculum.
     Values thinking is pictured as taking place on four levels:
     theoretical, conceptual, transactional, and transformational.
     The proper focus of study for understanding the valuing process
     is the interaction between the transactional and
     transformational levels.

94. Montefiore, Alan. "Moral Philosophy and the Teaching of
     Morality." Harvard Educational Review, 35 (1965): 435-449.

     Two positions concerning the purposes of moral education are
     presented: the autonomist argument that morality is essentially
     the concern of the free autonomous individual; and the
     naturalist argument that morality involves an acceptance of some
     authority as ultimate. The implications of both points of view
     for education are outlined, and a third, intermediate, position
     is hinted at.

95. Montefiore, Alan. "Philosophy and Moral (and Political)
     Education." Journal of Philosophy of Education, 13 (1975):
     21-32.

     Explores the question of what is the relationship, if any,
     between philosophical reflection upon morals and practical moral
     thought. The inseparability of moral and political questions is
     argued, and the essentially subversive nature of philosophical
     inquiry is discussed.

96. Moon, Robert P. "Altruism in Moral Theory and Education."
     Ph.D. dissertation, University of Minnesota, 1979. 40/02, p.
     736.

     Presents a philosophical and psychological analysis of the
     concept of altruism. Analyzes the role of altruism in major
     theories of moral education (Durkheim, Dewey, Peters and
     Kohlberg). Finally, argues the necessity for the social basis
     of morality.

97. Morgenbesser, S. "Approaches to Ethical Objectivity."
     Educational Theory, 7 (1957): 180-186.

     Rejects the notion that a theological basis is necessary for
     ethical objectivity. Suggests instead discussion and
     interchange of experience by students so that each can test his
     own ethic but not impose it on others.

98. Morgenson, Donald. "Values and Humanistic Psychology." Reflections on Values Education (item 1510), pp. 179-199.

Discusses the malaise besetting contemporary life: loneliness, meaninglessness and alienation. Suggests that humanistic psychology, with its commitment to human becoming, can help to solve the contemporary crises of values. Sees values education in collaboration with humanistic psychology as a means to create a liveable world.

99. Nelson, Thomas W. "What Is or Should Be Moral Teaching?" Theory into Practice, 14 (1975): 286-291.

Argues that although it is logically possible to avoid moral teaching, it is not practically possible. Presents three ways that teachers botch opportunities for moral teaching.

100. Nettleship, R.L. The Theory of Education in Plato's Republic. London: Oxford University Press, 1935.

Contains many helpful insights into Plato's view of moral education.

101. Newsome, George L. "Normative Discourse and Education." Education and Ethics. Edited by William G. Blackstone and George L. Newsome. Athens: University of Georgia Press, 1969.

Argues that the schools teach a simplified version of conventional middle=class morality and that the value system taught in schools is vague, ambiguous, inconsistent, and often hypocritical. The bureaucracy of the school often compromises the values professed. A philosophic analysis of pedagogical knowledge may be useful in explicating the meaning of moral concepts and in elucidating moral reasoning in education.

102. Niblett, W.R. "Some Problems in Moral Education Today," Moral Education in a Changing Society (item 1515), pp. 13-30.

Discusses reasons why moral education is so difficult today. Urges that the principles of moral education include recognition of the common humanity of young and old, the fostering of identity, the power of choice at many levels, and a greater encouragement of initiative and of assuming responsibility.

103. Ohan, Farid E. "Moral Education: Its Possibility in the Schools." Ph.D. dissertation, University of Toronto, 1976. 38/06, p. 3256.

Attempts to demonstrate that a non-cognitivist approach is an inadequate basis for moral education. Proceeds to show how a cognitivist approach is preferable.

104. O'Neal, W.F. "Existentialism and Education for Moral Choice."
     Phi Delta Kappan, 46 (1964): 48-53.

     Presents six insights for moral education derived from
     existential philosophy: man is potentially autonomous, the basic
     function of school is normative, the school should be concerned
     with moral education rather than moral training, there exists no
     irreconcilable conflict between self-interest and the interests
     of others, free choice entails self-discipline, and moral
     content cannot be separated from the moral procedures that are
     used to establish and maintain classroom discipline.

105. Pai, Y. "The Free Will Problem and Moral Education."
     Educational Theory, 16 (1966): 135-150.

     Suggests that moral freedom means acting from a sense of duty
     to a principle. Moral education, then, should involve not only
     a knowledge of rule but the development of a character. Its
     fundamental task is to aid children in holding a passionate
     devotion to their beliefs.

106. Park, Joe, and R. William Barron. "Can Morality Be Taught?"
     Morality Examined (item 1528), pp. 3-23.

     Contains a sketchy account of differing perspectives on the
     meaning of morality and approaches to teaching for morality.

107. Paske, Gerald. "Is Value Education Possible?" Philosophy of
     Education 1973: Proceedings of the Twenty-Ninth Annual
     Meeting of the Philosophy of Education Society. Carbondale
     and Edwardsville, IL: Philosophy of Education Society,
     Southern Illinois University, 1973, pp. 53-60.

     Argues that moral rules can be rationally justified but moral
     principles cannot. Shows that empathy--the basis for the
     construction of a fully developed morality--can be inculcated
     without engaging in indoctrination.

108. Pemberton, Janette E. "Discussions on Aristotle's Ethics:
     Implications for Teachers and Administrators." Largo, MD:
     Prince George's Community College, 1980. ED 185 551.

     Presents Aristotle's views on ethics and moral education and
     discusses their implications for practice.

109. Peters, R.S. "Democratic Values and Educational Aims."
     Education and Values (item 1525), pp. 67-86.

     Attempts to articulate some major aims for education that
     follow from the basic values distinctive to democratic society.
     Democracy is characterized as placing high value on the

development of reason and principles such as freedom,
truth-telling, impartiality, and respect for persons.

110. Peters, R.S. "Education as Initiation." Philosophical Analysis
      and Education. Edited by R.D. Archambault. New York: The
      Humanities Press, 1965, pp. 87-111.

      After rejecting traditional ways of characterizing education,
      Peters concludes that education is a process aimed at motivation
      of a certain kind. It is properly concerned with the intitation
      of the young into activities, modes of conduct, and thought,
      which have public standards written into them.

111. Peters, R.S. "Moral Education and the Psychology of Character."
      Philosophy, 37 (1962): 35-56.

      Character is described as primarily those traits which man can
      choose and applies only to rule-following behavior. Questions
      of moral education are posed: Which rules should the child be
      taught? How can they be taught so they will be rationally
      judged? How do we acquire judgment in applying rules? How do
      we explain the "executive gap"? Also in Psychology and Ethical
      Development (item 311).

112. Peters, R.S. "Moral Education--Tradition or Reason?" Let's
      Teach Them Right (item 424), pp. 100-110.

      Argues that in their early moral education, children must
      learn to do what is right without properly understanding why.
      Parents and teachers must lay down a firm foundation of moral
      rules and encourage children, as they develop, to strike out on
      their own and discover where they stand on controversial issues.

113. Phenix, Phillip H. Education and the Common Good: A Moral
      Philosophy of the Curriculum. New York: Harper, 1961.

      Organized around the major problems in contemporary culture,
      the book discusses the sort of curriculum needed for today's
      schools. Each topic is considered from the point of view of the
      values at stake; moral concern is the keynote.

114. Phenix, Phillip H. "The Moral Imperative in Contemporary
      Education." Readings in Values Clarification (item 1504), pp.
      38-48.

      Urges that educators seize upon the current social crisis and
      opportunity for developing moral education. What is needed is a
      moral theory, a vision that justifies and animates educators'
      actions. Presents three moral theories (anomic, autonomic, and
      heteronomic) and rejects them in favor of the teleonomic theory:
      the moral demand is grounded in a comprehensive purpose that is
      objective and normative and forever transcends concrete

institutional embodiment or ideological formulation. The moral imperative in education requires the nurturance of intelligence in concrete decision making.

115. Plato. Protagoras. Many editions.

Presents one of the classic discussions of the oft-recurring question, "Can virtue be taught?" Socrates argues against Protagoras' view that virtue can be taught. Virtue is not knowledge. Virtue is learned like a language--from everyone--in the streets, playground, marketplace, etc.

116. Price, Kingsley. "Love Yes, But Maybe Not Sex: Kohlberg, Plato and Proudfoot." Philosophy of Education 1980 (item 1509), pp. 317-320.

Argues (against Proudfoot item 117) that sexual love cannot be relied on to make us good--it involves possession. Spiritual love seems to offer more possibilities in this area.

117. Proudfoot, Merrill. "How Sex Can Make Us Good: Plato's Eros and Moral Education." Philosophy of Education 1980 (item 1509), pp. 307-316.

In a mild critique of Kohlberg, argues that moral education proceeds most surely where there is continuing interaction of intellect and passion. Eros provides the motor for moral life, and the steering wheel of Kohlberg can undoubtedly be useful. Justice has a great deal to do with how we conceptualize goodness, and love with how we attain it.

118. Purpel, David, and Kevin Ryan. "Moral Education in the Classroom: Some Instructional Issues." Moral Education ... It Comes with the Territory (item 1519), pp. 55-67.

The authors discuss and reject indoctrination as a method of moral education. They note the differences between a direct and indirect approach to moral education.

119. Ravitch, Diane. "Moral Education and the Schools." Commentary, 56 (September 1973): 62-67.

Argues that the goal of moral education must fit somewhere between indoctrination and the abdication of all values. Regardless of what we think, schools cannot avoid being involved in the transmission of values. Kohlberg's methods, especially the "just community" concept, are seen as a viable approach.

120. Reagan, Gerald M. "Moral Education in Theory and Practice." Theory into Practice, 14 (1975): 221-223.

In introducing this special issue of Theory into Practice Reagan poses 11 important questions for those interested in moral education.

121. Reeves, Marjorie E. "Moral Education in Early Maturity." Moral Education in a Changing Society (item 1515), pp. 157-171.

Children need to be brought up against hard moral realities--the givenness of much of our social and moral life. Teachers need to instill an inner control in children that will allow to them the long and maintained effort necessary for success.

122. Rich, John M. "Teaching the Justifications for the Moral Life." Educational Theory, 14 (1964): 308-313.

Argues that moral education must begin with the question, "Why be moral?" Concludes that the rightness of an act provides a sufficient reason for its performance.

123. Salk, Jonas. "The Survival of the Wisest." Phi Delta Kappan, 56 (1975): 667-669.

Argues, based on population growth, that if man is to survive, a complete inversion of values is required from survival of the fittest to an ethic of cooperation.

124. Scheffler, Israel. "Moral Education and the Democratic Ideal." Reason and Teaching. London: Routledge and Kegan Paul, 1973, Chapter 11.

Stresses the connections between moral, scientific, and democratic education and the centrality to all three of the habits of critical thought. Argues that moral schooling should pervade the whole of the school experience. The point of moral education in a democracy is not merely to shape; it is rather to liberate.

125. Scriven, Michael. Student Values as Educational Objectives, Publication #124. Lafayette, IN: Social Science Education Consortium, Purdue University, 1966.

Argues that teaching must be value-directed and value-affecting. We should teach the truth, i.e., the best supported theory. In doing so we will be teaching the general value of objectivity--science as the best way of arriving at the truth--and how to apply this general method to socially and practically important issues. See also items 250 and 251 for other dimensions of Scriven's argument.

126. Scriven, Michael. "Values in the Curriculum." SSEC Newsletter, 2 (1966): 1-3.

Argues that the goal of values education should be the straightforward development of cognitive skills for handling value disputes. The reasons given for this point of view are that there are no final answers and the best we can hope for is greater clarity about the facts of the situation and the nature of the value concepts.

127. Shane, Harold G. "The Future Mandates New Moral Directions." Emerging Moral Dimensions in Society: Implications for Schooling. Edited by Robert R. Leeper. Washington, D.C.: Association for Supervision and Curriculum Development, 1975, pp. 1-10.

Traces some of the reasons why there is a renewed interest in moral education and suggests some possible directions that can be taken. Kohlberg receives the most attention.

128. Shinn, Roger L. "Education in Values: Acculturation and Exploration." Education and Values (item 1525), pp. 111-122.

Argues that education in values serves two functions. It should inculcate the values of the society, but it should also encourage exploration into the worth of those values. Shinn shows how in a pluralistic society both processes are controversial.

129. Sokolow, H. Michael. "The Intersection of Coercion and Moral Education." Educational Philosophy and Theory, 12 (1980): 51-63.

Analyzes the concept of coercion as it relates to moral education and argues that coercion may be necessary to inculcate certain rudimentary virtues. However, it should not be used in such a way as to shape behavior without giving justification for that behavior for this will develop external morality not internal morality (seeing the need for rules).

130. Spencer, Herbert. Education: Intellectual, Moral and Physical. New York: A.L. Burt Co., n.d.

Believes that moral education can be taught through a science curriculum. Gives content of this curriculum based on utilitarian view of ethics. Describes how to apply the natural consequence theory to teaching moral values.

131. Stott, L.J. "Teaching a Sense of Responsibility." Educational Forum, 40 (1976): 431-436.

Argues that the essence of responsibility is to acknowledge one's respect and feeling for others. Not to hold students responsible is to teach them that they are not accountable.

132. Strike, K.A. "Freedom, Autonomy and Teaching." Educational
     Theory, 22 (1972): 262-277.

     Explores the question of whether freedom can be taught.
     Concludes that since teaching is causing, and since there is
     something wrong about causing something to be uncaused, freedom
     (or moral autonomy) cannot be taught.

133. Susky, J.E. "Compassion and Moral Development." Journal of
     Thought, 14 (1979): 227-234.

     Holds that long before a child can reason and establish
     principles of moral behavior the direction of ethical life has
     been set by the environment. Schooling should focus on
     developing humanness (compassion and empathy), for ultimately it
     is these factors which will control our choices in morally
     difficult situations. Justice will be transcended by kindness,
     love, and compassion.

134. Sword, John. "The Impossibility of Teaching a Private
     Morality." Journal of Moral Education, 6 (1976): 8-13.

     In a response to Straughan (item 938), Sword argues that
     because public morality is challengeable, it does not follow
     that decision making is exclusively private. The morality is
     public (what society requires) as is the challenge.

135. Vandenberg, Donald. "The Ontological Foundation of Moral
     Education." Ph.D. dissertation, University of Illinois, 1966.
     27/03, p. 713.

     Argues for the need, prior to teaching moral rules, to ground
     those rules ontologically in contemporary social life in order
     to make them authentic to the student.

136. Wall, Grenville. "Moral Autonomy and the Liberal Theory of
     Moral Education." Proceedings of the Philosophy of Education
     Society of Great Britain, 8 (July 1974): 222-236.

     Argues against the liberal notion that construes moral freedom
     as the right to make up your own mind about moral questions, no
     matter how you make it up. Argues instead that using procedures
     of moral thinking is similar to using principles of mathematical
     thinking--one still must come up with correct conclusions.

137. Watkins, James W. "Forming a Value Curriculum: Two
     Philosophical Issues to Consider," Moral Education ... It
     Comes With the Territory (item 1519), pp. 11-19.

     Discusses four possible approaches to moral education: do
     nothing, clarify values, teach a specific set of values, or
     teach a process for valuing. These four approaches are analyzed

from three philosophical approaches to education that have implications for moral education: idealism or realism, pragmatism, and existentialism. Finally, Watkins discusses the implications of three metaethical positions for values education: naturalism, emotionism, and prescriptivism.

138. Watt, A.J. Rational Moral Education. Melbourne: Melbourne University Press, 1977.

Argues that moral skepticism poses no major problems to the pursuit of moral education. Seeks out the primary principles that should inform the content and shape the form of moral education. Considering other people's interests is accorded a primary position.

139. Weber, Deborah. "History and Humanity: Reflections of a High School Senior." Moral Education Forum, 6 (Spring 1981): 17-19.

Argues that educators should allow students to feel that they have power over their future rather than impressing them with the powerless incompetencies of man's past.

140. Weldhen, Margaret. "The Existentialists and Problems of Moral and Religious Education: 1. Bultmann and Heidegger." Journal of Moral Education, 1 (1971): 19-26.

First of three articles dealing with the moral concepts developed by six existential thinkers. Discusses Bultmann's concepts of demythologizing and responsible freedom, and Heidegger's distinction between authentic and unauthentic existence.

141. Weldhen, Margaret. "The Existentialists and Problems of Moral and Religious Education: 2. Tillich and Jaspers." Journal of Moral Education, 1 (1972): 97-101.

Discusses Tillich's view that moral judgment is based on "creative intuition" and Jaspers' emphasis on the autonomy of the individual.

142. Weldhen, Margaret. "The Existentialists and Problems of Moral and Religious Education: 3. Bonhoeffer and Sartre." Journal of Moral Education, 1 (1972): 187-194.

Bonhoeffer's and Sartre's emphases on choice in morality are discussed, and implications for religious and moral education are drawn.

143. White, J.P. "The Moral Objectives of a Uniform Curriculum." Progress and Problems in Moral Education (item 1530), pp. 60-73.

Argues against the conservative tradition that proposes a
diversity of objectives for moral education. Instead, moral
education requires, by its very nature, common standards. Moral
objectives must be placed at the apex, with individualistic aims
properly subordinated to them.

144. Wilson, John. "Establishing a Dialectic in Moral Education."
     Progress and Problems in Moral Education (item 1530), pp.
     87-92.

     If teachers have a grasp of the nature of the task of moral
     education and its importance, they should naturally desire as
     much hard argument as possible. Philosophers can assist us in
     reaching a clearer understanding of what it means to be "morally
     educated".

145. Wilson, John. "First Steps in Education, Morality and
     Religion." Philosophy of Education 1977 (item 1527), pp.
     29-48.

     Urges plain talk to ensure we know what we are talking about
     before we try to go further.

146. Wilson, John. "The Methodology of Moral Education." The
     Humanist, 38 (November/December 1978): 15-16.

     Discusses moral education from the perspective of educating
     people in morality. Claims that the business of moral education
     has nothing to do with what any society may or may not approve
     of or practice. Appropriate moral education is based on
     philosophic principles, not on what public image or supposed
     experts maintain.

147. Wilson, John. "Motivation and Methodology in Moral Education."
     Journal of Moral Education, 10 (1981): 85-94.

     Two worries about moral education are considered. To the
     first--whether or not there are fundamental principles of reason
     and procedure--Wilson says don't worry, there are. To the
     second--how and in what direction pupils should be motivated to
     attend to such principles--Wilson argues that the proper object
     of motivation is allegiance to certain principles of rationality
     and justice. Personal benevolence is regarded as desirable but
     too fragile.

148. Wilson, John. "Practical Moves in Moral Education: An
     Introduction." Development of Moral Reasoning (item 1495),
     3-13.

Argues that the most practical first step for moral education is to achieve clarity about the aims of moral education. He goes on to spell out in very general terms some common interpretations of moral education and the practical moves entailed.

149. Wilson, John. "Two Types of Teaching." Philosophical Analysis and Education. Edited by R.D. Archambault. New York: The Humanities Press, 1965, pp. 157-170.

Argues that the context and manner of instruction are crucial factors in describing the activity of education. This is especially important in the area of moral education.

150. Zorter, Gary H. "Ethical Decision Making and Moral Education." Ph.D. dissertation, Washington University, 1973. 34/08, p. 5005.

Develops a rationalist position on the appropriate goals and methods of moral education.

Ethical Theory: Conceptions of Moral Responsibility,
Moral Justification, and the Moral Good

151. Aiken, H.D. "The Concept of Moral Objectivity." Morality and
      the Language of Conduct (item 169), pp. 69-105.

      Argues that there can be no definitive criterion of moral
      objectivity and, hence, no definitive principle of moral right
      and wrong. When there is serious question regarding a moral
      statement, there is simply a further obligation to examine it in
      light of other obligations, such as searching for further facts.

152. Aiken, H.D. "Moral Philosophy and Education." Harvard
      Education Review, 25 (1955): 35-39.

      Outlines developments in "analytic ethics" that have been
      ignored in education.

153. Amioka, Shiro. "A Study of John Dewey's Theory of Value and Its
      Implications for Education." Ph.D. dissertation, University
      of Illinois, 1959. 20/08, p. 3116.

      Dewey's attempt to abolish dualisms, especially that of
      fact/value, is discussed. Argues that it is possible to ground
      value statements in much the same way one grounds factual
      claims. The implications of Dewey's theory of value for
      education are presented.

154. Aristotle. Nichomachean Ethics. Many editions.

      Discusses the role of habituation and practical reasoning in
      the attainment of morality. The virtues that comprise the
      essence of morality are discussed at length.

155. Ayer, A.J. Language, Truth and Logic. New York: Dover Publica-
      tions, 1952.

      Sets forth starkly the implications of logical positivism for
      ethics. Ethical statements are seen as pseudo-concepts having
      no cognitive significance; at best they serve to express or
      arouse emotions of approval or disapproval. Sets forth the
      emotive theory of ethics.

156. Baier, K. <u>The Moral Point of View</u>. New York: Random House, 1965.

Argues that when one asks what is the best thing to do one commits oneself to the moral point of view. One also commits oneself to abiding by the outcome of one's deliberations. When committing oneself to the moral point of view, one also commits oneself to rationality, and this means that the rules one follows must be for everyone and must not be self-frustrating, self-defeating, or morally impossible. This approach is sometimes referred to as the "good reasons" approach to morality.

157. Baier, Kurt. "Moral Reasons and Reasons to Be Moral." <u>Values and Morals</u>. Edited by A.I. Goldman and J. Kim. Dordrecht, Holland: D. Reidel Publishing Co., 1978, pp. 231-256.

Poses an answer to the question "Why be moral?" that does not presuppose that duty and interest coincide. Baier disagrees with Prichard (item 242) on this point.

158. Baier, Kurt. "What Is Value? An Analysis of the Concept." <u>Values and the Future</u>. Edited by Kurt Baier and Nicholas Rescher. New York: The Free Press, 1969, pp. 33-67.

Attempts to become clear on the meaning of the concept value. Holds that values are tendencies of persons to promote certain ends because these ends are taken to make a favorable difference in people's lives. To say one values something entails a willingness to take protective action in defense of what is valued. The article contains many useful references to conceptions of the value concept.

159. Bailey, Charles. "Morality, Reason and Feeling." <u>Journal of Moral Education</u>, 9 (1980): 114-121.

Argues that morality has much to do with reason and little to do with feelings or affections.

160. Beardsmore, R.W. <u>Moral Reasoning</u>. London: Cambridge University Press, 1973.

Ties moral concepts to the conditions under which they are learned. Because holders of a particular moral outlook learn 'right' and 'wrong' in connection with particular things the meaning of these terms is connected with those things. The position espoused is one of conceptual relativism of moral concepts.

161. Berofsky, Bernard, ed. Free Will and Determinism. New York: Harper and Row, 1966.

A collection of readings exploring the various dimensions of free will, determinism, and man's responsibility for his actions.

162. Bhattacharya, N.C. "Inquiry, Values and Growth: A Reassessment of Dewey's Theory of Valuation." Educational Theory, 25 (1975): 92-101.

Points out some of the difficulties with Dewey's theory of valuation, but they are not held to be fatal.

163. Bok, Sissela. Lying: Moral Choice in Public and Private Life. New York: Pantheon Books, 1978.

Discusses the extent and depth of lying as a phenomenon of modern life. Argues that the pervasiveness of lying constitutes a threat to the stability of social life.

164. Brandt, Richard. "Rationality, Egoism and Morality." The Journal of Philosophy, 49 (1972): 681-697.

Argues that the rational egoist will act most often in accordance with the moral system of his society. Attacks the notion that somehow egoism is at variance with society. A rational egoist will advocate a moral system that is nonegoist.

165. Brandt, Richard B. A Theory of the Good and the Right. Oxford: Clarendon Press, 1979.

Argues that it is possible to identify certain likes/dislikes or desires/aversions as mistaken or irrational. Hence it is possible to ascertain the "correct" social moral code for an individual, i.e., the one that has been criticized by facts and logic as far as possible. Brandt argues for a rule utilitarian system of ethics.

166. Brandt, Richard B. "Toward a Credible Form of Utilitarianism." Morality and the Language of Conduct (item 169), pp. 107-143.

Develops a form of utilitarianism which holds that an act is right if and only if it conforms with that learnable set of rules the recognition of which as morally binding by everyone in the society of the agent would maximize intrinsic value.

167. Brandt, Richard B., ed. Value and Obligation: Systematic Readings in Ethics. New York: Harcourt, Brace and World, 1961.

One of the better collections of readings in ethical theory. Papers reflect a variety of positions on what is worthwhile, which acts are right, the justification of ethical beliefs, ethical relativism, human rights, the morality of institutions, and the issue of free will.

168. Candlish, Stewart. "The Origins of Subjectivism." Journal of Moral Education, 4 (1975): 191-200.

Exposes the absurdity of the slogan "a man acts rightly if he does what he thinks is right." The sources of its pervasiveness and persistence are exposed.

169. Castaneda, N.H., and G. Nakhnikian, eds. Morality and the Language of Conduct. Detroit: Wayne State University Press, 1963.

A collection of essays not published elsewhere on the nature of morality and the nature and function of the language of conduct.

170. Chazan, Barry I. "The Moral Situation: A Prolegomenon to Moral Education." Moral Education (item 171), pp. 39-49.

Chazan attempts to present a comprehensive picture of the moral situation. He develops a framework that distinguishes the moral from the non-moral.

171. Chazan, Barry I., and Jonas F. Soltis, eds. Moral Education. New York: Teachers College Press, 1973.

This volume of readings is designed to bridge the gap between the moral philosopher and the moral educator by providing discussions of themes in moral philosophy in a way that will enable those in moral education to understand more fully the complex nature of their task. Contains a general introduction by the editors (pp. 1-15), which discusses analytic and synthetic moral philosophy, common assumptions and problems of moral philosophy, and the limits of moral philosophy's contribution. Book contains sections on moral justification, principles, autonomy, and teaching and morality.

172. Coffey, Patrick J. "Personal and Impersonal Moral Reasoning." Ph.D. dissertation, St. Louis University, 1967. 28/08, pp. 3218.

Attempts to make the nature of practical moral reasoning more clear. Contrasts the processes by which moral experts and individuals reach moral decisions.

173. Cox, Harvey, ed.   The Situation Ethics Debate.   Philadelphia:
     The Westminster Press, 1968.

     Contains a collection of letters and articles critical of
     Fletcher's situation ethics (item 185).   Fletcher delivers a
     sharp reply.

174. Crittenden, Brian S., ed.   "The Shape of the Moral Domain."
     Moral Education: Interdisciplinary Approaches   (item   1492),
     pp. 290-327.

     Narveson, Baier, Edel, Gouthier, Kohlberg, Scriven, Melden,
     Sullivan, et al. discuss issues such as uses of the word moral
     and morality as justice.   There is a penetrating and excellent
     discussion among the authors on the role of rationality in moral
     judgment and action.

175. Daneke, Gregory A.   "Toward a Theory of Moral Instruction."
     Theory into Practice, 14 (1975): 247-257.

     An excellent discussion of three major trends in moral
     thought: scientific, humanistic, and principalistic.   These
     trends are discussed, inherent difficulties are pointed out, and
     implications for moral instruction are presented.

176. Daniels, N., ed.   Reading Rawls: Critical Studies on Rawls's "A
     Theory of Justice."   New York: Basic Books, 1974.

     Contains a collection of 14 papers critiquing various aspects
     of Rawl's theory of justice (item 244).

177. Dewey, John.   Democracy and Education.   New York: Macmillan,
     1961.

     In chapter 18 he distinguishes between valuation and
     evaluation; argues for the location of valuing in an
     experimental matrix and for a concomitant necessity for all
     educating to be of intrinsic as well as instrumental work.   In
     chapter 26 he discusses dualistic theories of morals; rejects
     dichotomies of duty/interest, intelligence/character,
     social/moral; suggests that these are to be understood as phases
     of a complete act of thought.

178. Dewey, John.   The Quest for Certainty.   New York: Capricorn,
     1960.

     In chapter 10 he distinguishes between subjective and
     objective value theory and criticizes both.   Argues that there
     are no absolutes in values; values are created by man in his
     environment.

179. Dewey, John. <u>Theory of the Moral Life</u>. New York: Holt,
      Rinehart and Winston, 1960.

      Contains part 2 of Dewey and Tuft's <u>Ethics</u>. Dewey almost
      obliterates the distinction between fact and value, between is
      and ought. In making moral choices we are guided by con-
      siderations that we express in statements of an ordinary
      empirical kind, statements that presuppose the agent's purposes
      but do not differ from empirical statements.

180. Dewey, John. ˙ <u>Theory of Valuation</u>. International Encyclopedia
      of Unified Science, Vol. 2, No. 4. Chicago: University of
      Chicago Press, 1966.

      Attempts to argue that questions of fact and questions of
      value are one and the same. The means-ends distinction in
      values is seen as inseparable. Both the end and the means
      interconnect in such a way as to be dependent on each other.

181. Diller, Ann L. "Rules and Moral Education." Ed.D. disserta-
      tion, Harvard University, 1971. 33/03, p. 1076.

      Considers what it means to follow, to formulate, and to
      acquire a moral rule and how the activities referred to by these
      concepts enter into moral education. R.S. Peters provides much
      of the framework of analysis used. For an action to be moral it
      must be based on reasons, and those reasons must be based in
      turn on moral rules.

182. Dworkin, Gerald, ed. <u>Determinism, Free Will and Moral Responsi-
      bility</u>. Englewood Cliffs, NJ: Prentice-Hall, 1970.

      A collection of papers exploring the meaning of, and
      interrelationships among, determinism, free will, and moral
      responsibility.

183. Ernst, Katherine. "A Comparison of John Dewey's Theory of
      Valuation and Abraham Maslow's Theory of Value." <u>Educational
      Theory</u>, 24 (1974): 130-141.

184. Falk, W.D. "Morality, Self and Others." <u>Morality and the
      Language of Conduct</u> (item 169), pp. 25-67.

      Analyzes different uses of the word "ought" in moral discourse
      and concludes that only the socially grounded ought is properly
      moral.

185. Fletcher,   Joseph.   Situation Ethics.   Philadelphia: The
     Westminster Press, 1966.

     Removes morality from a system of law and holds that only the
     ethic   of   love   is   relevant   to   deciding   one's   moral
     responsibilities.

186. Foot,   Philippa,   ed.   Theories of Ethics.   London: Oxford
     University Press, 1967.

     An excellent collection of 12 articles that examine from a
     variety   of   perspectives   the   naturalistic   fallacy   and
     utilitarianism.   The themes covered are the nature of moral
     judgment and the part played by social utility in determining
     right and wrong.

187. Frankena, William K.   "Ethical Theory."   Philosophy.   Edited by
     R.M. Chisholm et al.   Englewood Cliffs, NJ: Prentice-Hall,
     1964.

     Presents   an   overview   of   contemporary   ethical   theory.
     Discussed are intuitionism, ethical naturalism, pragmatic
     ethics, noncognitive theories, analytic approaches, religious
     ethics and existentialism, and normative ethics and social
     philosophy.

188. Frankena, William K.   Ethics.   2nd ed.   Englewood Cliffs, NJ:
     Prentice-Hall, 1974.

     The most concise, clear, and thorough introduction to ethical
     theory available.

189. Frankena, William K.   "Morality and Moral Philosophy."   Moral
     Education (item 171), pp. 19-29.

     This is a section of Frankena's Ethics.   In this section
     Frankena provides a clear framework for understanding the domain
     of moral philosophy.   Included are sections on the nature of
     moral philosophy, the nature of morality, factors in morality,
     and kinds of moral judgment.   Especially valuable is an outline
     of the kinds of normative judgment.

190. Frankena,   William   K.   "Recent   Conceptions   of   Morality."
     Morality and the Language of Conduct (item 169), pp. 1-24.

     Argues that there are three main conceptions of morality in
     recent philosophy.   Position A characterizes morality and the
     moral point of view in formal and individualistic terms, B in
     formal and social terms, and C in material and social terms.
     Arguments for and against each of the positions are analyzed.

191. Frey, R.G. "Moral Experts." The Personalist, 59 (1978): 47-52.

      Argues that moral expertise involves more than the capacity
      for critical inquiry into moral questions, the normative ethic
      of philosophers' judgment must be defensible.

192. Gert, B. The Moral Rules. New York: Harper and Row, 1966.

      Argues that rational man will want everyone else to obey rules
      prohibiting or causing specific evils to himself and those for
      whom he is concerned. To get other rational men to accept the
      rules he must advocate that the rules be obeyed by everyone
      including himself. The 10 rules that all rational men should
      accept are presented and explained.

193. Gibson, Rex. "In Defence of Ambiguity." Journal of Moral
      Education, 9 (1979): 17-22.

      Argues for the importance of ambiguity in language as an
      aspect of moral growth. The context, rather than the language,
      of social interaction is often the key to interpreting
      communication.

194. Gouinlock, James. "Dewey's Theory of Moral Deliberation."
      Ethics, 88 (1978): 216-228.

      Dewey's ethical theory is defended against attacks by White
      and Stevenson. Argues that Dewey has been misunderstood and
      that if anyone has a better solution to moral problems than
      social intelligence it should be presented.

195. Gouinlock, James. The Moral Writings of John Dewey. New York:
      Hofner Press, 1976.

      Presents a compilation of Dewey's writings on value and
      morality.

196. Green, Thomas F. The Activities of Teaching. New York:
      McGraw-Hill, 1971.

      Through an analysis of language Green tries to demonstrate
      that judgments of value are at least partially empirical or
      truth-functional in nature (pp. 173-192). The use of evaluative
      criteria is seen as especially important.

197. Guttchen, R.S. "On Ethical Judgment in Education." Educational
      Theory, 12 (1962): 65-72.

      Relates four basic questions of ethical theory to education.
      Formulates meanings of major ethical and educational terms.

198. Hampshire, Stuart. Thought and Action. New York: Viking Press, 1967.

Analyzes the relationships between thought and action. Holds that thought and action are distinctly separated, with thought seen as an introduction to action. Thought follows its own path without the will's intervention, governed by its own universal rules.

199. Hardwig, John R. "Autonomy and Rationality in Moral Decisions." Ph.D. dissertation, University of Texas at Austin, 1975. 36/02, p. 936.

Concludes that complete moral autonomy and complete moral rationality are incompatible. Both are essential to an adequate ethical theory, but a tension exists between them.

200. Hare, R.M. "Decisions of Principle." Moral Education (item 171), pp. 99-102.

In a section taken from The Language of Morals (see item 203) Hare argues for a purely formal conception of moral principles. The moral principle is a prescriptive statement that guides moral decision making. Moral education consists of educating people to choose and act on moral principles in general.

201. Hare, R.M. Freedom and Reason. New York: Oxford University Press, 1963.

Moral judgments are seen as having two important logical features: they are prescriptive and universalizable. Their function is to guide judgment, and when making a particular moral judgment one commits oneself to a moral rule governing all cases relevantly similar to the one he/she is judging. Moral judgments are therefore rational in that the judger is able to accept the universal prescription implicit in each.

202. Hare, R.M. "Language and Moral Education." New Essays in the Philosophy of Education (item 219), pp. 149-166.

Argues that there are two formal properties of moral language that must be understood if we are to make anything of the moral education of our successors. The implications of "prescriptivity" and "universalizability" for moral education are discussed. We need to get children committed to the formal character of language; if we do so there will be little need to worry about the content. A brief, neat summary of ideals presented at greater length in The Language of Morals (item 203) and Freedom and Reason (item 201). Also in The Domain of Moral Education (item 30).

203. Hare, R.M. The Language of Morals. New York: Oxford University
     Press, 1964.

     Stresses that moral judgments contain a prescriptive element.
     Presents a detailed analysis of the meaning of moral language
     and concludes that a moral judgment entails the imperative.

204. Hare, R.M. "A Rejoinder." The Domain of Moral Education (item
     30), pp. 115-119.

     Replies to Warnock (item 269) and defends his claim that
     universalizability and prescriptivity are crucial to moral
     language and have implications for moral education.

205. Harmon, Gilbert. "What Is Moral Relativism?" Values and
     Morals. Edited by A.I. Goldman and J. Kim. Dordrecht,
     Holland: D. Reidel Publishing Co., 1978, pp. 143-161.

     Proposes that there are three plausible versions of moral
     relativism: normative moral relativism, moral judgment
     relativism, and metaethical relativism. The first is a thesis
     about moral agents, the second a thesis about the form of
     meaning of moral judgments and the third a thesis about the
     truth conditions or justification of moral judgments.

206. Hook, Sidney, ed. Determinism and Freedom. New York: Collier
     Books, 1970.

     Contains readings on the issues of determinism and freedom.

207. Hook, Sidney. Education for Modern Man: A New Perspective.
     New York: Knopf, 1963, pp. 177-185.

     Argues that we ought to take a scientific approach to value
     judgments. This involves grasping the consequences of our value
     judgments, anticipating their effects on the original problem,
     and rating their bearing on other values to which we are
     implicitly committed.

208. Hudson, W.D., ed. The Is/Ought Question. London: Macmillan,
     1969.

     Contains papers on a topic of central interest to moral
     education: Can we derive ought statements about our moral
     obligations from purely factual considerations?

209. "Humanist Manifesto II." The Humanist, 33 (September/October
     1973): 4-9.

Sets forth a non-theistic, humanistic set of principles designed to provide guidance in an age of crises. The signers represent all disciplines and include many of the leading intellectuals of the 20th century. This document is frequently pointed to by religious critics of secular moral education as an indication that if moral education is not religious, it is atheistic.

210. Jackson, Jennifer. "Virtues with Reason." Philosophy, 53 (1978): 229-246.

Explores whether it is always reasonable to submit to moral restraints. Discusses also whether self-interest is always at the foundation of giving reasons for being moral. How these questions relate to the processes of childrearing and education is also discussed.

211. Joh, Jason N. "Respect for Persons." Theory into Practice, 14 (1975): 271-278.

Argues that respect for persons as a moral principle is not simply a vague moral sentiment, but provides more definite, though still general, procedural principles in teaching situations. It implies the recognition and acceptance of others as moral co-agents and sets out conditions governing rational thinking and moral and attitudinal considerations.

212. Jones, Clive. "The Contributions of Science to Moral Education." Journal of Moral Education, 5 (1976): 249-256.

Argues that there are significant connections between science and morality in the areas of logic, relevant knowledge, perspectives, and virtues of the will. These can be of value for moral education.

213. Jones, W.T., et.al., eds. Approaches to Ethics. New York: McGraw-Hill, 1962.

An extensive, topically arranged collection of readings on ethical theory.

214. Kant, Immanuel. Fundamental Principles of the Metaphysics of Morals. Many editions.

The principle of the "categorical imperative" is presented. One ought to act in a given way only if one is willing to make it a rule for all people to act in the same manner. The concept of duty is therefore rationally derived from the concept of a rational being.

215. Kleinberger, A. F. "The Social-Contract Strategy for the
     Justification of Moral Principles." Journal of Moral
     Education, 5 (1976): 107-126.

     Rawls' arguments in defense of his claim to derive principles
     of morality and justice from his hypothetical original position
     are critically examined and found unconvincing.

216. Koutsouvilis, A. "Universalism or Moral Skepticism." Journal
     of Moral Education, 2 (1972): 17-24.

     Two approaches to the understanding of the nature of moral
     judgment are discussed: R.M. Hare (universalism) and Socrates
     (moral skepticism). Argues that universalism is not a
     satisfactory and viable position.

217. Ladd, John. "The Issue of Relativism." The Monist, 47 (1963):
     585-609.

     Sets forth some of the major considerations involved in the
     question of whether or not cultural relativism of morals
     undermines morality itself. Argues that the facts of cultural
     relativity have a special relevance to practical activities that
     they do not have to theoretical knowledge (ethics) as such.

218. Lange, Deborah. "The Role of Rules and Justified Judgments in
     Moral Education." Philosophy of Education 1976 (item 1529),
     pp. 260-269.

     Shows how each different theory about the role of moral rules
     requires a different logic for the justification of moral
     judgments. Theories of justification and their attending logic
     are worthy of attention.

219. Langford, Glen, and D.J. Connor, eds. New Essays in the
     Philosophy of Education. London: Routledge and Kegan Paul,
     1973.

     Contains essays on topics related to moral education.

220. Mabbott, J.D. An Introduction to Ethics. Garden City, NY:
     Anchor Books, 1966.

     A brief, lucid introduction to ethics intended for the
     beginner. Each of the major contemporary theories of ethics is
     presented and followed by a critique.

221. McConnell, Terrance C. "Moral Dilemmas and Consistency in
     Ethics." Canadian Journal of Philosophy, 8 (1978): 269-287.

Explores the question whether an adequate ethical theory must
allow for genuine moral dilemmas or must rule out such cases in
order to avoid incoherence.   Concludes that an adequate moral
theory must rule out genuine dilemmas.

222. MacIntyre, Alasdair. After Virtue. South Bend, IN: University
      of Notre Dame Press, 1981.

      Argues that we are living through a new moral dark age. We
      lack moral resources and a living moral consensus rooted in the
      shared cultivation of virtues.   Virtues are defined as those
      dispositions which permit a person to function successfully in
      social settings. MacIntyre remains optimistic that we can again
      arrive at "a community united in a shared vision of the good for
      man."

223. MacIntyre,   Alasdair.   A Short History of Ethics.   London:
      Routledge and Kegan Paul, 1967.

      A sociological view of the history of ethical thinking from
      the Homeric age to the 20th century.

224. MacLagon, W.G. "Respect for Persons as a Moral Principle--I."
      Philosophy, 35 (1960): 193-217.

      Presents   a   scheme   of   affective-cognitive   development
      consisting of four stages: animal sympathy, passive sympathy,
      active sympathy, and agape (extending active sympathy to all
      persons).

225. MacLagon, W.G. "Respect for Persons as a Moral Principle--II."
      Philosophy, 35 (October 1960).

      Extends and elaborates upon arguments presented in item 224.

226. Mahon, Joseph.   "Responsibility, Moral Judgment and Moral
      Obligation." Journal of Moral Education, 1 (1972): 195-201.

      Examines and critiques the attitude that people, because they
      are products of their environments, may not be held responsible
      for what they do.

227. Mandelbaum, Maurice.   The Phenomenology of Moral Experience.
      Baltimore: Johns Hopkins Press, 1969.

      Argues that a phenomenological description of moral experience
      and judgment is essential if an adequate theory of ethics is to
      be developed.   Recent philosophy has been too linguistic in
      orientation. Any "contentual" standard is impossible. He
      presents a quasi-intuitionist position.

228. Midgley, Mary. "Is 'Moral' a Dirty Word?" _Philosophy_, 47
      (1972): 206-228.

      Argues that the central job done by the word "moral," the job
      for which it is worth preserving, is to mark a certain sort of
      seriousness and importance, as in the remark, "we can't just do
      what we fancy here; there is a moral question involved."
      Pinning the word "moral" to recognizing practices is a dead end.
      The main debate in ethics is between the people who stress the
      autonomy of morals and those who stress the continuity of morals
      with other topics. This paper represents an erudite, enter-
      taining, and illuminating attempt to find a dialectic.

229. Mill, John Stuart. _Utilitarianism_. Many editions.

      Presents the position that an act is right if and only if it
      tends to produce as much good as any other act might produce. A
      good act produces the greatest happiness for the greatest
      number.

230. Mitias, Michael H. "Dewey on Moral Obligation." _Southwestern
      Journal of Philosophy_, 7, 1 (1976): 75-82.

      Analyzes Dewey's concept of moral obligation. The focus is on
      two points: (1) for Dewey, the distinction between "is" and
      "ought" is a distinction between two basic types of experience,
      evaluative and descriptive; and (2) "ought" originates in the
      process of moral reflection, it is not a part of the facts of
      the situation.

231. Moore, G.E. "The Indefinability of Good." _Moral Education_
      item 171), pp. 63-71.

      In this section of his _Principia Ethica_ (item 232) Moore
      argues that the source of ethical objectivity lies in the
      intuitive sphere of human life. "Good" is a nonnatural,
      nonanalyzable, simple property of things that is perceived
      intuitively.

232. Moore, G.E. _Principia Ethica_. Oxford: Cambridge University
      Press, 1903.

      Attempts to distinguish those ethical judgments susceptible to
      proof by evidence from those that are not. Moore argues that it
      is fallacious to attempt to define good in terms of a natural
      object--the naturalistic fallacy. Good, like yellow, is held to
      be unanalyzable.

233. Morgenbesser, Sidney. "Approaches to Ethical Objectivity."
     <u>Moral Education</u> (item 171), pp. 72-79.

     Morgenbesser attacks all attempts to postulate a transcendent
     moral sphere. He argues that such efforts create unnecessary
     and nonexistent mechanisms or present inaccurate and simplistic
     pictures of the nature of reality. Objectivity in ethics
     results because similar people in similar situations hold
     similar moral views and attitudes--the voluntary sharing of
     attitudes among like-minded people.

234. Nakhnikian, George. "On the Naturalistic Fallacy." <u>Morality
     and the Language of Conduct</u> (item 169), pp. 145-158.

     Argues that although Moore's attack on naturalism does not
     show that naturalism is in principle impossible, it still
     contains six errors which ought to be avoided by all attempting
     to give a true account of moral discourse.

235. Nowell-Smith, Patrick H. <u>Ethics</u>. Baltimore: Penguin Books,
     1969.

     Argues that it is a mistake to assume that ethical words have
     only one function to perform. Presents a detailed description
     of the jobs, meanings, and implications of typical moral words
     in different contexts. Moral words sometimes assert what is
     true and false, but usually the primary job is something like
     praising or advising.

236. Perry, James F., and Phillip G. Smith. "Levels of Valuational
     Discourse in Education." <u>Philosophy of Education 1969</u>,
     Proceeding of the Twenty-fifth Annual Meeting, Philosophy of
     Education Society, 1969, pp. 105-112.

     Elucidates four levels of valuational discourse by showing
     distinctive features, interrelationships, and educational
     implications.

237. Perry, Thomas D. <u>Moral Reasoning and Truth</u>. Oxford: Clarendon
     Press, 1976.

     Takes aim at Hare's claim that prescriptivism and universalism
     are the key features of moral judgment (item 203). His view
     revolves around description of the existing standard of good
     moral reasoning and a "non-moral validation of that standard."

238. Peters, Richard S. "Concrete Principles and the Rational
     Passions." <u>Moral Education: Five Lectures</u> (item 1524), pp.
     28-55.

Peters discusses the role of concrete principles in morality
and moral education. He holds that concrete principles can
enter the moral life in a manner perfectly consistent with its
complexity and concreteness. Moral education must involve both
a commitment to what is worthwhile and possess depth and breadth
of understanding. Also in Psychology and Ethical Development
(item 311).

239. Peters, R.S.   Ethics and Education.   Glenview, IL: Scott,
      Foresman, 1966.

      Discusses the application of ethics and social philosophy to
      the problems of education. Presents a view of education as the
      transmission of worthwhile activities. The principle of justice
      is derived as the principal consideration in morality. It is
      seen as embedded in the matrix of moral language.

240. Peters, R.S. "Moral Principles and Moral Education." The
      Domain of Moral Education (item 30), pp. 120-134.

      An edited version of "Concrete Principles and the Rational
      Passions" (item 238).

241. Pincoffs, E. "Quandary Ethics." Mind, 80 (1971): 552-571.

      Argues that without compassion and commitment, the essence of
      life will remain a never ending quandary.

242. Prichard, H.A. "Does Moral Philosophy Rest on a Mistake?"
      Mind, 21 (1912): 21-37.

      Argues that it is a mistake to separate the formal (abstract)
      from the substantive (concrete) in ethics. What is obligatory
      is known only in specific situations where there are choices to
      be made.

243. Prichard, H.A. Moral Obligation: Essays and Lectures. London:
      Oxford University Press, 1949.

      Holds that when we say something is a duty we are reporting
      something that is self-evident and immediately apprehended. One
      discerns one's moral obligations through intuition.

244. Rawls, John A. A Theory of Justice. Cambridge, MA: Harvard
      University Press, 1971.

      Argues for the rationality of two principles of justice: "All
      social primary goods--liberty and opportunity, income and
      wealth, and the bases of self respect--are to be distributed
      equally unless an unequal distribution of any or all of these
      goods is to the advantage of the last favored" (p. 143).
      Contends that based on these principles rational men would

choose from the original position, ignorance with respect to one's position within the social matrix.

245. Rescher, Nicholas. <u>Introduction to Value Theory</u>. Englewood Cliffs, NJ: Prentice Hall, 1969.

   Presents a philosophical analysis of values as they are dealt with in everyday life. Questions of definition and the role of values in decision making and explaining behavior are discussed. Also included are chapters on evaluation and the logic of preference and the dynamics of value change. An extensive bibliography on the theory of value is appended.

246. Rich, John M. "Moral Education and the Emotions." <u>Journal of Moral Education</u>, 9 (1980): 81-87.

   Argues that the emotions should have a more central place in moral education than recent theorists have accorded them. Fear and guilt are used as examples to explain how emotions are learned. A developmental schema for education of morally relevant emotion is outlined.

247. Ross, W.D. <u>The Right and the Good</u>. Oxford: Clarendon Press, 1930.

   In a key section, posits a kind of compromise between extreme formalism and utilitarianism. Holds that certain kinds of situations create <u>prima facie</u> obligations that we ought to carry out unless there is a conflicting obligation.

248. Ryle, Gilbert. "On Forgetting the Difference Between Right and and Wrong." <u>Essays in Moral Philosophy</u>. Edited by A.I. Meldin. Seattle: University of Washington Press, 1958, pp. 147-159.

   Argues that moral virtue is not skill or expertness of any sort; rather it is in essence a matter of tastes, likings, preferences, and relishings. Knowledge of the difference between right and wrong includes an inculcated caring, a habit of taking certain sorts of things seriously.

249. Sartre, Jean-Paul. "Existentialism and Ethics." <u>Moral Education</u> (item 171), pp. 80-93.

   Sartre gives up completely on the search for an objective moral standard. The justification for an action is the fact of its being freely chosen and done. Society may judge such an action as "immoral," but it is supremely "moral," regardless of the outcome, if it is an expression of the agent's own choice and effort.

250. Scriven, Michael. Morality, Publication #122. Lafayette, IN:
     Social Science Education Consortium, Purdue University, 1966.

     Presents an ethical system based on the principle of equal
     consideration. Holds that morality is based on the long-term
     practical consequences of actions for the welfare of members of
     that society. What is in the interest of members of a society
     is seen as rationally determined.

251. Scriven,   Michael.   Value Claims in the Social Sciences,
     Publication #123. Lafayette, IN: Social Science Education
     Consortium, Purdue University, 1966.

     Outlines four types of value claims and concludes that value
     claims are not different from factual claims.

252. Sellars, W.S., and John Hospers, eds. Readings in Ethical
     Theory, 2nd ed. New York: Appleton-Century-Crofts, 1970.

     An excellent collection of papers on the major 20th-century
     philosophical questions concerning ethics.

253. Sichel, Betty A. "John Rawls' Theory of Moral Development."
     Philosophy of Education 1977 (item 1527), pp. 247-256.

     Analyzes and amplifies sections 70-75 of Rawls's A Theory of
     Justice (item 244). Argues that Rawls's stages have much
     greater merit than those of other developmentalists in that he
     provides a philosophic framework missing from other moral
     development theories. Rawl's stage theory, and the moralities
     of authority, of association, and of principles, are discussed.

254. Singer, Marcus G. Generalization in Ethics. New York:
     Atheneum, 1971.

     Attempts to determine the basis of morality and to resolve the
     problem of the justification of moral principles. The criteria
     of the right are seen to derive from the generalizability
     inherent in any such principle. Also central to Singer's
     argument are the principles of consequences, of the categorical
     imperative, of justification and of correlated moral principles.

255. Singer, Marcus G. "Moral Rules and Principles." Moral
     Education (item 171), pp. 103-111.

     Singer focuses on the formal aspects of moral principles, that
     is, on the nature and function (rather than content) of
     principles in moral life and education. He argues that there
     are, in spite of apparent diversity, universalizable moral prin-
     ciples at the core of all moral life.

256. Singer, Peter. "Moral Experts." *Analysis*, 32 (1972): 116-117.

Argues that philosophers are moral experts by virtue of their advanced knowledge and skill relative to critical inquiry into questions of morality.

257. Smart, J.J.C., and Bernard Williams. *Utilitarianism: For and Against*. New York: Cambridge University Press, 1973.

Smart presents an outline of utilitarian ethics, and Williams offers a critique.

258. Soltis, Jonas F. "Men, Machines and Morality." *Moral Education* (item 171), pp. 30-38.

The objective of this paper is to analyze the meaning of morality by focusing on common language usages of the term "morality." He argues that the very language used to talk about morality is a key to the basic clarification of what is to be included and excluded from the moral sphere.

259. Stevenson, Charles L. *Ethics and Language*. New Haven: Yale University Press, 1944.

Insists that the central function of ethics is not so much to express emotions as to influence other people. At bottom, ethical judgments rest on subjective feelings and attitudes.

260. Sullivan, Roger J. *Morality and the Good Life: A Commentary on Aristotle's Nicomachean Ethics*. Memphis, TN: Memphis State University Press, 1977.

A clear, readable introductory interpretation of and commentary on the *Nichomachean Ethics*. A useful guide to understanding the ethical theory of Aristotle.

261. Taylor, P.W. *Normative Discourse*. Englewood Cliffs, NJ: Prentice-Hall, 1961.

Identifies four general phases in the enterprise of justifying value judgments: verification, validation, vindication, and rational choice. The first consists of checking to see if the choice conforms to an acceptable, more general rule or standard. The other steps involve ensuring logical consistency to general conceptions of a way of life (a hierarchy of value systems).

262. Tomlinson, Thomas S. "The Use of Principles in Moral Reasoning." Ph.D. dissertation, Michigan State University, 1980. 41/07, p. 3143.

Argues that the application of moral concepts requires the use of moral judgments, but this process is not clarified by the appeal to principle. Instead, the appeal should be to the indefinite body of particular moral convictions that underlie our understanding of principles.

263. Toulmin, Stephen. The Place of Reason in Ethics. Cambridge, England: Cambridge University Press, 1970.

Following an evaluation of three traditional theories of ethics--imperative, objective, and subjective--Toulmin concludes that all are lacking. The central questions for him are: How is one to decide which ethical arguments are to be accepted? What kinds of reasons for moral decisions constitute good reasons? What is needed, according to Toulmin is a descriptive account of ethical concepts; it is from this that we will gain our understanding of what constitutes "good reasons." The book is lucidly written and abounds with useful insights.

264. Trianosky-Stillwell, Gregory. "Should We Be Good? The Place of Virtue in Our Morality?" Ph.D. dissertation, University of Michigan, 1980. 41/01, p. 287.

Argues that the concept of virtue is at the core of right action. A call for a new concept of virtue--spiritual virtue--is issued. Spiritual virtue is seen as that which harmonizes the components of our inner life.

265. Ungoed-Thomas, J.R. "Conditions for Dialogue in Moral Education Between Teachers and Educational Philosophers." Progress and Problems in Moral Education (item 1530), pp. 77-92.

Argues that for effective curricular planning to occur in moral education there must be a constructive dialogue between philosopher and teacher. If educational philosophers wish to establish dialogue with teachers the conditions are: first, that their philosophies clearly define their functions; second, that they reveal operational realism; and third, that they display understanding of the logic of scientific research.

266. Veath, Henry B. Rational Man: A Modern Interpretation of Aristotelian Ethics. Bloomington, Indiana University Press, 1970.

Contains an insightful analysis of Aristotelian thought which reaffirms the primacy of practical reason and moral virtues in the moral life.

267. Waddington, C.H. The Ethical Animal. Chicago: University of Chicago Press, 1967.

Attempts to establish a framework within which ethical beliefs can be evaluated and criticized. Holds that human evaluation depends on the transmission of information from one generation to the next and that this is possible only if the young child is ready to accept this information from authority. The world of living things reveals a general evolutionary direction similar to healthy growth. Any ethical beliefs advanced can be meaningfully judged according to their efficacy in furthering this generally evolutionary direction.

268. Wallace, G., and A.D.M. Walker, eds. The Definition of Morality. London: Methuen, 1970.

A collection of papers that exemplify the topics and treatment characteristic of contemporary moral philosophy.

269. Warnock, G.J. "Morality and Language: A Reply to R.M. Hare." The Domain of Moral Education (item 30), pp. 107-114.

A reply to Hare (item 204), arguing that prescriptivity and universalizability are not only not unique to moral language but are also not of great importance in moral language and moral education.

270. Warnock, Mary. Ethics Since 1900. 3rd ed. Oxford: Oxford University Press, 1978.

A brief but thorough overview of 20th-century ethical theory. A very readable book with chapters on G.E. Moore, intuitionism, the emotive theory, moral psychology, and existentialism.

271. Westermark, Edward. Ethical Relativity. New York: Harcourt, Brace, 1932.

Argues that values are moral emotions that indicate only approval or disapproval. Morality, therefore, is relative, and moral principles have no objective validity.

272. Wilson, John. "Understanding Reasons." Journal of Moral Education, 9 (1980): 110-113.

Examines the question of what it is to understand and use a reason. Argues that this is chiefly a matter of knowing a rule and its application. Stages of moral reasoning may be backgrounds which encourage certain preferences for this or that type of reason.

The Nature of Moral Character and the
Morally Educated Person

273. Attfield, David G. "Motivation in Moral Education: The Case for Virtue." Journal of Moral Education, 7 (1978): 158-165.

274. Attfield, David G. "Problems with Virtues." Journal of Moral Education, 7 (1978): 75-80.

   Four problems in the teaching of virtues are discussed: (1) determining which virtues to teach; (2) indoctrination; (3) problems with single-track and multitrack virtues; and (4) virtues and the guidance of action. Concludes that the problems are not insurmountable.

275. Bertocci, Peter A. "A Personalistic Philosophy of Education." Education and Values (item 1525), pp. 87-110.

   Argues that as individuals reason about the relations among values, they discover a mutually supportive patterning among those values that discourages fruitless conflict. The ideal personality orchestrates the value-experiences of life, he does not scale them.

276. Beversluis, Eric. "Moral Education as Education in Practical Reasoning." Philosophy of Education 1976 (item 1529), pp. 270-276.

   Attempts to explain the nature of practical reasoning and show that the moral person is the one who deliberates in accordance with the canons of practical reason and who acts in accordance with the results of such deliberation.

277. Brent, Allen. "Can Wilson's Moral Criteria Be Justified?" Journal of Moral Education, 2 (1973): 203-210.

   Argues that Wilson's list of moral components is unsound because it conflates two conflicting systems of ethical justification (prudential and utilitarian) in an illegitimate way.

278. Burch, Robert W. "Are There Moral Experts?" The Monist, 58 (1974): 646-658.

   Considers a variety of arguments against the claim for the existence of moral experts. Argues that all these arguments fail, but does not discuss in detail what the attributes of moral experts are.

279. Coombs, Jerrold R. "Attainments of the Morally Educated
     Person." Development of Moral Reasoning (item 1495), pp.
     14-29.

     Discusses those features of rational moral judgment that he
     sees as the desirable focus of moral education. Coombs then
     lists 11 attainments required of morally educated persons.
     These attainments relate to capacities necessary to reason about
     moral questions and to act morally: knowledge must be acquired,
     abilities, inclinations, sensitivities, and commitments formed,
     and emotions and imagination developed.

280. Coombs, Jerrold R. "Concerning the Nature of Moral Competence."
     The Teaching of Values in Canadian Education (item 1503), pp.
     7-20.

     Reviews various views on the nature of moral judgment in order
     to construct a justified view of the nature and aims of moral
     education. The position taken is that the task of moral
     education is to teach persons to make and act upon rational
     moral decisions. Wilson's components of moral competence
     receive careful attention, but Coombs concludes that his view is
     too narrow. Argues that we must have a defensible view of the
     nature of rational morality before we teach it, but no clear
     picture emerges from his analysis.

281. Crawford, A.B. "Teleological Principles and the Congruence of
     Obligation and Motivation: Its Implication for Moral
     Education." Educational Theory, 20 (1970): 40-43.

     Argues that in a teleological theory of obligation, the
     recognition or belief that one is obligated to do something is
     capable of moving one to comply with that obligation. The
     implications for moral education of this view, as opposed to a
     deontological view, are discussed.

282. Daniels, L.B., and S. Parkinson. "Role X'ing and Moral
     Education--Some Conceptual Speculations." Educational Theory,
     26 (1976): 329-336.

     Analyzes various meanings of role exchange ability with a view
     to becoming clearer about the nature of moral education.

283. DeLue, Steven M. "Aristotle, Kant and Rawls on Moral Motivation
     in a Just Society." American Political Science Review, 74
     (1980): 385-393.

     Argues that Rawls's position can best be seen as synthesizing
     aspects of Aristotle and Kant and providing a motive source for
     acting upon known just standards of conduct.

284. Dunlop, Francis. "Form, Content and Rationality in Morality and
      Moral Education." Proceedings of the Philosophy of Education
      Society of Great Britain, 11 (1977): 78-97.

      Critiques Wilson's theory of rational morality on the grounds
      that Wilson ultimately tends to undermine morality by his focus
      on means rather than submission to the moral law.

285. Dunlop, Francis. "Moral Procedures and Moral Education." The
      Domain of Moral Education (item 30), pp. 169-177.

      Questions John Wilson's position that it is only legitimate to
      transmit procedures for moral thinking. Argues that moral
      "content" is logically prior to procedures and methods.

286. Ferrett, Robert T. "Moral Conduct of Middle School Students:
      Evidence for a Multifactor Model." Ph.D. dissertation,
      University of California at Riverside, 1978. 39/02, p. 639.

      Proposes a comprehensive 14-factor model of moral behavior
      which serves as an appropriate rationale for moral/citizenship
      education. A preliminary validation effort was undertaken with
      moral reasoning proving to be a significant factor.

287. Fingarette, Herbert. On Responsibility. New York: Basic Books,
      1967.

      A person is not responsible for what he or she does until s/he
      shows signs of genuine acceptance of responsibility. Since
      psychopaths lack the kind of understanding (as caring) essential
      for moral agency they do not share with others the relevant
      "form of life." Moral education cannot take place without moral
      concern.

288. Fraenkel, Jack R. "The Relationship Between Moral Thought and
      Moral Action: Implications for Social Studies Education."
      Theory and Research in Social Education, 9 (1981): 39-54.

      Argues that although the level of moral reasoning may relate
      to the likelihood of moral behavior's occurring, moral reasoning
      is only one of many factors that may affect when and where moral
      behavior will occur.

289. Gardner, Peter. "On Some Paradoxes in Moral Education."
      Journal of Philosophy of Education, 15 (1981): 65-76.

Analyzes R.S. Peters' formulation of the conflict between the need to develop moral habits in children and the need at the same time to foster rationality. Argues that Peters and Aristotle have different views on the issue and that Peters' formulation raises many other questions. Holds that Peters' resolution of the paradox does not deal adequately with the many issues raised by his formulation.

290. Gouthier, David P. "Moral Action and Moral Education." Moral Education: Interdisciplinary Approaches (item 1492), pp. 138-146.

There are three clearly distinguishable aspects of conscious moral behavior: (1) the acquisition of dispositions to action, (2) the conceptualization of a policy of action, and (3) moral awareness--learning to bring moral sensitivity to bear on all those areas affected by our activities.

291. Hamm, C. "The Content of Moral Education, or In Defense of the Bag of Virtues." School Review, 85 (1977): 219-229.

Demonstrates how important content is in moral education and presents examples of such content with which all can surely agree. Also in The Teaching of Values in Canadian Education (item 1503), pp. 37-46.

292. Hamm, C. "The Role of Habit in Moral Education." Educational Theory, 25 (1975): 417-428.

Analyzes Peters' (item 310) paradox of moral education and concludes that there is no paradox, i.e., reason and habit are logically unrelated and operate on different planes.

293. Hare, William. "Education and Character Development." Journal of Moral Education, 2 (1973): 115-120.

Argues that character assessment and moral assessment need not involve each other. Of the two, character is the much broader concept. Habit training is neither a necessary nor a sufficient condition of character development.

294. Hemming, James. "Another Prospect on Moral Education." Journal of Moral Education, 9 (1980): 75-80.

Argues against Wilson that moral education is more a context of social experience than a list of items to be worked over. Makes suggestions for a broader contextual approach to moral education.

295. Jackson, Michael. "Appreciation: A Suggestion about Teaching Religion and Values." The Teaching of Values in Canadian Education (item 1503), pp. 55-61.

Elucidates the educationally relevant features of the concept of appreciation and shows why that concept is suitable for expressing the goals of the teaching of values. Appreciation is seen as an intellectual achievement in which a variety of considerations must be balanced.

296. Jarrett, James L. "What Passes for Moral?" Philosophy of Education 1978 (item 1499), pp. 244-253.

Argues that human beings respond to the world in certain characteristic ways. In line with Jung's point of view most people are essentially what might be called non-intellectual in their approach to life. Moral philosophy, however, has been dominated by intellectual types. Sensory and intuitive types also have ethical values. The highest value is, according to Jarrett and Jung, self-actualization.

297. Jones, Reynold. "An Aspect of Moral Education." Journal of Philosophy of Education, 14 (1980): 63-71.

Reviews the moral problem of weakness of will (akrasia) and agrees that objectivity, if taught in schools, will strengthen the will and people will become better able to do what they feel is right.

298. Kazepides, Tasos. "The Alleged Paradox of Moral Education." The Domain of Moral Education (item 30), pp. 155-166.

Attempts to play down the paradox of moral education as described by R.S. Peters (item 310) that non-rational habituation must be used in the moral education of young children when the ultimate goal of moral education is the development of autonomous moral agents. Uses Aristotle extensively to show that paradox is not as sharply drawn as Peters would have us believe.

299. Kazepides, Arastasios. "A Philosophical Analysis of the Concept of Habit and Its Place in Moral Education." Ed.D. dissertation, Temple University, 1966. 28/03, p. 1003.

Attempts to resolve the habit-reason paradox in Aristotle and shows the relevance of different senses of 'habit' to the different problems of moral education.

300. Kennedy, Dale. "R.S. Peters' Concept of Character and the Criterion of Consistency for Actions." Educational Theory, 25 (1975): 54-64.

Argues contra Peters that most of the time the idea of
conformity is not appropriate in discussion of an individual's
regulation of his own conduct. Argues instead that the proper
focus of moral education is to ensure consistency of action with
respect to knowledge of good and evil.

301. Knitter, William C. "Reason and Action as Related to
     Character." Ph.D. dissertation, University of Chicago, 1980.
     41/07, p. 2991.

     Examines Hume's, Dewey's, and Sartre's views on the relation
     of reason to character. Shows how all see the use of reason as
     embedded within a set of factors organized by the concept of
     character.

302. Lee, Don. "Toward a Methodological Theory of Moral Education."
     Ph.D. dissertation, Wayne State University, 1974. 35/07, p.
     4050.

     Attempts to develop a comprehensive theory of moral education
     by focusing on the integration of thought and action through
     habit.

303. Loukes, Harold. "What Is Moral Education?" Let's Teach Them
     Right (item 424), pp. 111-122.

     Argues that with the current moral confusion in society what
     is needed is a conception of the morally educated man as
     distinct from the morally trained man. Wilson's moral
     components (item 324) are offered as an acceptable set of
     criteria for the morally educated man.

304. Melden, A.I. "Moral Education and Moral Action." Moral
     Education: Interdisciplinary Approaches (item 1492), pp.
     115-137.

     Places a great deal of emphasis on the role of understanding
     in truly moral behavior. Draws a distinction between moral
     training (involving conditioning in the young child) and moral
     education.

305. Miller, Peter. "Who Are the Moral Experts?" Journal of Moral
     Education, 5 (1975): 3-12.

     An analysis of moral expertise, both cognitive and know-how,
     is presented. It is concluded that one has achieved relative
     moral expertise when one does some things well to some benefit
     to some others as well as oneself while leading a relatively
     non-destructive life.

306. Mills, Ian. "Moral Decision-Making, Religious Reinforcement and
      Some Educational Implications." Journal of Moral Education, 6
      (1977): 162-169.

      Examines the concept of akrasia (weakness of the will) and
      moral educations failure to address this problem adequately.
      Argues the reinforcement for doing what is right must be
      provided. This is best accomplished by teachers who themselves
      take morality seriously.

307. O'Leary, P.T. "Moral Education, Moral Character, and the
      Virtues." Journal of Educational Thought, 15(1981): 41-46.

      Argues that moral virtues and judgment are indispensable to
      each another and to the development of moral character.
      Self-control is a virtue and essential to judgment. The desire
      to do the impulsive must be overcome before one can behave
      rationally.

308. Pahel, Kenneth. "Moral Motivation." The Domain of Moral
      Education (item 30), pp. 135-144.

      Contends that moral growth involves a gradual development of
      moral understanding; moral maturity involves the gradual
      acquisition of a number of feeling dispositions; and there ought
      to be a kind of harmony or fit between moral understanding or
      reasoning on the one hand and the feeling dispositions on the
      other. For moral education to have an impact on behavior the
      program must give equal stress to both moral reasoning and to
      opportunities for relevant emotive and evaluative experience.
      Also in Journal of Moral Education, 5 (1976): 223-230.

309. Peters, R.S. "Form and Content in Moral Education."
      Adolescents' Development and Education (item 1512), pp.
      96-102.

      Argues that although Kohlberg says nothing about the learning
      of the content of morality, this is an important dimension of
      moralization. Argues that social learning theory, even though
      it smacks of authoritarianism, is the only possibility for
      explaining the early internalization of moral character. Also
      in The Monist, 58 (1974); Psychology and Ethical Development
      (item 311); and The Domain of Moral Education (item 30).

310. Peters, R.S. "Reason and Habit: The Paradox of Moral
      Education." Moral Education in a Changing Society (item
      1515), pp. 46-65.

The paradox of moral education is that while it is desirable to develop people who conduct themselves rationally and intelligently, the brute facts of child development reveal that at the most formative years of a child's development he is incapable of this form of life and impervious to the proper manner of passing it on. Children can and must enter the palace of Reason through the courtyard of Habit and Tradition. Discusses the necessity of habit in moral life and argues that there is no necessary contradiction between habit and the use of intelligence in moral life. Also in Psychology and Ethical Development (item 311).

311. Peters, R.S., ed. Psychology and Ethical Development. London: George Allen and Unwin, 1974.

A collection of papers by R.S. Peters. Contains seven papers, all published elsewhere, on the nature of ethical development.

312. Plato. The Meno. Many editions.

How is virtue acquired? Begins by considering what virtue is. Argues that virtue is never really taught. Virtues of great men are merely right opinions granted as the capricious gifts of the gods.

313. Pritchard, Michael S. "Responsibility, Understanding, and Psychopathology." The Monist, 58 (1974): 630-645.

Argues that becoming a moral agent involves more than knowledge of morality or the ability to reason about moral questions. It has as its essential ingredient accepting a "form of life," that is, caring about morality.

314. Pugh, George E. "Behavioral Science and the Teaching of Human Values." International Review of Education, 26 (1980): 103-120.

Presents a brief overview of the findings of sociobiology and ethology and interprets these findings in such a way as to illustrate their compatibility with commonsense ethical concepts. Argues that behavioral science is not in conflict with the foundations of ethics; specifically, it does not conflict with the ideal of free will.

315. Rawls, John. "Towards the Cultivation of Moral Sentiments." The Domain of Moral Education (item 30), pp. 145-154.

Moral attitudes involve the acceptance of specific moral virtues, and the principles which define these virtues are used to account for the corresponding feelings. Moral attitudes appeal ultimately to sound principles of justice and right. This essay is taken from A Theory of Justice (item 244), section 73.

316. Reddiford, G. "Moral Imagining and Children." Journal of Moral Education, 10 (1981): 75-84.

Imagining is defined as putting to one side one's own descriptions of the world in order to understand a situation in terms of another person. It is seen as a necessary condition of acting from a moral point of view. The conditions of learning to be imaginative are discussed, as are the relations of moral imagining to sympathy, compassion, and concern.

317. Rich, John M. "Ryle and the Teaching of Virtue." Philosophy of Education 1977 (item 1527), pp. 324-332.

Argues that virtue is best understood in terms of excuses and excuse making. The reason people find it difficult to lead a moral life can be observed in the grounds offered in self-exoneration. The excuse making of three types of persons is examined. Argues that virtue can be taught easily only to certain types of individuals. The need for a differential approach to moral education depending upon the excuses given by different individuals is discussed.

318. Roth, John K. "A Portrait of the Morally Educated Person: Some Sketchbook Impressions." Counseling and Values. 25 (1980): 9-39.

Through an analysis of the lives and thoughts of M.L. King, Albert Camus, and Elie Wiesel, Roth concludes that the morally educated person is the one who recognizes, supports, emulates, and extends the good in others.

319. Ryle, G. "Can Virtue Be Taught?" Education and the Development of Reason. Edited by R.F. Dearden, P.H. Hirst, and R.S. Peters. London: Routledge, Kegan Paul, 1972, pp. 434-447.

After discussing and rejecting Plato's and Aristotle's views on the question (can virtue be taught?), Ryle argues that learning a virtue means coming to treat certain things (e.g., honesty, compassion for others) as of overwhelming importance. Virtue is hence more a function of one's heart than one's head.

320. Schulte, John M., and Stanton M. Teal. "The Moral Person." Theory into Practice, 14 (1975): 224-235.

Presents an argument regarding the goals of moral education,
that is, what is required of a person to be moral. Argues that
a person must both understand the nature of his/her actions and
have been able to act otherwise. The nature of moral principles
is also discussed . The implications for educational practice
of the authors' viewpoint is presented.

321. Schwartz, Adina.   "Aristotle   on   Education   and   Choice."
     Educational Theory, 29 (1979): 97-107.

     Seeks to understand the relations between Aristotle's view
     that persons can be virtuous only if they choose to do virtuous
     acts and his claim that individuals must be cultivated by means
     of habits. Holds that there is no conflict; however, there are
     limits on the creativity of the ideal choosing agent. The man
     of practical wisdom creates a life that exemplifies an ideal.

322. Stevenson, Leslie.   Seven Theories of Human Nature.   Oxford:
     Clarendon Press, 1974.

     Presents seven theories of human nature. Included are the
     views of Plato, Christianity, Marx, Freud, Sartre, Skinner, and
     Lorenz.

323. Suttle, Bruce B.   "Moral Education and Incontinence: An
     Attempted Defense of the Socratic Dictum That One Cannot
     Knowingly Do That Which Is Wrong."   Ph.D. dissertation,
     University of Illinois, 1980. 41/12, p. 5022.

     Argues that cases of moral incontinence are not instances of
     psychological weakness but rather involve questions dealing with
     what it means to act obligatorily.

324. Wilson, John.   "Assessing the 'Morally Educated' Person."
     Moral Education (item 171), pp. 125-130.

     Wilson presents a comprehensive list of cognitive, affective,
     and behavioral components, which, taken together, define the
     nature of the moral person. These components in turn define the
     objectives and contents of moral education programs. The focus
     is on thoughts, motivations, and feelings rather than on
     behavior.

325. Wilson, John.   "Moral Components and Moral Education: A Reply to
     Francis Dunlop." The Domain of Moral Education (item 30), pp.
     178-186.

     Discusses Dunlop's (item 285) misunderstanding of his position
     and urges that moral educators get on with the job and not be
     sidetracked by such controversy.

326. Wilson, John. "Motivation and Morality." Journal of Moral
     Education, 2 (1972): 25-29.

     Argues that behavioral conceptions of motivation are too
     prevalent in the field of moral behavior. Researchers need to
     begin to realize the importance of reasons in guiding behavior.

327. Wilson, John. "Rationality and Moral Education." Proceedings
     of the Philosophy of Education Society of Great Britain, 11
     (1977): 98-112.

     Replies to Dunlop's criticism that he focuses only on means to
     the exclusion of the moral law. Argues that there is a moral
     content, but that it is a rational content and only through
     following the methods of moral reasoning will one end up with
     moral actions.

328. Woods, John, and Douglas Walton. "Moral Expertise." Journal
     of Moral Education, 5 (1975): 13-18.

     An expert is defined as one who predicts or explains better
     than the layman. This definition is then applied to the moral
     domain. Argues that moral philosophers neglect moral
     argumentation about specific moral issues: it is at this contact
     point with reality that the possibility of moral expertise lies.

329. Wright, Derek. "Motivation and Morality: A Response to John
     Wilson." Journal of Moral Education, 2 (1972): 31-34.

     Argues that the antithesis between reason and cause is not as
     sharp among experimental psychologists as John Wilson supposes.
     What is needed is an understanding of the conditions which
     facilitate the integration of reason and action.

Questions Regarding Indoctrination and Neutrality

330. Atkinson, R.F. "Instruction and Indoctrination." Philosophical Analysis and Education. Edited by R.D. Archambault. New York: The Humanities Press, 1965, pp. 171-183.

Defines the contrasting teaching contexts in which instruction and indoctrination take place. The recognition of the conflict between manner (how we should teach) and moral imperatives (what we should teach) and the search for ways of containing and accommodating it in a rational fashion are the concerns of the moral educator. Also in Concepts of Indoctrination (item 367).

331. Bailey, Charles. "Rationality, Democracy and the Neutral Teacher." Cambridge Journal of Education, 2 (1971): 68-76.

Argues that the practice of teacher neutrality, set up in the name of rationality, may in fact lead to the protection of irrationalities.

332. Benson, Thomas L. "The Forms of Indoctrinary Method." Philosophy of Education 1977 (item 1527), pp. 333-334.

Argues that there are two forms of indoctrinary method: one in which information is presented in a biased manner and one in which the individual is denied the opportunity to withhold assent from what is presented. Both methods are analyzed.

333. Bricker, David C. "Moral Education and Teacher Neutrality." School Review, 80 (1972): 619-627.

Argues that teachers should not remain affectively neutral in their presentation of moral dilemmas in class. Teachers should be a model of the affective concern necessary in order for serious morality to occur.

334. Casement, William R. "Indoctrination and Contemporary Approaches to Moral Education." Ph.D. dissertation, Georgetown University, 1980. 42/02, p. 734.

After defining indoctrination, this study concludes that values clarification successfully avoids it while the cognitive-developmental approach may well result in indoctrination.

335. Counts, George S. "Should the Teacher Be Neutral?" Phi Delta Kappan, 51 (1969): 186-189.

In a response to Junnell (item 352), Counts argues that the question is not whether or not schools should impose values on children, but rather what values should they impose? The answer for Counts is the basic American ideals of freedom, justice, and equal opportunity.

336. Crittenden, B.S. "Neutrality in Education." Educational Philosophy and Theory, 12 (June 1980), pp. 1-18.

Discusses the issue of neutrality from the perspective of Freire, who holds that education can never be neutral, and if it attempts to be so it is in fact oppressive. Crittenden argues that the all-or-nothing position on neutrality overstates the case and that a partial neutrality is possible and desirable.

337. Crittenden, Brian S. "Teaching, Educating and Indoctrinating." Educational Theory, 18 (1968): 237-52.

The relationship of the concept of indoctrination to political and religious beliefs as well as to the concepts of teaching and educating is discussed. Argues that whether an action is indoctrination or not depends on both what is taught and the pedagogical procedures used. The intentions of the teacher are not a significant indicator of indoctrination. A teacher or parent can be mis-educating regardless of his/her intentions. Also published as "Indoctrination as Mis-education" in Concepts of Indoctrination (item 367).

338. Davey, A.G. "Education or Indoctrination." Journal of Moral Education, 2 (1972): 5-15.

Argues that the only acceptable means by which to differentiate between education and indoctrination is empirical criteria. The author then cites evidence that many people who have been educated behave similarly to those who have been indoctrinated. Argues that teachers need to look more closely at their relationships with students when they are educating them.

339. Dusoir, Celia. "Neutrality in School." Progress and Problems in Moral Education (item 1530), pp. 134-140.

Replies to Wilson (item 381), Warncock (item 374), and Stenhouse (item 370).

340. Eckstein, J. "Is It Possible for the Schools to Be Neutral?" Educational Theory, 19 (1969): 337-346.

In a critique of Ennis (item 342) attempts to show that it is possible for the schools, both ontologically and ethically, to be neutral.

341. Elliott, John. "The Concept of the Neutral Teacher." Cambridge
      Journal of Education, 2 (1971): 60-67.

      Argues that for teachers to remain neutral and not state their
      opinion can have many potentially harmful educational effects.

342. Ennis, R.H. "The 'Impossibility' of Neutrality." Harvard
      Educational Review, 29 (1959), pp. 128-136.

      Argues that the dispute about neutrality is essentially a
      verbal dispute. An interpretation does not presuppose intent is
      presented, for if neutrality is based on intent alone, schools
      can be neutral. The real question, according to Ennis, is what
      stand, if any, the schools should take on social questions.

343. Ennis, R.H. "The Possibility of Neutrality." Educational
      Theory, 19 (1969): 347-356.

      Comments on Eckstein's critique (item 340) of his original
      article on neutrality (item 342).

344. Ennis, Robert H. "Reply to Mary Anne Raywid." Studies in
      Philosophy and Education, 2 (1962): 96-103.

      Ennis defends himself against Raywid's attack (item 361) and
      restates his analysis of the issue of neutrality (item 342).

345. Flew, Anthony. "What Is Indoctrination?" Studies in Philosophy
      and Education, 4 (1966): 281-306.

      Summarizes the views of Wilson (item 379) and Hare (item 58)
      and then subjects their ideals to criticism. Objects to
      Wilson's view of content as the criterion of indoctrination.
      Both aim and content must be accounted for in any adequate
      analysis of indoctrination. He concludes by distinguishing
      between primary and secondary senses of the concept of
      indoctrination. Also published as "Indoctrination and
      Doctrines" in Concepts of Indoctrination (item 367).

346. Flew, Anthony. "'What Is Indoctrination?' Comments on Moore
      and Wilson." Studies in Philosophy and Education, 5 (1967):
      273-283.

      Flew discusses papers by Moore (item 359) and Wilson (item
      378) who in turn were reacting to a paper by Flew (item 345).
      Flew disagrees with Moore on the centrality of method and argues
      that whatever the method, distinctions of content are essential.
      He disagrees with Wilson in arguing that all religions
      indoctrinate. Published as "Indoctrination and Religion" in
      Concepts of Indoctrination (item 367).

347. Gatchel, Richard H. "The Evaluation of the Concept." Concepts
      of Indoctrination (item 367), pp. 9-16.

      Demonstrates how the concept of indoctrination has evolved
      over the years and has only lately acquired the pejorative
      connotation that most writers now assume it has. He regards
      indoctrination as essentially a method of teaching. Originally
      appeared as "Evolution of Concepts of Indoctrination in American
      Education." Educational Forum, 23 (1959).

348. Green, Thomas F. "Indoctrination and Beliefs." Concepts of
      Indoctrination (item 367), pp. 25-46.

      Suggests that beliefs can be held "evidentially" or
      'nonevidentially' and the manner in which one holds one's
      beliefs is the distinguishing characteristic of indoctrination.
      Argues that the only beliefs which must be rejected are those
      which prevent us from being open to reasons and evidence.
      Originally appeared as "A Topology of the Teaching Concept."
      Studies in Philosophy and Education, 3 (1964): 284-319.

349. Gregory, I.M., and R.G. Woods. "Indoctrination: Inculcating
      Doctrines." Concepts of Indoctrination (item 367), pp.
      162-189.

      In a critique of White (item 376) they argue that
      indoctrination is intimately bound up with doctrines. It is the
      inculcation of doctrines.

350. Hall, Robert. "Indoctrination Revisited." The Humanist, 38
      (November/December 1978): 23-25.

      Suggests that there are three ways in which the absolute
      freedom (relativism) in moral education may be justifiably
      qualified without becoming indoctrinative: (1) moral education
      should teach rational thought; (2) there must be certain values
      built into any school; (3) there must be positive but critical
      promotion of those values on which there is wide social
      agreement.

351. Hoffman, D.C. "The Schools and Neutrality: In Response to
      Professor Robert H. Ennis." Educational Theory, 14 (1964):
      182-185.

      Argues that the effort of schools can be like that of a
      referee in a basketball game--they can be neutral (non-position)
      but we cannot say they are neutral (without effect). This is
      the role Dewey had in mind when he talked about the possibility
      of schools' being neutral but having social consequence.

352. Junnell, Joseph S. "Do Teachers Have the 'Right' to
      Indoctrinate?" Phi Delta Kappan, 51 (1969): 182-185.

Argues that teachers inevitably must load the dice in favor of the values society wishes to perpetuate. The many problems involved in this view are discussed.

353. Kilpatrick, William H. "Indoctrination and Respect for Persons." Concepts of Indoctrination (item 367), pp. 47-54.

Argues that indoctrination means the implanting of doctrines that are to be held uncritically. It is the parents intention that determines whether or not s/he is indoctrinating. If s/he intends to make the child critical of most standards as soon as possible, then s/he is not indoctrinating. This is an excerpt from Kilpatrick's Philosophy of Education (New York: Macmillan, 1951).

354. Kleinig, John. "Principles of Neutrality in Education." Educational Philosophy and Practice, 8 (October 1976): 1-16.

Argues that there are a great plurality of principles of neutrality, difficult to formulate in any satisfactory manner. Concludes that the question is much more complex than commonly assumed.

355. Litke, Robert. "What's Wrong with Closing Minds?" Values Education: Theory/Practice/Problems/Prospects (item 1511), pp. 87-94.

Argues that to close someone's mind is to curtail power of rationality which in turn is to limit his ability to be free--which is to assault or commit violence on him. Various ways of closing people's minds are discussed, and teachers are warned to examine frequently what they are doing.

356. Marantz, Haim. "Leslie Smith on Indoctrination." Journal of Moral Education, 4 (1975): 117-120.

Argues that while Smith's (item 365) rejection of four theses to account for indoctrination seems correct, his arguments in support of his conclusions seem inadequate.

357. Mesa, James P. "Moral Indoctrination and the Virtue of Prudence." Ph.D. dissertation, Saint Louis University, 1978. 40/05, p. 2735.

Develops a Thomistic account of moral indoctrination. Asserts that there exists genuine knowledge in morality, and the development of the morally virtuous person is the aim of moral education. There exists a true and knowable content for moral education.

358. Meynell, Hugo A. "Moral Education and Indoctrination." Journal of Moral Education, 4 (1974): 17-26.

Claims that there is no distinction between moral education
and indoctrination. "Moral education" is simply the term we use
for such moral influencing of the young as we approve of. At
the end of the paper he attempts to rescue himself from this
position through an epistemological analysis of moral knowledge.

359. Moore, W. "Indoctrination as a Normative Concept." Studies in
     Philosophy and Education, 4 (1966): 396-403.

     Presents a distinction between liberal and authoritarian
     indoctrination, with the latter intending that the belief remain
     fixed always in the learner. The liberal perspective holds that
     indoctrination is necessary early in life, but these beliefs
     later are allowed, and even encouraged, to be challenged.
     Argues that there are times when indoctrination is justifiable
     and even necessary. Published as "Indoctrination and Democratic
     Method" in Concepts of Indoctrination (item 367).

360. Raywid, Mary A. "The Discovery and Rejection of
     Indoctrination." Educational Theory, 30 (1980): 1-10.

     Presents the changing historical conceptions of the concept of
     indoctrination. In an analysis of the Progressive Era's
     response to the challenge of indoctrination, it is concluded
     that Dewey's experimentalism emphasizing the method of
     intelligence is in principle the best response made to that
     concern and a perspective of great utility today.

361. Raywid, Mary A. "Language and Concepts in Education." Studies
     in Philosophy and Education, 2 (1962): 86-96.

     Uses Ennis' article on neutrality (item 342) as a vehicle to
     question whether Oxford-style analytic analysis of issues has
     any use for members outside the group. Concludes that it
     probably does not.

362. Rembert, Andrew. "Teaching about Values: Remaining Neutral vs.
     Advocating One's Own View." Peabody Journal of Education, 53
     (1976): 71-75.

     The issue of advocacy versus neutrality is explored, but
     Rembert can't seem to make up his mind. He does, however, feel
     that the burden of proof should fall on those who advocate
     advocacy. On the other hand, with some values of great
     importance, advocacy might be warranted ... maybe.

363. Scolnicov, Samuel. "Truth, Neutrality and the Philosophy
     Teacher." Growing Up with Philosophy (item 1507), pp.
     392-404.

Argues that one should wish to develop critical thought and philosophical understanding, and that remaining neutral is frequently required to this end. However, since we want children to care about truth and rationality, they must reveal that they too have this concern.

364. Smart, Patricia. "The Concept of Indoctrination." New Essays in the Philosophy of Education (item 219), pp. 33-46.

Rejects Wilson's (item 379) opinion that it is subject matter and not method that constitutes indoctrination. Argues that indoctrination involves teaching half-truths as whole truths either by giving only one point of view or by suppressing other possible points of view.

365. Smith, Leslie. "Indoctrination and Intent," Journal of Moral Education, 3 (1974): 229-233.

Argues that indoctrination is understood better in terms of the impact of the educational practice on the student than in terms of the intention(s) of the teacher.

366. Snook, I.A. "The Concept of Indoctrination." Studies in Philosophy and Education, 7 (1970): 65-108.

In a wide-ranging discussion of the concept of indoctrination, concludes that it is dependent on the intentional bringing about of undesirable states of mind of a specified sort. Intentions are paramount, but method and content are also important. Also published as "Indoctrination and Moral Responsibility" in Concepts of Indoctrination (item 367).

367. Snook, I.A., ed. Concepts of Indoctrination: Philosophical Essays. London: Routledge and Kegan Paul, 1972.

A collection of philosophical essays on the topic of indoctrination. Most of the essays were originally published elsewhere under different titles.

368. Snook, I.A. Indoctrination and Education. London: Routledge and Kegan Paul, 1972.

In a short and readable book Snook puts forth his view that intention, not method or content, is the paramount consideration in the definition of indoctrination.

369. Snook, I.A. "Neutrality and the Schools." Educational Theory, 22 (1972): 278-285.

Argues that neutrality is possible and, overall, desirable because it is necessary for the development of reason.

370. Stenhouse, Lawrence. "Neutrality as a Criterion in Teaching:
     The Work of the Humanities Curriculum Project." Progress and
     Problems in Moral Education (item 1530), pp. 123-133.

     Chastises Wilson (item 379) and Warnock (item 374) for not
     discussing the empirical findings of the Humanities Curriculum
     Project in their discussions of neutrality. Stenhouse was the
     director of the Humanities Curriculum Project, which, among
     other goals, attempted to define the role of the neutral
     chairmanship in leading discussions on controversial
     issues--human issues of universal concern.

371. Suttle, Bruce. "The Need and Inevitability of Moral
     Indoctrination." Educational Studies, 12 (1981): 151-161.

     Following a critical analysis of the three major
     interpretations of indoctrination, Suttle argues that moral
     indoctrination is pernicious only when it is in fact avoidable.
     Argues that at times it is unavoidable; inducting children into
     mathematical principles is offered as an analogy.

372. Wagner, Paul A. "Indoctrination and Moral Education." Ph.D.
     dissertation, University of Missouri, 1978. 39/10, p. 6019.

     Argues that indoctrination is inevitable in moral education
     and that the existing programs of Kohlberg, Simon, and Lipman,
     since they refuse to recognize this, are flawed. Two procedural
     and one substantive principle that should be indoctrinated are
     presented.

373. Wall, Grenville. "Moral Authority and Moral Education."
     Journal of Moral Education, 4 (1975): 95-99.

     Argues that the moral educator cannot be morally neutral but
     must be morally committed. The moral educator must be a moral
     authority.

374. Warnock, Mary. "The Neutral Teacher." Progress and Problems in
     Moral Education (item 1530), pp. 103-112.

     Argues that teachers cannot and should not be neutral. It is
     a valuable learning experience for children to experience how
     adults draw moral conclusions from evidence. The student
     response to teacher moral pronouncements is seldom
     nonreversible, if reversibility is deemed necessary by the
     student.

375. Watkins, James W. "Can Moral Instruction Avoid Indoctrination."
     Ed.D. dissertation, University of California, Los Angeles,
     1972. 33/10, p. 5620.

Three views on indoctrination are considered (those of Hare, Atkinson, & Peters). Concludes that ethical theories exist that make non-indoctrinated moral education conceptually possible.

376. White, J.P. "Indoctrination." The Concept of Education. Edited by R.S. Peters. London: Routledge and Kegan Paul, 1967, pp. 177-191.

Argues against Wilson's view (item 379) that indoctrination is distinguished only by the content of the student's belief. Instead, White argues that the intention of the person must be considered. It is also a mistake to assume that indoctrination must assume an ideology. Also in Concepts of Indoctrination (item 367) as "Indoctrination and Intentions."

377. White, J.P. "Indoctrination Without Doctrines?" Concepts of Indoctrination (item 367), pp. 190-201.

In a reply to Gregory and Woods (item 349) White argues that their concept of a "doctrine" is not all that clear and cannot be sustained. Reiterates that intention is the key to understanding the concept of indoctrination.

378. Wilson, J. "Comment on Flew's 'What Is Indoctrination?'" Studies in Philosophy and Education, 4 (1966): 390-395.

Responds point by point to Flew's critique (item 345) of Wilson's earlier paper (item 379). He elaborates on the distinction between indoctrination and conditioning, and agrees that in any full account of indoctrination, aim, method, and intention must play a part. Published as "Indoctrination and Freedom" in Concepts of Indoctrination (item 367).

379. Wilson, John. "Education and Indoctrination." Aims in Education (item 69), pp. 24-46.

The difference between education and indoctrination lies not in method but in subject matter: education deals only with beliefs that have the weight of available evidence in their favor. The implications of the concept of indoctrination for teachers and the freedom of youth are discussed.

380. Wilson, John. "Indoctrination and Rationality." Concepts of Indoctrination (item 367), pp. 17-24.

Distinguishes indoctrination from conditioning by arguing that indoctrination has an intimate connection with belief rather than behavior. People are indoctrinated to believe something, conditioned to do something.

381. Wilson, John. "Teaching and Neutrality." <u>Progress and Problems</u>
      <u>in Moral Education</u> (item 1530), pp. 113-122.

      Responds to Warnock (item 374) by elaborating upon and
      attempting to clarify the positions she presents.

Questions Regarding Relationships Among Religion,
Religious Development, and Moral Development

382. Anders-Richards, Donald. "Love and Morality." Journal of Moral
Education, 3 (1974): 129-133.

Answers criticisms of his perspective that morality and
religion (agapism) are identical (see item 383).

383. Anders-Richards, Donald. "Moral and Religious Education."
Journal of Moral Education, 1 (1972): 103-108.

Argues that morality does not depend upon religion, but that,
properly conceived, the two are identical: the agapeistic life
of Christ is suggested as the moral life.

384. Archibald, Helen A. "The Naturalistic Fallacy." Religious
Education, 75 (1980): 152-164.

Raises the question of whether George Albert Coe--the father
of the religious education movement--committed the naturalistic
fallacy in deriving his views in religious education from
scientific analysis.

385. Bailey, Charles. "Moral Judgment and Religious Commitment I."
Cambridge Journal of Education, 10 (1980): 75-82.

Argues that moral reasoning does not depend on religious
understanding or commitment to any religious perspective. To
place morality on a religious perspective is to destroy one's
moral agency.

386. Bartley, W.W. Morality and Religion. London: Macmillan, 1971.

Reviews many differing views on the relationship between
morality and religion from the time of Plato to the present in a
clear and insightful manner. Discusses attempts to reduce
morality to religion and other attempts to reduce religion to
morality. It is held that the two concepts are inseparable.

387. Beck, George Andrew. "Aims in Education: Neo-Thomism." Aims in
Education (item 69), pp. 109-132.

The implications of the writings of Thomas Aquinas for education are discussed. The purpose of the educator should be to
guide the developing nature of the child to that unique perfec-
tion that makes the self complete in its inner life. The inner
core of conscience is seen as more important than the externals
of behavior. A good society is a society of fully developed
persons.

388. Chazan, Barry. "Jewish Education and Moral Development."
      Moral Development, Moral Education and Kohlberg (item 1514),
      pp. 298-325.

      Examines the relationship between Jewish education and
      Kohlberg's theory of moral development and moral education.
      Concludes, following an explination of traditional Jewish views
      of morality and character education, that the Kohlberg model is
      too Platonic, too individualistic, and too traditionless to be
      applicable to the Jewish educational world.

389. Chazan, Barry. "Who Is Moral Man?" Religious Education, 71
      (1976): 27-39.

      Argues that the conclusions of analytic moral philosophy,
      Kohlberg, and values clarification present non-theological and
      non-speculative support for the liberal religious notion of
      morality.

390. Cogdell, Gaston. "Religion and Moral Education." The Humanist,
      38 (November/December 1978): 22-23.

      Argues that schools should teach morality only in those areas
      where there is complete agreement. In all other areas the
      school should remain scrupulously neutral. In some areas there
      is agreement within the religious and secular communities
      regarding values, and schools are rightly involved in teaching
      these values. But where secular humanism and religion disagree
      (e.g., on sex education), unless both sides are presented, such
      subjects should not be in the curriculum.

391. Conn, Walter E. "Moral Development as Self-Transcendence."
      Horizons, 4 (1977): 189-205.

      Argues that a criterion of self-transcendence is implicit in
      both the psychological developmental perspective of man and in
      religious experiences. Both authentic morality and genuine
      religion are expressions of a single radical dynamism of the
      human spirit.

392. Dykstra, Craig R. "Christian Education and the Moral Life: An
      Evaluation of and Alternative to Kohlberg." Ph.D. disserta-
      tion, Princeton Theological Seminary, 1978. 39/03, p. 1454.

      Rejects Kohlberg as a basis for moral education for the
      Christian community, as too juridical. Argues that Christian
      morality, and moral education, must flow from the love of God
      made concrete with others.

393. Elliott, John, ed. "Fundamental Issues Underlying Religious and
     Moral Education." Cambridge Journal of Education, 10 (Easter
     Term 1980).

     Presents the proceedings of a conference for teachers held at
     the Cambridge Institute of Education in March 1980. The papers
     focus on the relationships between moral judgment, understand-
     ing, and religious commitment.

394. Elliott, M. "Religion and Moral Education: A Reply to C.M.
     Hamm." The Domain of Moral Education (item 30), pp. 46-53.

     Agrees that within the very restricted ground Hamm (item 407)
     has defined, he is successful, but Hamm has failed to refute the
     idea that a more thoughtful and less literally understood
     religion might serve as a decisive factor in moral deliberation.
     Thus he has not proven that moral education must proceed without
     reference to religion.

395. Foster, Arthur L. "Valuing as Religious Experience." Values
     in an Age of Confrontation. Edited by J.W. Canning. Columbus:
     Charles E. Merrill, 1970, pp. 119-123.

     Argues that valuing is essentially a religious experience of
     making contact with the Godhead.

396. Fowler, James. "Faith and the Structuring of Meaning." Toward
     Moral and Religious Maturity (item 403), pp. 51-85.

     Presents the theory of stages of faith development and
     discusses each of the seven stages separately. The aspects
     (dimensions) of each of the faith stages is presented in a lucid
     manner.

397. Fowler, James. "Moral Stages and the Development of Faith."
     Moral Development, Moral Education and Kohlberg (item 1514),
     pp. 130-160.

     Discusses the authors efforts to broaden Kohlberg's theory by
     presenting a stage theory of structural approaches to the
     forming and maintenance of faith visions. Faith is defined as
     the process by which we engage in constructing frames of meaning
     for our lives by making tacit and/or explicit commitments to
     value and power centers that promise to sustain our lives and
     meanings. Presents a chart that relates the relationships
     between stages of faith and stages of moral development.

398. Fowler, James. "Stage Six and the Kingdom of God." Religious
     Education, 75 (1980): 231-248.

Since stage six of his stages of faith represents the culmination of growth in faith, it is argued that it is the way toward encounter with the character and intention of ultimate reality.

399. Fowler, James W. "Stages in Faith: The Structural-Developmental Approach." Values and Moral Development (item 1501), pp. 173-223.

Fowler describes his six stages in faith development and how he has researched this area. He explains the parallels between his developmental stages and those of Piaget, Kohlberg and Erikson.

400. Fowler, James W. Stages of Faith. San Francisco: Harper and Row, 1981.

Presents an analysis of the human phenomena of religious faith as seen from the framework of a structural-developmental theory. Six stages of faith development are posited and their relationships to other developmental stage theories explored. An extensive case study illustrates Mary's pilgrimage through the stages. Appendices include the research interview and the methods of analysis of the interview data.

401. Fowler, James W. "Toward a Developmental Perspective on Faith." Religious Education, 69 (1974): 207-218.

Presents the view that faith is a way of knowing and construing that follows a developmental sequence. Six stages of faith are presented.

402. Fowler, J., and S. Keen. Life Maps. Waco, TX: Word Books, 1978.

Argues that the activity of faith has a direct bearing on the construction of meaning. This construction of meaning is held to occur in developmental stages. Contains detailed description of the stages, with illustrative passages from interviews scored at each stage.

403. Fowler, J., and A. Vergote, eds. Toward Moral and Religious Maturity: The First International Conference on Moral and Religious Development. Morristown, NJ: Silver-Burdette, 1980.

Contains a collection of papers which constitute the best single source of information on recent thought on the interplay between religious and moral development.

404. Friedman, Maurice. "The Source of Moral Authority: Can Modern
     Man Be Ethical Without Being Religious?" Religious Education,
     57 (1962): 410-415.

     Argues that modern man cannot be ethical without being
     religious, for all ethics must rest on an attitude toward
     reality that ultimately is of religious depth.

405. Gardner, P. "Religious Education: In Defense of Non-Commitment."
     Journal of Philosophy of Education, 14 (1980): 163-164.

     Argues that while it is paradoxical to oppose moral education
     on the ground that we lack criteria of truth in morals, those
     who oppose religious education on the ground that we lack
     criteria of truth in religion face no similar paradox.

406. Hall, Robert T. "Morality and Religion in Public Education: A
     Dialogue." Religious Education, 72 (1977): 273-292.

     Presents a response to a statement by Pennsylvania bishops
     lamenting that secularism in schools is in fact resulting in the
     de facto teaching of secular values. Hall argues that there is
     good reason for recent Supreme Court decisions removing religion
     from schools. He reviews these decisions and presents an
     approach to values that is secular yet that affirms basic human
     values.

407. Hamm, Cornel. "Moral Education Without Religion." The Domain
     of Moral Education (item 30), pp. 35-45.

     Argues that morality and religion are logically distinct forms
     of discourse; that morality cannot be based on religion and,
     therefore, that it is a serious mistake to attempt to substitute
     religious for moral instruction.

408. Hamm, Cornel M. "Morality and Religion: A Rejoinder." The
     Domain of Moral Education (item 30), pp. 54-57.

     Argues that Elliott's reply (item 394) to his original article
     (item 407) is unconvincing. Still, when one goes for moral
     advice it is moral not religious advice one seeks.

409. Hauerwas, Stanley. "Character, Narrative, and Growth in the
     Christian Life." Toward Moral and Religious Maturity (item
     403), pp. 441-484.

     Provides a constructive account of character and narrative as
     crucial categories for understanding the moral life and moral
     growth. An Aristotelian view of the acquisition of virtue is
     seen as a more adequate conception of the essentials of the
     moral life than developmental perspectives.

410. Hemming, James, and Howard Marrott. "Humanism and Christianity: The Common Ground of Moral Education." Let's Teach Them Right (item 424), pp. 138-165.

      In a paper issued in 1965 by a group of Christians and Humanists on religious and moral education in county schools, attempts to find a common ground without concealing differences of principle. Argues that in a pluralistic society, even when a completely secular approach is adopted, children must be allowed to consider a variety of viewpoints, some of which may be religious. Generally it is held that moral education should move ahead on those points on which there is agreement.

411. Hirst, Paul. "The Foundations of Moral Judgment." Let's Teach Them Right (item 424), pp. 123-129.

      Attempts to develop a non-religious foundation for morality. Argues that there are moral principles that should guide us, but situation ethics has a point in emphasizing that these principles should not be rigidly and mechanically applied.

412. Hirst, Paul. Moral Education in a Secular Society. London: University of London, University Press, 1974.

      Discusses the significance of the secularization of contemporary society for moral life. Argues that there is a secular approach to the justification of morality and moral education that is compatible with Christianity. According to Hirst, this approach has the rationally autonomous individual as its goal.

413. Hirst, Paul H. "Morals, Religion and the Maintained School." Let's Teach Them Right (item 424), pp. 8-24.

      Seeks answers to two questions: Is man's moral understanding dependent on religious knowledge and belief; and Are religious propositions simply beliefs? These questions are posed to ascertain if there is a domain of publicly justifiable religious knowledge that can be taught in public schools. Concludes that such a body of knowledge does not yet exist, but still some teaching about religion can be defended in public schools.

414. Jarvis, Peter. "Religious Education as a Vehicle for Moral Education?" Journal of Moral Education, 2 (1972): 69-73.

      Finds that many junior high teachers conduct moral education under the banner of religious education. Argues that this is an artificial and inefficient vehicle because much of it is both beyond the conceptual level and outside the experience of children.

415. Jaspard, Jean-Marie. "The Relation to God and the Moral
      Development of the Young Child." Toward Moral and Religious
      Maturity (item 403), pp. 137-164.

      Reports on the results of longitudinal data with young
      children on the motivational dynamisms that conjointly and
      reciprocally form the basis for the relationship between
      conceptions of God and the formation of moral attitudes.

416. Joy, Donald M. "Moral Development: Evangelical Perspectives."
      Religious Education, 75 (1980): 142-151.

      Delineates the common ground shared by evangelicals and
      Kohlberg. Four presuppositions held by evangelicals regarding
      morality are presented: morality is supra-human, justice
      originates in the righteousness of God, human morality is "the
      image of God," and moral failure, too, belongs in the domain.

417. Kegan, Robert. "There the Dance Is: Religious Dimensions of a
      Developmental Framework." Toward Moral and Religious Maturity
      (item 403), pp. 403-440.

      Presents a broad conception of development involving total
      persons in motion, a creative motion, the notion of life itself.
      Argues that the developmentalist perspective can help us to
      understand three empirical phenomena: yearnings for agency and
      inclusion, loss and recovery of meaning and coherence, and
      movement to active partner in the "ultimate environment." The
      educational implications for religious education are briefly
      discussed.

418. Kohlberg, Lawrence. "Education, Moral Development and Faith."
      Journal of Moral Education, 4 (1974): 5-16.

      Kohlberg presents his own moral development perspective and
      then compares it with Fowler's faith stages.

419. Kohlberg, Lawrence, and Clark Power. "Moral Development,
      Religious Thinking and the Question of a Seventh Stage."
      The Philosophy of Moral Development (item 676), pp. 311-372.

      Discusses the relationship of moral and faith development,
      drawing heavily on the work of Fowler (item 400). Argues that
      there is a close empirical relationship between faith and moral
      development. A seventh stage is presented in which the
      interests of self and others are seen as in harmony (agape).
      One moves beyond justice to an attitude of acceptance, humility,
      and forgiveness. This is the most extensive exposition of stage
      7 extant.

420. Lee, James Michael. "Christian Religious Education and Moral
      Development." Moral Development, Moral Education and Kohlberg
      (item 1514), pp. 326-355.

      Argues that Kohlberg's theory holds that man is basically good
      through a fundamental orientation toward increasing higher
      levels of moral development. Suggests that God works in and
      through the process of human development. Discusses how a
      social science approach to religious education, entailed by
      Kohlberg's theory, challenges traditional theological approaches
      to Christian education and suggests reasons why a social science
      approach is justifiable.

421. McCaffrey, Jane D. "The Relationship Between Moral Education
      and Religious Education in the Writings of George Albert Coe."
      Ph.D. dissertation, The Catholic University of America, 1979.
      40/03, p. 1526.

      Analyzes Coe's view of the place and nature of moral education
      within religious education. No separation between religious and
      moral education is seen.

422. McDonagh, Edna. "Moral Theology and Moral Development." Toward
      Moral and Religious Maturity (item 403), pp. 320-342.

      Questions whether developmental theory isn't the denial or
      reincarnation of Natural Law. Also questioned is developmental
      theory's easy optimism about human goodness. Argues that
      development needs to be anchored in community and virtues, not
      just in classroom discussion. An attempt to integrate moral
      theology and moral education is presented.

423. Macquarrie,   John,   ed.   A Dictionary of Christian   Ethics.
      Philadelphia: The Westminster Press, 1967.

      A compendium of Christian ethical teaching, with articles
      contributed by some 80 authorities. Useful in determining the
      meaning of terms and concepts that make up the basis of
      Christian ethical teaching.

424. Macy,   Christopher,   ed.   Let's Teach Them Right.   London:
      Pemberton Publishing, 1969.

      Consists of a series of papers on religious education,
      religious and moral education together, and moral education.
      The papers on purely religious education are not listed
      separately in this bibliography.

425. Mischey, E.J., and E.V. Sullivan. "Faith Orientation: Motive to
      Be Moral." Contemporary Education, 48 (Fall 1976): 35-41.

Reviews Fowler's stages of faith theory (item 399) and reports the preliminary results of a study to assess the relationships between moral stages, faith stages, and identity stages.

426. Motet, Dan. "Kohlberg's Theory of Moral Development and the Christian Faith." Journal of Psychology and Theology, 6 (1978): 18-21.

Describes some analogies between Kohlbergian theory and scriptural passages. Different orientations to salvation are analyzed from a stage perspective. It is concluded that Jesus Himself gauged his audience and spoke appropriately to all stages. Even Jesus, it turns out, was a developmentalist.

427. Mullen, Peter F. "Education for Moral and Spiritual Development." Ed.D. dissertation, University of Massachusetts, 1977. 38/10, p. 5983.

After critiquing Piaget and Kohlberg, suggests that there are spiritual stages parallel to Kohlberg's moral stages. Outlines a teacher-training program designed to educate teachers adept at facilitating both moral and spiritual development.

428. Nielsen, Kai. Ethics Without God. New York: Pemberton, 1973.

Argues that morality based on religion or God is grossly mistaken. Moral obligation cannot follow from God's commands for one can always reasonably ask, "Why should I obey God?" One should obey God only if he is perfect and the only way one can know that is with a prior sense of goodness, Therefore, knowledge of goodness is prior to God.

429. O'Donohoe, James A. "Moral and Faith Development Theory." Toward Moral and Religious Maturity (item 403), pp. 373-401.

Sketches some of the basic concepts of the nature and task of Roman Catholic theological ethics and outlines the implications of Kohlberg and Fowler for this area of inquiry. Finally, some observations on the phenomenon of religious conversion are offered. The ability of conversion to bring together the cognitive and the affective in development is suggested.

430. Oser, Fritz. "Stages of Religious Judgment." Toward Moral and Religious Maturity (item 403), pp. 277-315.

Presents the results of a study in which stages of religious development were detected through the use of the Paul dilemma.

431. Outka, G., and J. Reeder, eds. Religion and Morality. Garden City, NY: Anchor, 1973.

Contains a collection of essays on the relationship between religion and morality. Topics covered include definitions of religion and morality, traditions in Judaism and Christianity, and modern discussions of the dependency, or non-dependency, of morality on religion.

432. Palmer, Gwen. "Religious Education and the Primary School." Cambridge Journal of Education, 4 (1974): 123-133.

Argues that religious education can fulfill important needs of children in primary schools.

433. Paton, J.M. "Moral and Religious Education--We Have No Choice." Education Canada, 2 (1971): 15-19.

Argues that schools have no choice but to tackle moral and religious education. Feels that moral and religious education go hand in hand.

434. Phenix, Philip H. "Ethics and the Will of God." Moral Education (item 171), pp. 55-62.

In dealing with the question of moral justification Phenix rejects the notion of a naturalistic conception of morality but retains objectivity in the moral order by positing an objective, non-natural, ideal moral order rooted in a God notion. Ethical objectivity has its roots in an ideal and Divine God.

435. Power, F. Clark, and Lawrence Kohlberg. "Religion, Morality, and Ego Development." Toward Moral and Religious Maturity (item 403), pp. 343-372.

Presents a case that morality can, in principle, be derived rationally apart from divine revelation. The relationship of ego development to moral and religious understanding is explored. Demonstrates that religious conceptions depend on moral structures. Concludes that morality offers us a reasonable way of resolving interpersonal conflicts, but cannot offer us a reason for being and for purposeful human activity.

436. Rogers, William R. "Interdisciplinary Approaches to Moral and Religious Development. A Critical Overview." Toward Moral and Religious Maturity (item 403), pp. 11-50.

Lays out a structure of the various approaches that can be taken to moral and religious development. This is accomplished in a historical framework. The paper concludes by setting forth a paradigm in which these approaches can be most constructively viewed.

437. Sell, A.P.F. "Christians, Humanists and Common Ground." Journal of Moral Education, 1 (1972): 177-186.

Although some have tried to find a common ground between Christians and Humanists, it is argued that the gulf is fixed. How the two may work together in moral education is discussed. In the same issue H.J. Blackman responds.

438. Sizer, Theodore, ed. Religion and the Public Schools. Boston: Houghton Mifflin, 1967. NI

A collection of readings featuring 17 articles on such topics as teaching about religion; the challenge of religion to our educational system; the relationships among secularism, pluralism, and religion, and theological perspectives on public education.

439. Smith, John. "The Concept of the Moral, Moral Relativism, the Nature of Moral Norms and the Sources of Moral Authority." Religious Education, 57 (1962): 445-448.

Argues that there are three sources of moral authority: society, individual duty, and love of God. Only the latter, it is suggested, is adequate to motivate moral life.

440. Straughan, Roger. "Religion, Morality and the Curriculum." London Educational Review, 3 (Autumn, 1974): 73-79.

Attempts a reconciliation with regard to the position that regards religious education and moral education as rival candidates in the school curriculum.

441. Ury, Zalman F. "The Ethics of Israel Salanter and Moral Education in Jewish Schools." Ph.D. dissertation, University of California, Los Angeles, 1966. 27/12, p. 4176.

Salanter's ethic is analyzed critically from an educational perspective, and implications for moral education in Jewish schools in America are explored. Salanter's use of ecstasy and self- and group analysis in bridging the thought-action gap are discussed.

442. Wallwork, Ernest. "Morality, Religion, and Kohlberg's Theory." Moral Development, Moral Education and Kohlberg (item 1514), pp. 269-297.

Argues against Fowler and with Kohlberg that religion is neither necessary nor sufficient for the justification of morality. Religion can be shown to have a positive influence on morality through the motivation and practical reasons it provides for moral action.

443. Ward, Keith. "Moral Judgment and Religious Commitment II: A Reply to Charles Bailey." Cambridge Journal of Education, 10 (1980): 83-87.

Argues that what morality is embodies, necessarily, an ideological commitment. It is a mistake to assume that there is a non-ideological basis for morality, which is what Bailey has argued (item 385) in saying there is a non-religious basis for morality.

444. Wilson, John. Education in Religion and the Emotions. London: Heinemann, 1971.

Argues that religious emotions such as awe are of special importance in education. Education in religion and the emotions should not be a matter of inculcating or persuading people. Rather it must be a matter of helping them to become more reasonable in the spheres of religion and emotion. The book contains a first sketch of a taxonomy of the emotions and a brief chapter on techniques and tools for educating the emotions.

445. Wilson, John. "The Logical Basis of Moral and Religious Education." Let's Teach Them Right (item 424), pp. 93-99.

Argues that any "basis for moral education" should consist of impacting those skills that are necessary to make good or reasonable moral decisions and act on them. His moral components and their relationship to religious education are discussed.

446. Wright, Jason S. "Morality and Hebraic Christian Religion." Journal of Moral Education, 11 (1981): 32-40.

Moral development in the Old and New Testaments is discussed. Religion and morality were held to be one. Argues that true morality flows from the essential nature of persons who are in harmony with objective divine reality.

Critiques of the Enterprise of Moral Education

447. Bereiter, Carl. "The Morality of Moral Education." Hastings Center Report, 8 (April 1978): 20-25.

     Argues that the cognitive-development approach and values clarification, contrary to their claim of neutrality, do in fact teach values. In classrooms this means the majority opinion will prevail. If the teacher does not teach the child what to believe, someone else will.

448. Bereiter, Carl. Must We Educate? Englewood Cliffs: Prentice-Hall, 1973.

     Argues that the school should do what it does well, develop skills, and leave the rest alone. Especially moral education should be left to the family.

449. Bereiter, Carl. "Schools Without Education." Harvard Educational Review, 42 (1972): 390-413.

     Argues that since schools are not successful in influencing the way children turn out anyway, they shouldn't try to influence such things as values. Schools should concentrate only on providing child care and skill training.

450. Blocher, D.H. "Toward an Ecology of Student Development." Adolescents' Development and Education (item 1512), pp. 490-496.

     Warns against narrow views of human development. Suggests that the total development of the person is the proper concern of education and this requires an ecological view of the schooling process.

451. Broughton, J.M. "Beyond Formal Operations." Teacher's College Record, 79 (1977): 87-97.

     Presents five reasons why educating people up to the final stage of operational thought may not be justifiable as the central aim of postchildhood education.

452. Broughton, John M. "Dialectics and Moral Development Ideology." Readings in Moral Education (item 1522), pp. 298-307.

     Analyzes existing critiques of Kohlberg and offers his own Marxian perspective.

453.   Broughton, John M.   "The Limits of Formal Thought." Adolescents'
       Development and Education (item 1512), pp. 49-60.

       Argues that if we are to have a comprehensive of adolescent
       and adult rationality we must broaden the construct of formal
       operations as a mode of consciousness. As it is construed by
       Piaget it is a mode of consciousness involving only logical
       empiricism. Formal operations should be seen as the culmination
       of a destructive socialization that alienates our thinking and
       being.

454.   Crabtree, Walden.   "Establishing Policy in the Values Education
       Controversy." Contemporary Education. 46(1974): 24-27.

       Argues that the thing to do with parents who object to schools
       meddling with their childrens values is to train the parents to
       accept what is going on.

455.   Cragg, A.W.   "Moral Education in the Schools." Canadian Journal
       of Education, 4 (1979): 28-38.

       Introducing moral education exacerbates the problem of the
       hidden curriculum rather than reducing it. Each approach to
       moral education is based on philosophic conception of morality
       which is not openly debated.

456.   Cragg, A.W.   "Moral Education in the Schools: The Hidden Values
       Argument." Interchange, 10 (1978/ 79): 12-25.

       Argues that inspite of new moves into moral education the
       hidden curriculum will still be with us, it will simply take a
       new shape for there are also hidden values in Kohlberg and
       values clarification.

457.   Crittenden, Brian.   Bearings in Moral Education, Australian
       Educational Review No. 12. Hawthorn, Victoria: Australian
       Council for Educational Research, 1978.

       Consists of a brief critical review of recent work in moral
       education. Reviews recent shifts in moral philosophy and
       concludes by urging the need for a wider perspective on moral
       education.

458.   Delattre, Edwin J. and William J. Bennett. "Where the Values
       Movement Goes Wrong?" Change, 11 (1979): 38-43.

       Argues against current approaches to values education. Claims
       that the goal of values education should not be to develop
       skilled youth at thinking about morality, but rather to develop
       youth who are moral. In spite of rapid social change there
       still exist core values. Teachers should present moral ideals
       with conviction, not with tentativeness.

459. Eger, Martin. "The Conflict in Moral Education: An Informal
      Case Study." The Public Interest, 63 (1981): 62-80.

      Examines the question of whether great harm is being done by
      teaching values by probing the connection between a values
      education program and the social conflict to which it gave rise.
      The case centers on the teaching of values clarification in 1979
      in Spencer-Van Etten school district in upstate New York. A
      series of questions on adequate training of teachers, parental
      control of schools, academic freedom, exclusion of competing
      moral positions, etc. are posed.

460. Floy, Joseph. "Can Children Do Moral Philosophy?" Growing Up
      With Philosophy (item 1507), pp. 145-157.

      Argues that moral education is itself immoral. Childhood is a
      stage of life that must be protected in all its innocence and
      dependence--it is a world organized and stabilized by adult
      authority. Ethics introduced too early can fragment this world
      and lead only to cynicism, skepticism, boredom and alienation.

461. Gordon, David. "Free-Will and the Undesirability of Moral
      Education." Educational Theory, 25 (1975): 407-416.

      Argues that in order for a teacher to develop pupils' autonomy
      they must reject moral education. Moral education is taken to
      mean the development of a pupil's inclination to do what is
      right.

462. Grant, Gloria. "Values/Diversity in Education: A Progress
      Report." Educational Leadership, 35 (1978): 443-448.

      Argues that the progress toward integrating educational
      resources into schools which represent diverse social and
      cultural values and norms has been slow and inadequate.

463. Hyland, Eddie. "Towards a Radical Critique of Morality and
      Moral Education." Journal of Moral Education, 8 (1979):
      156-167.

      Argues that there is no deductive justification possible for
      moral rules, therefore no reason for being moral. In morality's
      place he argues for an analysis of needs and wants as a
      foundation for a fuller and richer value system.

464. Lerner, Michael P. "Marxism and Ethical Reasoning." Social
      Praxis, 2 (1974): 63-88.

      It is argued that a historical analysis of the function of
      ethics reveals its centrality in the struggle between dominant
      classes and those that challenge them. Lerner claims that the
      "good-reasons" approach of Kai Nelson's Reason and Practice in

Ethics has ideological use in justifying an established order. An alternative view of ethics more complimentary to those involved in the struggle for social change is presented.

465. Martin, Jane R. "Moral Autonomy and Political Education." Growing Up With Philosophy (item 1507), pp. 174-194.

Argues that traditional philosophy, which prepares children for intellectual autonomy, fails to acquaint children with the social, economic and political realities of which they are a part. If the existing social system is unjust then true education must produce youthful social critics. Philosophical inquiry will lead to only abstract ideals without apparent application to real social and moral issues.

466. Nielsen, Kai. "Class Conflict, Marxism and the Good-Reasons Approach: A Response to Michael Lerner." Social Praxis, 2 (1974): 89-112.

Argues that the 'good-reasons' approach does not have the conservative ideological--implications attributed to it by Michael Lerner (item 464). Examines the problems of morality embedded in Marxist ideology and offers a resolution of those problems.

467. Ofstad, Harold. "Education versus Growth in Moral Development." The Monist, 58 (1974): 581-599.

Argues that moral agency can not be brought about through educational procedures such as instruction or rational dialogue. If the posited ten conditions of moral agency are to come about at all it is more than likely the lucky outcome of a developmental process in which social growth and interaction have been of decisive importance.

468. Oliver, Donald W. and Mary Jo Bane. "Moral Education: Is Reasoning Enough?" Moral Education ... It Comes With the Territory (item 1519), pp. 349-369.

Questions whether or not most people engage in the kind of moral reasoning advocated by moral education curriculum and if so whether or not this kind of reasoning is a significant part of something we might call the moral personality. Discusses the limits of reason and the need to encourage students to confront the irrationality in life and think metaphorically. Also in Moral Education: Interdisciplinary Approaches (item 1492).

469. Phillips, D.Z. "Is Moral Education Really Necessary?" British Journal of Educational Studies, 27 (1979): 42-56.

Criticized the view that moral education should make explicit the values in an academic curriculum. The view that education should be value free is also criticized. The proper focus should be the values enbedded with the subjects being taught. Claims that what is not necessary is moral educationists, especially those who corrupt education by their focus on values in schools rather than in subjects.

470. Reid, Herbert and Ernest Yanarella. "Critical Political Theory and Moral Development: On Kohlberg, Hampden-Turner and Habermas." Theory and Society, 4 (1977): 505-541.

It is shown that Kohlberg's stages are little more than a continuation of the ideological hegemony of Lockean-Liberalism. When faced with the prospect of their critique becoming merely a demystifying hermeneutics, the possibilities and limits of existential radicalism--Hampden-Turner and Habermas--are explored. It is concluded that "the pragmatics of communicative competence must be recontextualized within a larger critical and more deeply dialectical theory of totality and temporality, hopefully illuminating radically democratic modes of struggle with the hegemony of alienating institutions and their 'historical blocks'."

471. Ruscoe, Gordon C. "Moral Education in Revolutionary Society." Theory into Practice, 14 (1975): 221-223.

Examines some of the features of the moral context in which education in a revolutionary society operates. Discusses the need for changing habitual forms of moral behavior. The inevitable conflicts between economic and ideological concerns is discussed.

472. Ryan, Kevin. "Is it Going to be Just a Word Game?" The Humanist, 38 (November/December 1978): 21.

Argues that although we know that for moral and value education to take root there must be some affective commitment and involvement yet our intellectual approach to moral education does little to develop these dispositions.

473. Sullivan, Edmund V. "Can Values Be Taught?" Moral Development and Socialization (item 542), pp. 219-243.

Argues that institutions project certain kinds of values into education. This projection of values also pervades the content of curriculum which is introduced into schools. It is incumbent on the believer in moral education that he/she address the institutional question when considering moral education. A postcritical approach to moral education is proposed which involves subjecting ones values to "critical awareness." Five broad guidelines for postcritical education are offered.

474. Sullivan, Edmund V. "The Scandalized Child: Children, Media and
      Commodity Culture." Toward Moral and Religious Maturity (item
      403), pp. 549-573.

      Argues that mass media with its legitimation of mass culture
      (seen as a commodity culture assults basic human dignity) is so
      pervasive and influential in the moral socialization that the
      only way to morally educate children is by means of developing a
      post critical perspective in children. This involves developing
      in children a "critical awareness" of their environment.

475. Wallen, Norman E. "Can Moral Behavior Be Taught Through
      Cognitive Means?--No." Social Education, 41 (1977): 329-331.

      Argues that reasoning alone is merely an intellectual
      exercise. Thought must be linked with strong emotions if it is
      to affect behavior.

476. Walzer, Michael. "Teaching Morality." The New Republic, 178
      (June 10, 1978): 12-14.

      Points to the fatal weakness in "American liberal approach to
      moral life" as it affects education. One posture relegates
      values to private life and leads to intense subjectivity. The
      other posture reduces values to quantifiable cost/benefit analy-
      sis and leads to a radical objectivity. Neither conforms to the
      realities of our common moral life. Neither can be realized by
      any imaginable form of social life.

477. Welton, M. "Is Moral Education Possible in Advanced Capitalist
      Consumer Society." The History and Social Science Teacher, 13
      (1977): 9-22.

      Presents a neo-Marxist analysis and concludes that liberal
      capitalist ideology and its value structure fail to justify the
      state and the institutions in it--schools do not escape this
      "legitimation crisis." The interest on form rather than content
      is seen as merely a diversion from the fact that schools teach
      values that justify societal immorality--capitalism.

478. Wynne, Edward. "Adolescent Alienation and Social Policy."
      Teacher's College Record, 78 (1976): 23-40.

      Cites data to show that our social and political institutions
      are becoming less effective at socializing our young to become
      mature, wholesome, and committed citizens. The situation is
      analyzed from a Durkheimian perspective and interpreted as one
      of increasing social fragmentation. Values education should be
      on an affective level as opposed to using more formalism,
      cognition and legalism.

Moralization: The Learning of Morality

General Accounts of Moralization

479. Adkins, D.C., F.D. Payne and J.M. O'Malley. "Moral Development." Review of Research in Education, Vol. 2. Itasca, IL: F.E. Peacock, 1974, pp. 108-144.

   Consists of a review of empirical research on cognition, emotion, and behavior as they relate to moral development.

480. Ausabel, David P. "Psychology's Undervaluation of the Rational Components in Moral Behavior." Moral Education: Interdisciplinary Approaches (item 1492), pp. 200-227.

   Moral obligation, a feeling that one ought to do what is right, is a core value of the moral system that organizes all other values within an integrated and coherent system. Ausabel describes the age-developmental history of moral obligation. The discrepancy between moral belief and behavior can be explained on the following grounds: (1) moral belief is too often assumed to be synonymous with moral knowledge; (2) expressed beliefs are confused with true beliefs; (3) there often exist genuine moral confusion, inconsistency, and conflict.

481. Baltes, P.B., and J.R. Nesselroade. "Cultural Change and Adolescent Personality Development: An Application of Longitudinal Sequences." Developmental Psychology, 7 (1972): 244-256.

   Presents evidence that suggests that adolescent trait change is dictated less by age-related components than by the type of social change patterns that set the environmental milie for adolescents.

482. Baumrind, Diana. "A Dialectical Materialist's Perspective on Knowing Social Reality." New Directions for Child Development, No. 2: Moral Development (item 1497), pp. 61-82.

Presents a Marxist approach to moral development that embraces cultural relativism and rejects the Western view of justice. Advocates that the study of social cognition and moral reasoning should involve interviewing and observation in naturally occurring conflicts and crises.

483.   Bowlby, John.   Child Care and the Growth of Love.   Baltimore: Penguin Books, 1968.

Presents the conclusion, based on an extensive summary of research, that maternal deprivation is a major factor in the development of anti-social personalities. This book is adapted from the more extensive study conducted by Bowlby for the World Health Organization, Maternal Care and Mental Health.

484.   Bradburn, E. "Children's Moral Knowledge," Educational Research, 9 (1967): 203-207.

Using projective techniques with a population of 600 ten year olds it was found that most children perceive that their parents think it is good to take responsible action for the sake of others. Children apparently have a high degree of moral knowledge--they know what is generally accepted.

485.   Brim, Orville G., and Stanton Wheeler.   Socialization after Childhood: Two Essays.   New York: John Wiley, 1966.

Brim, in his paper "Socialization Through the Life Cycle," reviews the need for socialization after childhood and concludes that the task of effective socialization is to socialize so that the work of society gets done while allowing individuals to gradually transform the social system. Wheeler, in his paper "The Structure of Formally Organized Socialization Settings," attempts to analyze the properties of socializing organizations that may influence socialization outcomes.

486.   Bronfenbrenner, Urie. "The Role of Age, Sex, Class, and Culture in Studies of Moral Development." Religious Education, 57 (July-August 1962): S3-S17.

Examines the acquisition of values as a function of age, sex, class, and culture.

487.   Bronfenbrenner, Urie. Two Worlds of Childhood: U.S. and U.S.S.R. New York: Russell Sage, 1970.

Compares and contrasts childrearing practices in the U.S. and the U.S.S.R. Observes that Soviet practices, through the emphasis on collective effort in schools, result in children manifesting prosocial behavior. American children, on the other hand, the product of affluent neglect, seem to be brought up by

their peers and by television. Some practical suggestions for
improving education in the U.S. are offered.

488. Brown, Laurence B., and Mansur Lalljee. "Young Persons'
      Conceptions of Criminal Events." Journal of Moral Education,
      10 (1981): 165-172.

      Students in the 15 to 17 age range were asked to list crimes
      they had heard of, the source of information about each crime,
      appropriate punishment, and circumstances under which the
      punishment should be reduced. The results of the questionnaire
      reveal a wide variety of accounts of criminal events.

489. Brown, Roger. "The Acquisition of Morality." Chapter 8 in
      Social Psychology by Roger Brown. New York: The Free Press,
      1965, pp. 350-417.

      Reviews psychoanalytic, learning by imitation (identifica-
      tion), and Piagetian conceptions of moral development. In a
      creative synthesis Brown posits that moralization proceeds in
      three dimensions--knowledge, conduct, and feeling--and involves
      four kinds of learning.

490. Brown, Roger, and Richard J. Herrnstein. "Moral Reasoning and
      Conduct." Psychology, by R. Brown and R.J. Herrnstein.
      Boston: Little, Brown, 1975, pp. 287-340.

      Presents a preliminary model of the relationship between moral
      reasoning and moral conduct where the individual's perceptions
      of the situation play a key role.

491. Bull, Norman. Moral Judgment from Childhood to Adolescence.
      Beverly Hills, CA: Sage Publications, 1969.

      Following a review of existing conceptions of the formation of
      character, a four-stage theory of moral development is
      presented: anomie, heteronomy, socionomy, and autonomy. The
      relationship between these stages and sex, intelligence, S.E.S.,
      and religion is then experimentally examined using primary,
      secondary, and college-age youth as subjects.

492. Clausen, John A., ed. Socialization and Society. Boston:
      Little, Brown, 1968.

      An excellent collection of papers on the dynamics of
      socialization. All the papers are useful in understanding the
      socialization process, but only the Maccoby paper (item 572)
      directly discusses the socialization of morality.

493. Crittenden, Brian J., ed. "The Cognitive and the Affective in
      Moral Action," Moral Education: Interdisciplinary Approaches
      (item 1492), pp. 372-402.

Aronfreed, Scriven, Kohlberg, et al., discuss issues such as punishment, affective control, and moral sensitivity.

494.   DePalma, David J., and Jeanne M. Foley, eds. Moral Development: Current Theory and Research. Hillsdale, NJ: Lawrence Erlbaum Associates, 1975.

Contains a collection of papers originally presented at a symposium on moral development at Loyola University of Chicago in 1973.

495.   Dyer, Prudence, and Richard D. Brooks. "Expressed Values: A Structural Model and a Report of a Ten Year Study with Elementary and Secondary Students, A Summary Report." Des Moines, Drake University, 1976. ED 133 237.

Student compositions over a ten-year period were analyzed for student values. It was found that students' values change as they grow older and that grade-level values can change from year to year.

496.   Edwards, J.B. "Chosen Ideal Person, Least Ideal Person, and Judgments about Moral Wickedness." Journal of Moral Education, 3 (1973).

Age developmental trends are detected as children move from very specific ideals of what is bad, based on immediate social context, to a more universal and realistic view of righteousness and wickedness. How educators could use these perspectives is briefly discussed.

497.   Edwards, J.B. "Some Studies of the Moral Development of Children." Educational Studies, 7 (1965): 200-211.

A review of mostly pre-1960 literature on the development of morality in children.

498.   Friesen, J.W. "Value Orientation of Modern Youth: A Comparative Study," Adolescence, 7 (1972): 265-275.

Finds using value indicators that youth culture is not separate and apart from adult society. The cultural continuity theory is supported.

499.   Gerson, Randy P., and William Damon. "Moral Understanding and Children's Conduct." New Directions for Child Development, No. 2: Moral Development (item 1497), pp. 41-59.

Presents the theoretical and conceptual background for a not-yet-completed study. Argues that predicting the social conduct of children entails unraveling the complex interactions between the child's capacity for social understanding, personal objectives, and contextual details of daily life.

500. Grahm, Douglas. Moral Learning and Development: Theory and Research. New York: Wiley-Interscience, 1972.

Presents the theory and relevant research on the three main theories that have influenced thinking about moral learning and development in recent years: psychoanalytic theory, learning theory, and cognitive developmental theory. Contains a good set of references on each of the theoretical orientations.

501. Grinder, R.E., and E.A. Nelson. "Moral Development in Early Adolescence: Perspective on a Perplexing Issue." The High School Journal, 63 (1980): 228-232.

Reviews the literature on early adolescent moral development and argues that the intellective and emotive facets of morality are complementary and become increasingly integrated during early adolescence. Ethical behavior during this period is enhanced by contact with adults who emphasize accepting responsibility for conduct and self-appraisal of conduct.

502. Hample, Dole J. "An Empirical Study of Value Argument." Ph.D. dissertation, University of Illinois, 1975. 36/09, p. 5635.

A model of value argument is created. Finds that Fishbein's equations (item 1126) do not predict adherence to value claims.

503. Harvard, Lesley C. "Questions from the Classroom." Journal of Moral Education, 3 (1974): 235-240.

A descriptive and anecdotal account of an exploration into the values of primary school youth.

504. Havinghurst, Robert J. "How the Moral Life is Formed." Religious Education, 57 (1962): 432-439.

Four phases of moral development during childhood are presented. Also discussed is the difficulty of predicting moral development and the effect of the situation on moral behavior.

505. Higgins, Elizabeth. "An Exploratory Investigation of the Valuing Process of Some Fourth Grade Pupils." Ph.D. dissertation, United States International University, 1968. 30/06, p. 2253.

In analyzing fourth grade children's writings using the Laswell Valuing Framework, finds that children mention more value enhancements than deprivations and that values shift from time to time.

506. Hoffman, Martin L. "Conscience, Personality and Socialization
      Techniques." Human Development, 13 (1970): 90-126.

      The relationships between children's moral orientations,
      personality traits, and parents' discipline techniques are
      explored.

507. Hoffman, Martin L. "Development of Moral Thought, Feeling and
      Behavior." American Psychologist, 34 (1979): 958-965.

      Following a review of relevant literature, concludes that
      there exist three somewhat independent moral internalization
      processes, each with its own experiential base: fear of
      ubiquitous authority, motive to consider others, and the
      cognitive processing of information.

508. Hoffman, Martin L. "Moral Development." Carmichael's Manual of
      Child Psychology, 3rd ed. Edited by Paul H. Mussen. New
      York: John Wiley and Sons, 1970, pp. 261-359.

      A broad and detailed overview of the factors contributing to
      moral development. Contains an extensive analysis of the
      relationship of parental child rearing and disciplinary
      practices in moral development.

509. Hogan, Robert. "Dialectical Aspects of Moral Development."
      Human Development, 17 (1974): 107-117.

      Summarizes and reviews three standard models of moral
      development and proposes an alternative viewpoint which
      incorporates a dialectical perspective.

510. Hogan, Robert. "Moral Development and the Structure of
      Personality." Moral Development: Current Theory and Research
      (item 494), pp. 153-167.

      Attempts to place moral development within a total personality
      structure comprised of five dimensions: autonomy, empathy,
      socialization, moral judgment, and moral knowledge.

511. Hogan, Robert; John A. Johnson; and Nicholas P. Emler. "A
      Socioanalytic Theory of Moral Development." New Directions
      for Child Development. No. 2: Moral Development (item 1497),
      pp. 1-18.

      Argues that the development of moral character must be viewed
      within a comprehensive theory of personality and culture. Takes
      a Durkheimian social evolutionary view of the nature of
      morality. Discusses three phases of the evolution of character
      structure: rule attainment, social sensitivity, and autonomy.

512. Holbrook, David. "Are We Losing the Next Generation? A Strange
      Experience on a Poetry Course." Journal of Moral Education,
      10 (1981): 117-127.

      Argues that "pop" film and television causes student
      withdrawal from the adult world and therefore dissociation from
      the normal confrontation necessary to adolescent development.

513. Horowitz, Irving L. "Moral Development, Authoritarian Distemper
      and the Democratic Persuasion." Moral Development and
      Politics (item 1531), pp. 5-21.

      Argues that the development of morals is diametrically opposed
      to and categorically distinct from moral development. Moral
      development is seen as imposed but the development of morals
      presupposes a morally pluralistic society. A variety of
      theories of moral development are reviewed. Argues that
      morality entails responsibility, which in turn entails choice
      regarding one's morality.

514. Kitwood, Tom. "The Morality of Inter-Personal Perspectives: An
      Aspect of Values in Adolescent Life." Journal of Moral
      Education, 7 (1978): 189-198.

      A code of conduct relevant to relationships in mid-adolescence
      is described, together with an outline of the method by which it
      was abstracted from interview data. Some comments on the
      character and significance of the code are offered.

515. Kitwood, Tom. "What Does 'Having Values' Mean?" Journal of
      Moral Education, 6 (1977): 81-89.

      Explores the question of how values are "attached" to persons.
      Argues that there must be a clear conception of the person, as
      an individual, in a social setting. A model that meets these
      requirements is offered. Three applications of this model are
      presented.

516. Lasseigne, Mary W. "The Influence of Peer and Adult Opinion on
      Moral Beliefs of Adolescents." Ed.D. dissertation, Indiana
      University, 1963. 24/12, p. 5198.

      Analyzes the relative effectiveness of peer group influence
      and adult group influence upon the opinions of adolescents
      concerning moral beliefs. Finds that adolescents are more
      influenced by peers.

517. Lee, John, and Susan Dye Lee. "How Moral Values are Learned."
      Morality Examined (item 1528), pp. 83-102.

Briefly discusses Freudian, Piagetian, and social learning perspectives on the learning of morality. A very superficial analysis.

518. Lickona, Thomas. "Critical Issues in the Study of Moral Development and Behavior." Moral Development and Behavior (item 519), pp. 3-27.

Introduces the papers in his book. Contains sections on the meaning of morality, the thought-action problem, the role of affect in morality, and accounting for evil in the world.

519. Lickona, Thomas, ed. Moral Development and Behavior: Theory, Research, and Social Issues. New York: Holt, Rinehart and Winston, 1976.

A collection of high-quality papers dealing with such issues as how morality is learned, research into the psychological bases of moral thought and behavior, and morality and social issues. Contains papers by Kohlberg, Aronfreed, Bronfenbrenner, Mischel, Eysenck, Hoffman, Selman, Rest, et al.

520. Maccoby, Eleanor E. "The Development of Moral Values and Behavior in Childhood." Socialization and Society (item 492), pp. 228-269.

Reviews the developmental viewpoint of Piaget and Kohlberg and the social learning point of view on moral socialization. The two theories are contrasted, and it is observed that both theories are right up to a point. The paper concludes by examining the phenomenon of intergenerational change from both perspectives.

521. McKinney, John P. "Moral Development and the Concept of Values." Moral Development and Socialization (item 542), pp. 201-218.

Addresses the question of the nature of values and their relationship to morality. Argues that moral behavior is based on moral judgment and that moral judgment, in turn, is based on cognitive units (values). Values provide the social framework within which judgments are made. A prescriptive/proscriptive distinction in value orientations is presented and evidence cited in its support. The relationship between these orientations and child rearing practices is discussed.

522. Mitchell, J.J. "Moral Dilemmas of Early Adolescence." Adolescence, 10 (1975): 442-445.

Identifies areas of moral conflict for early adolescents and points out that they are often normal manifestations of growth.

States that moral growth involves adopting group rules as well as formulating personal rules.

523. Mitchell, J.J. "Moral Growth During Adolescence." Journal of Moral Education, 3 (1974): 123-128.

A review of trends in moral development during adolescence that does not mention Piaget or Kohlberg. Talks about abstractions, practice, and sociocentric and cognitive emphases.

524. Mussen, Paul, and Nancy Eisenberg-Berg. Roots of Caring, Sharing, and Helping: The Development of Prosocial Behavior in Children. San Francisco: W.H. Freeman, 1977.

A concise, readable inquiry into the antecedent determinants of prosocial behavior. Separate chapters examine the contributions of biology, culture, person variables, the family, mass media, cognition, and situational factors.

525. O'Connor, John, and Lawrence S. Wrightsman. "Moral Development and the Development of Motives." Social Psychology in the Seventies by Lawrence S. Wrightsman. Monterey, CA: Brooks/Cole, 1973, pp. 99-129.

Presents a broad overview of the development of morality in Western culture. Sections of the chapter discuss Freudian theory, the neo-Freudian theory of Erickson, cognitive theories, research on morality, and the development of achievement motivation.

526. O'Connor, Robert E. "Parental Sources and Political Consequences of Levels of Moral Reasoning among European University Students." Moral Development and Politics (item 1531), pp. 237-255.

Using results from surveys of university students in England and France, attempts to relate the students' moral development to childhood socialization. Also explores the relationship between political variables and moral reasoning. Finds that socialization within the home appears to be the major factor in the development of individuals with mature moral reasoning capabilities.

527. Peck, Robert F., and Robert J. Havinghurst. The Psychology of Character Development. New York: John Wiley and Sons, 1960.

Suggest a motivational theory of morality presented in terms of psycho-social development. They hypothesize five character types: amoral, expedient, conforming, irrational-conscientious, and rational-altruistic. Argues that these personality types constitute five primary types of moral motivation. Evidence is

presented to show that these character types represent a
developmental schema and that there is a relationship between
character type and moral behavior.

528. Prescott, James W. "Before Ethics and Morality." The Humanist,
      32 (November/December 1972): 19-21.

      Argues that without a definition of moral behavior one cannot
      define moral education. One fundamental principle of moral
      behavior is offered: the rejection of creeds, policies, and
      specific behaviors that inflict pain, suffering, and deprivation
      upon our fellow man. Shows how sensory experiences during the
      formative periods of development stimulate the brain to produce
      certain structural and functional neural characteristics
      necessary for moral behavior. Before a child's reason can
      establish moral principles the course of an ethical and moral
      life is set.

529. Robinson, Gail P. "The Acquisition of Values: A Theoretical
      Model." Ph.D. dissertation, Oregon State University, 1978.
      38/07, p. 4058.

      A values acquisition model is developed consisting of a
      personal construction system that becomes a personal value
      system after processing in an interaction component. The model
      developed suggests how to develop values "grammars" and how to
      carry out needed descriptive studies.

530. Simon, A., and L.O. Ward. "Children's Concepts of Good and
      Bad--A Pilot Study." Journal of Moral Education, 1 (1972):
      129-133.

      The study e;ocoted spontaneous judgments of what children
      thought were "good" and bad. Significant developmental trends
      in terms of idealistic versus materialistic emphasis were
      detected.

531. Simpson, Elizabeth L. Democracy's Stepchildren: A Study of Need
      and Belief. San Francisco, CA: Jossey-Bass, 1971.

      Explores the relationship between basic human needs and
      attitudes, values, motivation and behavior. Specifically, the
      relationship between psychological deprivation and the
      acceptance of political values is examined. It is found, using
      data from high school students in three communities, that social
      deprivation is related to political values. The appendix
      contains a copy of the instrument used to assess psychological
      deprivation.

532. Skeel, D.J. "How Do Children Rank Their Values?" Viewpoints,
      52, 1 (1976): 55-72.

Using Rokeach's Value Survey 12 groups of children in different geographic regions ranked their values. Some differences were found among children, but a marked difference was found between teachers' rankings and student rankings.

533. Stanton, Michael. "Judgments by Secondary School Pupils of Rules of Games and Social Actions." Journal of Moral Education, 5 (1975): 71-80.

It was found that younger children had the highest ratings for rule-keeping statements. In judging actions, both highly desirable and highly undesirable, there was found to be a generality in judgment.

534. Steward, John. "Modes of Moral Thought." Journal of Moral Education, 8 (1979): 124-134.

The Williams' (item 593) version of moral development is tested, and its main conclusions receive tentative support: i.e., development is cumulative rather than linear and takes place in four separate modes (expedient, altruistic, intuitive, and heteronomous).

535. Stone, Norma K. "The Development of Moral Thought in Children." Values, Feelings and Morals, Edited by Hearn D. Dewain. Washington, D.C.: American Association of Elementary-Kinder-garten-Nursery Educators, 1974, pp. 5-18.

Presents a brief overview of three theories of moralization: Freudian, social learning, and cognitive-developmental.

536. Straughan, Roger. "Private and Public Morality: Some Misconceptions Explored. A Reply to John Sword." Journal of Moral Education, 6 (1977): 158-161.

Reaffirms the position, taken in an earlier article (item 2029) and attacked by Sword (item 134), that morality can be learned only in the context of direct situational experience. Therefore, hypothetical dilemmas cannot provide a basis for moral education.

537. Tapp, June L. "A Child's Garden of Law and Order." Law in American Society. 2, 2 (1973): 13-16.

Reports the results of a cross-cultural study in the development of compliance. It was found that in defining rules, the prescriptive function was the most widely recognized, that is, rules are seen as guides to action. Across the seven cultures studied there was general agreement about the need for laws in society. Also in Psychology Today, 4 (December 1970).

538. Ungoed-Thomas, J.R. "Patterns of Adolescent Behavior and
      Relationships in Northern Ireland." Journal of Moral
      Education, 2 (1972): 53-61.

      Finds that compared with school, the home is relatively
      unimportant as a source of situations involving friendship,
      hostility, and moral conflict. Concludes that there is a great
      need to expand the social experiences of Ulster youth.

539. Wells, Leora W. The Acquisition and Development of Values:
      Perspectives on Research. Bethesda, MD: National Institute
      of Child Health and Human Development, National Institutes of
      Health, 1968, ED 066 414.

      Report of a conference held by NIH on research relating to how
      children acquire their systems of values and morality. The
      conclusions of various participants are summarized. Among those
      presenting were Bronfenbrenner, Kohlberg, Aronfreed, Gustafson,
      Edel, and Baier.

540. Wilder, Paul G. "The Moral of a Story: Preschoolers' Gradual
      Comprehension of a Narrative on Sesame Street." Moral
      Education Forum, 5 (Fall 1980), pp. 2-14.

      Traces the evolution of preschoolers' understanding of a
      Cookie Monster story. Finds that children sense certain
      interpersonal conflicts from an early age and that repeated
      viewing of the story added little to the children's
      understanding of the conflicts.

541. Williams, Norm, and Sheila Williams. The Moral Development of
      Children. London: Macmillan, 1970.

      Provides an introduction to the psychology of moral
      development. Contains chapters on concern, conscience, moral
      judgment, modes of moral thought, and moral development. A
      readable introduction to a complex subject.

542. Windmiller, Myra; Nadine Lambert; and Elliot Turiel, eds. Moral
      Development and Socialization. Boston: Allyn and Bacon, 1980.

      Nine papers on three current theories of moral development,
      issues that emerge from contradictions among the theories, moral
      development and the study of values, and the question whether or
      not morality or values can be taught.

543. Winnicott, D.W. "The Young Child at Home and at School." Moral
      Education in a Changing Society (item 1515), pp. 96-111.

      The very possibility of morality in adulthood depends on the
      fostering of a healthy, feeling, inward life in the young child.
      Trust and belief in ideas of right and wrong must develop from

the working of the individual child's inner processes. These
inner processes accommodate moral ideals to the extent that
early life instills a belief in reliability.

544. Withey, Stephen. "The Influence of the Peer Group on the Values
      of Youth."   Religious Education, 57 (July-August 1962):
      534-544.

      Presents a review of relevant literature on the subject.

545. Workie,   Abeinah.   "Deceptiveness   in   Cooperation   and
      Competition." Journal of Moral Education, 3 (1974): 159-165.

      It was found that youth are more deceptive in purely
      competitive situations than in purely cooperative ones.

546. Allinsmith, Wesley. "The Learning of Moral Standards." Inner
     Conflict and Defense. Edited by D.R. Miller and G.G. Swanson.
     New York: Schocken Books, 1966.

     In an empirical test of psychoanalytic conceptions of the
     development of morality it was found that the severity of guilt
     regarding transgression of norms was significantly related to
     timing of weaning and toilet training. Relationships between
     parental disciplinary styles and moral behavior are also
     discussed.

547. Bettelheim, Bruno. "Moral Education." Moral Education: Five
     Lectures (item 1524), pp. 85-107.

     It is middle-class morality alone that makes learning
     possible. It consists of the conviction that to postpone
     immediate pleasure in order to gain more lasting satisfactions
     in the future is the most effective way to reach one's goals.
     Conscience develops on the basis of fear, learning depends on
     the prior formation of a conscience. Fear must be used in the
     early development of children to get them to overcome their
     instincts for immediate gratification. The motivating power of
     irrational anxiety will steadily give way to more rational
     purpose.

548. Bettelheim, Bruno. "Psychoanalysis and Education." The School
     Review, 77 (1969): 73-86.

     Discusses the role of schools in the formation of the super-
     ego. Argues that schools have recently focused too much atten-
     tion on the id.

549. Blos, P. On Adolescence: A Psychoanalytic Interpretation. New
     York: The Free Press, 1962.

     The definitive treatment of adolescence from the psycho-
     analytic perspective. Contains a bibliography of the psycho-
     analytic literature on adolescence.

550. Bronfenbrenner, Urie. "Freudian Theories of Identification and
     Their Derivatives." Child Development, 31 (1960): 15-40.

     Reviews Freudian thought on the process of identification in
     personality development. Recent criticisms and modifications of
     Freud's theory of identification are discussed.

551. Ekstein, R. "Psychoanalysis and Education for the Facilitation
     of Positive Human Qualities." Journal of Social Issues, 28
     (1972): 71-86.

     Discusses the development of positive human qualities from the
     psychoanalytic perspective and concludes that the application of
     psychoanalytic insights to education can contribute to the de-
     velopment of these qualities.

552. Erickson, Erik H. "Identity and the Life Cycle." Psychological
     Issues, 1, 1 (1959).

     Presents a theory of human development derived from psycho-
     analytic ego psychology. Eight stages of development are
     described. Each stage includes a psychosocial crisis that
     represents the developmental task for that period of time. If
     the crisis of a given stage is inadequately resolved, its legacy
     lives on in the individual's movement through the other stages.
     Each of the stages influences one's capacity for moral behavior.
     The stages are: Trust vs. Mistrust, Autonomy vs. Shame,
     Initiative vs. Guilt, Industry vs. Inferiority, Identity vs.
     Identity Diffusion, Intimacy vs. Isolation, Generativity vs.
     Self-Absorption, and Integrity vs. Despair.

553. Flugel, J.C. Man Morals and Society. New York: International
     Universities Press, 1970.

     The definitive psychoanalytic perspective on the development
     of morality. Although no specific reference is made to moral
     education, the determinants of morality in society and the home
     are provocative insights for those concerned with schools and
     the moral education of youth.

554. Freud, Sigmund. Civilization and Its Discontents. New York:
     W.W. Norton, 1962.

     Discusses in broad strokes man's place in the world. Argues
     that civilization is made possible only through the repression
     of the instinctive life of man. Aggression and egoistic
     self-satisfaction must be repressed, which results in guilt.
     Conscience is seen as the result of instinctual renunciation.
     Man has two urges, one toward personal happiness, the other
     toward union with others.

555. Freud, Sigmud. The Ego and the Id. Many editions.

     Contains Freud's introduction of the term "superego." It is
     seen as a modification of the ego and the main force in the
     resolution of the Oedipal conflict. Through identification with
     the parents the child internalizes a system of values and
     prohibitions.

556. Gilligan, James. "Beyond Morality: Psychoanalytic Reflections on Shame, Guilt, and Love." Moral Development and Behavior (item 519), pp. 144-158.

Sees morality as a force antagonistic to life, a force causing illness and death. Morality is action and thought motivated by compulsion and obligation rather than by love, and by a negative wish to avoid shame and guilt rather than by a positive wish to express feelings of love. Psychoanalysis, unlike ethics, does not tell people what they should do, but asks them what they want to do. Discusses the differences between shame and guilt and how they impact on various dimensions of moral growth.

557. Hall, Calvin. A Primer of Freudian Psychology. New York: New American Library, 1954.

A concise, readable presentation of the organization, dynamics, and development of personality according to Freud. A good starting point for those unfamiliar with psychoanalytic theory.

558. Hartman, H., and R.M. Lowenstein. "Notes on the Superego." Psychoanalytic Study of the Child, 17 (1962): 42-81.

The most comprehensive attempt by far to define and conceptualize the scope and functions of the superego. In their view the ego-ideal and the conscience are subsumed under the superego.

559. Nass, M.L. "The Superego and Moral Development in the Theories of Freud and Piaget." Psychoanalytic Study of the Child, 21 (1966): 51-68.

Reviews psychoanalytic and Piagetian conceptions of the development of morality and concludes that the cognitive developmental and Freudian perspectives are intertwined. Holds that there is no basic incompatibility between the two positions; the psychoanalytic perspective is simply a broader vision.

560. Peters, R.S. "Freud's Theory of Moral Development in Relation to That of Piaget." British Journal of Educational Psychology, 30 (1960): 250-258.

Makes relevant conceptual distinctions and compares Piaget and Freud. Also in Psychology and Ethical Development (item 311).

561. Post, Seymour C., ed. Moral Values and the Superego Concept in Psychoanalysis. New York: International Universities Press, 1972. NI

A collection of papers dealing with the development of the
superego and the relationships among psychoanalysis, moral
values, and culture.

562. Sandler, J. "On the Concept of Superego." Psychoanalytic Study
      of the Child, 15 (1960): 128-162.

      Analyzes the superego concept in order to devise an indexing
      system for the abundant case material on the concept. In the
      process a wide range of perspectives on the superego are
      discussed.

563. Sears, Robert R.; Lucy Rau; and Richard Alpert. Identification
      and Child Rearing. Stanford, CA: Stanford University Press,
      1965.

      An extensive empirical inquiry into the identification
      process, using 4 year olds. Patterns of parental relations were
      used to examine the extent of identification. The results only
      partially confirm the psychoanalytic theory.

564. Sears, Robert R., et al. Patterns of Child Rearing. Evanston,
      IL: Row Peterson, 1957.

      Presents a Freudian interpretation of the formation of values
      during childhood. The formation of the ego-ideal and conscience
      through identification with the parents is discussed.

565. Tice, Terrence N. "A Psychoanalytic Perspective." Moral
      Development and Socialization (item 542), pp. 161-199.

      Presents the Freudian theory of moral development. An effort
      is made to show how the Freudian stages of psycho-sexual
      development complement other developmental theories. Also
      points out that the primary process involved in internalization
      of moral standards--identification--is a perspective also
      subscribed to by social learning theorists.

566. Aronfreed, Justin. Conduct and Conscience: The Socialization of Internalized Control over Behavior. New York: Academic Press, 1966.

     Posits an internal evaluative (cognitive) structure that mediates the acquisition process of socialization. Finds room for both social learning theory and cognitive psychology in the moralization process.

567. Aronfreed, Justin. "Moral Development from the Standpoint of a General Psychological Theory." Moral Development and Behavior (item 519), pp. 54-69.

     In what is basically a critique of Kohlberg's work on moral development Aronfreed presents a social learning perspective of moralization. He presents data that indicate that thought assumes its power over conduct only because of the affective loadings which become attached to the representational thought. He discusses how thought can become affectively loaded and how affectivity mediates cognitive control.

568. Aronfreed, Justin. "Some Problems for a Theory of the Acquisition of Conscience." Moral Education: Interdisciplinary Approaches (item 1492), pp. 183-199.

     The ultimate criterion for assessing moral maturity should be not judgment and reasoning, but a person's conduct or behavior. Moral judgments have not been shown to be a major determinant of social behavior. The proper focus of study should be on how the effects of social experience become represented in such a way that the child acquires internalized control over his behavior.

569. Bandura, Albert. Social Learning Theory. Englewood Cliffs, NJ: Prentice-Hall, 1977.

     Presents a concise overview of social learning theory. An interpretation of the development of moral reasoning is presented. With a little effort the reader will be able to construct a social learning interpretation of the origins of moral behavior, which, because of the general nature of the book, is not discussed explicitly.

570. Bandura, A., and F.J. McDonald. "The Influence of Social Reinforcement and the Behavior of Models in Shaping Children's Moral Judgments." Journal of Abnormal and Social Psychology, 67 (1963): 273-281.

Finds that children's bases for judging moral acts (by consequences or intentions) by Piagetian stages can be altered by modeling and reinforcement.

571.   Bandura, Albert, and R.H. Waters. Social Learning and Personality Development. New York: Holt, Rinehart and Winston, 1963.

Applies social learning theory to the socialization of children. The assumption is made that behavior is controlled directly by a stimulus, by consequence as revealed in feedback, and through central mediational processes that are involved in observational learning. Social learning is seen as the result of observing the behavior of others, imitating that behavior, and being reinforced for the new pattern of behavior.

572.   Berkowitz, Leonard. The Development of Motives and Values in the Child. New York: Basic Books, 1964.

This guide for parents and teachers focuses on modeling, discipline, and identification from a social learning perspective.

573.   Berkowitz, L. "Social Norms, Feelings and Other Factors Affecting Helping and Altruism." Advances in Experimental and Social Psychology, Vol. 6. Edited by L. Berkowitz. New York: Academic Press, 1972.

Reviews a wide range of research in order to identify the factors that influencing altruistic behavior. Concludes that norms play a minor role and situational conditions play a very important role. Situational factors influence awareness of others' dependency, recall of pertinent social ideals, judgments of the legitimacy of the others' dependency, and the willingness to accept the psychological costs.

574.   Brady, Gene H. "A Social Learning Explanation of Moral Development." Contemporary Educational Psychology, 3 (1978): 20-26.

Presents a social learning explanation of moral development in which children abstract an array of generative rules that guide moral judgments and behaviors.

575.   Bryan, J.H.; J. Redfield; and S. Mader. "Words and Deeds about Altruism and the Subsequent Reinforcement Power of the Model." Child Development, 42 (1971): 1501-1508.

Children who are preached at and rewarded exhibit the behavior requested to a greater degree than do those who are simply preached at.

576. Cowan, Philip A., et al. "Social Learning and Piaget's Cognitive Theory of Moral Development." Journal of Personality and Social Psychology, 11 (1969): 261-274.

Replicates Bandura and McDonald's study (item 622) of the influence of modeling on children's moral judgments. Similar results were obtained but it was concluded that neither study affirmed or denied Piaget's hypothesis. A reply by Bandura follows (pp. 275-279).

577. Crane, Valerie, and Bennie L. Bollif. "Effects of Adult Modeling and Rule Structure on Responses to Moral Situations of Children in Fifth Grade Classrooms." The Journal of Experimental Education, 41 (1973): 49-52.

Finds that fifth graders will more often imitate models who provide reasons for their responses to value conflict than models who do not provide reasons.

578. Eysenck, H.J. "The Biology of Morality." Moral Development and Behavior (item 519), pp. 108-123.

Offers an explanation for the origin of moral behavior by linking the acquisition of a "conscience" with the conditioning of anxiety. Conscience is a conditional reflex. Conditionability is linked to cortical arousal. Cortical arousal is genetically determined. Therefore, moral behavior is not the result of freely willed and responsible decision making but rather a combination of a genetically determined arousal level and conditioned social behavior.

579. Eysenck, H.J. "The Development of Moral Values in Children." British Journal of Educational Psychology, 39 (1960): 11-21.

Argues that conscience is, in fact, a conditioned response built up during the child's formative years by pairing anti-social behavior with punishment. If the hypothesis is correct, differences in conditionability should be related to moral behavior. Evidence is cited that indicate that this hypothesis is correct.

580. Hoffman, Martin L. "Empathy, Role Taking, Guilt and Development of Altruistic Motives." Moral Development and Behavior (item 519), pp. 123-143.

Presents a theoretical account of the development of the altruistic motive that emphasizes its dependence on empathy. The analysis emphasizes affective response to others' distress on the one hand and cognitive development and role taking on the other. States that socialization experiences can strengthen the naturally occurring altruistic capacities and offers hypotheses regarding ways of facilitating this development.

581. Miller, N.E., and J. Dollard. Social Learning and Imitation.
      New Haven: Yale University Press, 1941.

      Presents a drive reduction theory of social learning. Holds
      that reinforcement is the result of drive reduction. The
      behavior of others serves as a cue for imitation because
      imitation has been reinforced through drive reduction in the
      past.

582. Mischel, Walter. "Preference for Delayed Reinforcement and
      Social Responsibility." Journal of Abnormal Social Psychology,
      62 (1961): 1-7.

      Finds that subjects preferring immediate, smaller rewards show
      less social responsibility than subjects preferring larger
      delayed rewards.

583. Mischel, Walter, and Harriet N. Mischel. "A Cognitive Social-
      Learning Approach to Morality and Self-Regulation." Moral
      Development and Behavior (item 519), pp. 84-107.

      Discusses the topic of moral competence (how individuals
      acquire the potential for generating organized behavior of a
      moral character), the conditions relevant to the performance of
      moral conduct, the achievement of self-regulation, and basic
      issues in the organization and inter-relations of moral
      judgment, moral conduct, and self-regulation.

584. O'Leary, K.D. "The Effects of Self Instruction on Immoral
      Behavior." Journal of Experimental Child Psychology, 6
      (1968): 297-301.

      Children who instructed themselves concerning the rules prior
      to acting were found to cheat less than students who did not use
      self-instruction.

585. O'Neill, William F. "Behaving and Believing: An Exploration
      into the Role of Values in the Learning/Knowing Process."
      Values and the Curriculum (item 1494), pp. 41-73.

      Traces the behavioral origins of values. Argues that the
      distinction between truth and value cannot be justified. Values
      and goals can be determined objectively by studying what is and
      what is capable of becoming. Belief is a function of behavior;
      therefore, to change values one must change behavior. The
      volume also includes critical reactions to this paper.

586. Rushton, J. Philippe. Altruism, Socialization and Society.
      Englewood Cliffs, NJ: Prentice-Hall, 1980.

      Attempts to provide a fully integrated conceptual analysis of
      the vast literature on altruism. The literature is viewed

largely from a social learning perspective. Contains chapters
on the sociobiology of altruism, motivations to be altruistic,
the altruistic personality, learning to be altruistic, the
family, the mass media, and the educational system. A thorough
bibliography is presented.

587. Sieber, Joan E. "A Social Learning Theory Approach to
      Morality." Moral Development and Socialization (item 542),
      pp. 129-159.

      Presents behaviorist learning theory and applies it to the
acquisition of morality. Philosophical conceptions of morality
are explicated and applied to the phenomena of the learning of
moral behavior. Proposals for moral education are presented.
Cautions that too early an insistence on morally independent
behavior is likely to result in anxiety, confusion, and an
inability to be strong in moral crises.

The Cognitive-Developmental Perspective

588. Bearison, D.J. "The Construct of Regression: A Piagetian Approach." Merrill-Palmer Quarterly, 20 (1974): 21-30.

Argues that regression within the Piagetian model of cognitive development is best understood as applicable only to the functional aspects of behavioral analysis and not to the logical abstract components that constitute the formal aspects of the theory.

589. Boyd, Dwight R. "An Interpretation of Principled Morality." Journal of Moral Education, 8 (1979): 110-123.

Principled morality is interpreted philosophically and psychologically. Assumptions embedded in this notion are presented, as is a phenomenological account of how they might be reflected in the process of moral judgment.

590. Boyd, Dwight. "The Rawls Connection." Moral Development, Moral Education and Kohlberg, (item 1514), pp. 185-213.

Points out that much of Kohlberg's discussions about stage 6 are based on Rawl's theory of justice (see item 244) and attempts to present an outline of a position that is a correct and plausible interpretation of Kohlberg's comments about Rawls.

591. Boyd, D., and L. Kohlberg. "The Is-Ought Problem: A Developmental Perspective." Zygon, 8 (1973): 358-372.

Following the presentation of the cognitive-developmental approach to the study of moral reasoning, the implications of this approach for the is-ought problem are discussed. It is held that in fact there is only one arena in which the moral life is played; the facts of the situation and one's obligations are seen as inseparable.

592. Candee, Daniel; Richard Graham; and Lawrence Kohlberg. "Moral Development and Life Outcomes." Cambridge, MA: Harvard University, 1978. ED 165 036.

Attempts to study the types of lives led by persons who have naturally developed more sophisticated structures of moral thought. Finds that individuals at higher stages of moral reasoning are more likely to hold high-status jobs, although there is no evidence that they are more satisfied with them. Also, higher-stage individuals tend to use induction in their child-rearing practices.

593. Colby, Anne. "Evaluation of a Moral-Developmental Theory." New
      Directions for Child Development, No. 2: Moral Development
      (item 1497), pp. 89-104.

      Presents a history of the evolution of the moral judgment
      interview scoring procedures used to evaluate the reasoning of
      Kohlberg's original longitudinal sample and to validate the
      stage typology. Discusses the conceptual and procedural changes
      that have taken place. See also item 703.

594. Colby, Anne, Lawrence Kohlberg; and John Gibbs. "A Longitudinal
      Study of Moral Judgment." Paper presented at the biennial
      meeting of the Society for Research in Child Development, San
      Francisco, 1979. ED 172 946.

      Presents the results of Kohlberg's 20-year longitudinal study
      of the moral reasoning of 58 males. Protocols were scored using
      the latest scoring system. The sequential development through
      stages and the reliability and validity of the instrument were
      confirmed.

595. Crittenden, Brian S., ed. "The Theory of Developmental Stages
      in Moral Judgment," Moral Education Interdisciplinary
      Approaches (item 1492), pp. 355-372.

      Scriven, Kohlberg, Aronfreed, et al., challenge and examine
      the developmental conception of moral judgment.

596. Damon, William. The Social World of the Child. San Francisco:
      Jossey-Bass, 1977.

      Contains an extensive report on the development of children's
      thinking about their social world. Several aspects of the
      child's social world are examined: the child's acquisition of
      social-conventional knowledge and of justice reasoning, his
      relations with authority, his acquisition of sex-role knowledge,
      and his understanding of friendship. The research reported
      assesses children's thinking in hypothetical as well as
      real-life situations. Developmental stages in reasoning about
      the social world are identified.

597. Damon, William. "Structural-Developmental Theory and the Study
      of Moral Development." Moral Development and Socialization
      (item 524), pp. 35-68.

Reviews developmental theory on how morality is learned, consistency in moral life, and the ordering of moral thought. Damon's own analysis of the social-moral concerns of children, with its focus on concerns of positive justice and concerns of authority, is reported. Three conclusions about moral consistency are discussed. Damon argues, in conclusion, that the understandings engendered by developmental research are of great use to teachers--specific educational techniques are not necessary to justify such research.

598. Damon, William. "Studying Early Moral Development: Some Techniques for Interviewing Young Children and for Analyzing the Results." Values Education: Theory/Practice/Problems/ Prospects (item 1511), pp. 25-40.

Discusses efforts to study the important aspects of early morality: positive justice, concerns of authority, and concerns of responsibility and blame. The stage of positive justice found in young children's reasoning is reported and discussed.

599. Eisenberg-Berg, Nancy. "Development of Children's Prosocial Moral Judgment." Developmental Psychology, 15 (1979): 128-137.

Developmental trends in reasoning are noted in elementary and secondary school students on prosocial dilemmas: dilemmas where the needs of individuals conflict in a context where law, rules, and the like are minimized or irrelevant. Stereotypical reasoning decreased with age, while empathetic reasoning increased.

600. Erickson, V. Lois. "The Domains of Ego and Moral Development." Moral Education Forum, 2 (September 1977): 1-4.

Sets forth some of the key concepts of the domains of ego and moral development, shows how they overlap, and discusses related educational and research issues.

601. Faherty, John K. "Moral Judgment and the Cognitive-Developmental Approach to Socialization." 1979. ED 191 599.

Reviews cognitive-developmental theory and discusses relevant criticisms. Also comments on the contribution of social influences, child rearing influences, and parental role modeling on moral development. The effectiveness of schools in fostering moral development is also discussed.

602. Flavell, J.H.   "An Analysis of Cognitive-Developmental Se-
      quences." Genetic Psychology Monographs, 86 (1972): 279-350.

      Offers proposals concerning the classification and explanation
      of developmental sequences of cognitive acquisitions in which
      earlier-developing elements are related to later-developing ones
      by addition, substitution, modification, inclusion, or media-
      tion. Any sequence can be explained by appeal to one of the
      following three factors: structure of the organism, structure of
      the environment, and structure of items. Developmentalists are
      warned that human cognitive development may exhibit significant
      asequential features in addition to the sequential features.

603. Garbarino, James, and Urie Bronfenbrenner.   "The Socialization
      of Moral Judgment and Behavior in Cross-Cultural Perspective."
      Moral Development and Behavior (item 519), pp. 70-83.

      Attempts to reconcile Kohlberg's psychological stage theory
      with   Bronfenbrenner's   five   types   of   moral   judgment   on
      behavior--a social-psychological scheme.   The development of
      moral reasoning is placed within a broad conception of
      socialization. Argues that morally mature judgment and behavior
      are facilitated by a morally pluralistic society. Evidence is
      offered to support this claim.

604. Gibbs, John.   "The Piagetian Approach to Moral Development: An
      Overview."   Values   Education: Theory/Practice/Problems/
      Prospects (item 1511), pp. 51-64.

      Presents Piagetian theory and compares it with Kohlberg's
      extension of the theory. The research base for the development
      of moral reasoning is examined.

605. Gibbs, John; Lawrence Kohlberg; Anne Colby; and Betsy Speicher-
      Dubin.   "The Domain and Development of Moral Judgment: A
      Theory and a Method of Assessment."   Reflections on Values
      Education (item 1510), pp. 19-45.

      Presents an introduction to Kohlberg's theory. Discusses the
      nature of stages of moral reasoning, the domain of moral
      judgment-moral concerns and issues, how stage growth occurs, and
      how it is assessed through the moral interview format. Includes
      examples of the Moral Judgment Interview protocol.

606. Gilligan, Carol.   "In a Different Voice: Women's Conceptions of
      Self and of Morality." Stage Theories of Cognitive and Moral
      Development (item 655), pp. 52-88.

      Argues that Kohlberg's stage theory of moral development has
      not given adequate expression to the concerns and experience of
      women. From her own research data, consisting of interviews
      with women contemplating abortion, an alternative sequence for

the development of women's moral judgments is suggested. The hypothesized developmental sequence is based on self-sacrifice in the service of a morality of care rather than upon a conception of justice. Also in Harvard Educational Review, 47 (1977): 43-61.

607. Gilligan, Carol. "Justice and Responsibility: Thinking about Real Dilemmas of Moral Conflict and Choice." Toward Moral and Religious Maturity (item 403), pp. 223-249.

Argues that when one shifts from reasoning about hypothetical issues to thinking about real dilemmas of moral conflict and choice, the concept of moral agency is brought into the center of moral development. When judgment is tied to action, thinking shifts to issues of responsibility and care. Holds that the understanding of these concerns also follows a developmental sequence.

608. Gilligan, Carol, and John Murphy. "From Adolescence to Adulthood: The Moral Dilemmas of Reconciliation to Reality." Moral Education Forum, 4 (1979): 3-13.

Argues that as intellectual development continues beyond adolescence and into adulthood there occurs a shift from the metaphysics of logical justification to the empirical discovery of the consequences of choice. This requires a cognitive transformation from a formal to a dialectical mode of reasoning. What may appear as regression is in fact a dual-context form of reasoning. The bibliography is missing.

609. Golding, Gail, and Toni Laidlaw. "Women and Moral Development." Interchange, 10 (1979-80): 95-103.

Agreeing with Gilligan (item 606), the authors hold that caring concerns are more relevant to understanding the female approach to morality than are justice concerns.

610. Hennessey, Thomas C. "An Interview with Lawrence Kohlberg." Values/Moral Education: The Schools and the Teachers (item 1500), pp. 211-242.

Kohlberg discusses his childhood and education, philosophical influences, his research, applied moral education, and the relationship of moral reasoning to moral behavior.

611. Kegan, Robert. "Ego and Truth: Personality and the Piagetian Paradigm." Ph.D. dissertation, Harvard University, 1977.

Interprets the totality of human personality development from a Piagetian perspective.

612. Kegan, Robert. "The Piagetian Paradigm and the Person." Moral
     Education Forum. 2 (November 1977): 1-13.

     Applies the Piagetian paradigm to new areas of human
     development. Depression and mental breakdown are seen as
     reflections of disequilibrium in ego development. The positions
     argued are taken from the author's 1977 doctoral dissertation at
     Harvard University (item 611).

613. Keasey, Charles B. "Implications of Cognitive Development for
     Moral Reasoning." Moral Development: Current Theory and
     Research (item 494), pp. 39-56.

     Examines the relations between cognitive and moral stages and
     cites research to support the argument that attainment of
     concrete operations is a necessary precondition for stage 2
     reasoning and that the attainment of formal operations is a
     necessary precondition for the attainment of stage 5.

614. Keniston, Kenneth. "Student Activism, Moral Development and
     Morality." American Journal of Orthopsychology, 40 (1970):
     577-592.

     Argues that although there is room for optimism regarding the
     increasing degree of principled moral reasoning among youth,
     moral reasoning alone is not sufficient to account for virtuous
     behavior. There is a need to stop viewing the moral sector of
     development as separate from the other sectors.

615. Kohlberg, Lawrence. "The Child as a Moral Philosopher."
     Readings in Values Clarification (item 1504), pp. 49-61.

     A concise and clear statement of the cognitive-developmental
     approach to moral reasoning. Also in Psychology Today, 7
     (1968): 25-30.

616. Kohlberg, Lawrence. "The Claim to Moral Adequacy of a Highest
     Stage of Moral Judgment." The Journal of Philosophy, 70
     (1973): 630-646.

     Elaborates on the claim previously taken (item 626) that the
     higher stages are objectively preferable to lower stages. A
     Rawlsian (item 244) interpretation of stage 6 is presented.
     Also in The Philosophy of Moral Development (item 624).

617. Kohlberg, Lawrence. "A Cognitive-Developmental Analysis of
     Children's Sex-Role Concepts and Attitudes." The Development
     of Sex Role Differences. Edited by E. Maccoby. Stanford, CA:
     Stanford University Press, 1966, pp. 82-173.

Argues that family climates can either facilitate or impede "natural" developmental trends, but generalized reinforcement and identification mechanisms do not in themselves provide an adequate explanation for the sex-role attitudes in children. To adequately account for the development of sex-role attitudes one must take into account basic cognitive-developmental trends.

618. Kohlberg, Lawrence, ed. Collected Papers on Moral Development and Moral Education. Cambridge, MA: Center for Moral Education, Harvard University, 1973.

A collection of photocopies of 16 early papers by Kohlberg.

619. Kohlberg, Lawrence. "Continuities and Discontinuities in Childhood and Adult Moral Development Revisited." Life-Span Developmental Psychology: Research and Theory. Edited by B.P. Baltes and K.W. Schaie. New York: Academic Press, 1973.

Presents revisions in the theory based on apparent "regressions" to stage 2 among adults, new stage-scoring procedures, and further longitudinal interviews with subjects. Extensive attention is given to the relationships between stages of ego development and stages of moral development. The existence of a stage 7 is hinted at. Also in The Psychology of Moral Development (item 625).

620. Kohlberg, Lawrence. "The Development of Children's Orientations Toward a Moral Order Part 1: Sequence in the Development of Moral Thought." Vita Humana, 6 (1963): 11-33.

Presents an overview of Kohlberg's findings with regard to moral development. Argues that the evidence suggests a series of internally patterned or organized transformations of social concepts and attitudes rather than a simple internalization of external rules.

621. Kohlberg, Lawrence. "The Development of Modes of Moral Thinking and Choice in the Years 10 to 16." Ph.D. dissertation, University of Chicago, 1959.

Kohlberg's original extension of Piaget's work. The subjects of this study--75 males--are the data base from which Kohlberg's longitudinal data are derived.

622. Kohlberg, Lawrence. "Development of Moral Character and Moral Ideology." Review of Child Development Research. Edited by M. Hoffman and L. Hoffman. New York: Russell Sage Foundation, 1964, pp. 383-431.

Reviews traditional conceptions of moral character and moral conduct. This is followed by discussions on the development of moral ideology, the development of guilt, moral factors in

delinquency and neurosis, relation of moral ideologies to personality integration, and implications for concepts of moral
education.

623. Kohlberg, Lawrence. "Epilogue. Education for Justice: The
     Vocation of Janusz Korczak." The Philosophy of Moral
     Development (item 624), pp. 401-408.

     The life of a martyred Polish educator illuminates the
     centrality of education for justice in a "Stage 7" commitment to
     serving children.

624. Kohlberg, Lawrence. Essays on Moral Development. Volume 1: The
     Philosophy of Moral Development. New York: Harper and Row,
     1981.

     A collection of articles by Kohlberg in which the focus is on
     moral stages and justice. In these papers Kohlberg sets forth
     his philosophical positions on moral, political, and educational
     issues underlying his developmental theory. With the exception
     of one paper on stage 7, all of the papers have been previously
     published. Each paper has, however, been slightly modified with
     an introduction linking it to the other papers and to the theme
     of the book.

625. Kohlberg, Lawrence. Essays on Moral Development. Volume 2: The
     Psychology of Moral Development. New York: Harper and Row,
     forthcoming.

     A collection of mostly previously published articles trace the
     psychological theory from earlier formulations to the present,
     present the longitudinal data and the method of scoring it, and
     provide accounts of eras in the life cycle from a stage
     perspective.

626. Kohlberg, Lawrence. "From Is to Ought: How to Commit the
     Naturalistic Fallacy and Get Away with It in the Study of
     Moral Development." Cognitive Development and Epistemology.
     Edited by T. Mischel. New York: Academic Press, 1971.

     Argues that there is a parallelism between a theory of
     psychological development and a formalistic moral theory. The
     formal psychological development criteria of differentiation and
     integration, of structural equilibrium, map onto the formal
     moral criteria of prescriptiveness and universality. The higher
     stages, because they more completely and adequately deal with
     moral conflict, are judged therefore to be better. Also in The
     Philosophy of Moral Development (item 624).

627. Kohlberg, Lawrence. "The Future of Liberalism as the Dominant
     Ideology of the West." Moral Development and Politics (item
     1531), pp. 55-68.

Argues that his own theory of moral development substantiates the notion that liberalism will persist. Shows the utility of his developmental theory in understanding the present moral age. Also in The Philosophy of Moral Development (item 624).

628. Kohlberg, Lawrence. "Moral Development." International Encyclopedia of the Social Sciences. New York: Crowell, Collier and Macmillan, 1968, pp. 489-494.

Discusses and dismisses cultural (Durkheimian) and Freudian interpretations of the development of moral character. Presents and defends his developmental-stage theory.

629. Kohlberg, Lawrence. "Moral Development and Identification." Child Psychology, 62nd Yearbook of the National Society for the Study of Education. Edited by H. Stevenson. Chicago: University of Chicago Press, 1963.

In a thorough review of the research, psychoanalytic and social learning interpretations of the acquisition of morality are found not to adequately account for the existence of moral character. The developmental perspective on the origins of moral character is presented and defended.

630. Kohlberg, Lawrence. "Moral Psychology and the Study of Tragedy." Festschrift, Directions in Literary Criticism. Edited by S. Weintraub and P. Young. University Park, PA: Pennsylvania State University Press, 1973.

Analyzes conceptions of tragedy from the developmental-stage theory perspective. Contains interesting analyses of stages of moral reasoning represented in great literature. Also in The Philosophy of Moral Development (item 624).

631. Kohlberg, Lawrence. "Moral Stages and Moralization: The Cognitive Developmental Approach." The Psychology of Moral Development (item 625), Chapter 3.

Presents a recent summary of cognitive developmental theory, the nature of the six stages, and the methods of assessing the stages.

632. Kohlberg, Lawrence. "Psychological Approaches to the Study of Moral Development." The Psychology of Moral Development (item 625), Chapter 1.

The cognitive-developmental approach to studying moral development is placed in a historical survey of the basic schools of moral psychology and sociology. The theoretical perspective and empirical findings of each school are reviewed.

633. Kohlberg, Lawrence. "The Relations Between Moral Judgment and Moral Action: A Developmental View." Paper presented at Institute of Human Development, University of California at Berkeley, 1969.

Presents the argument that at the higher, principled stages, there is greater consistency between one's reasoning and one's actions. Since the higher stages are more moral, principled reasoners behave in a more moral manner.

634. Kohlberg, Lawrence. "Relationships Between the Development of Moral Judgment and Moral Conduct." Paper presented at biannual meeting of the Society for Research in Child Development, Minneapolis, 1965.

Presents the argument that at the higher, principled stages, there is greater consistency between one's reasoning and one's actions.

635. Kohlberg, Lawrence. "Sex Differences in Morality." Sex Role Development. Edited by E.E. Maccoby. New York: Social Science Research Council, 1964. NR.

636. Kohlberg, Lawrence. "Stage and Sequence: The Cognitive-Developmental Approach to Socialization." Handbook of Socialization Theory and Research. Edited by D. Goslin. New York: Rand McNally, 1969, pp. 347-480.

Probably Kohlberg's most extensive account of cognitive-developmental theory within a broad socialization perspective. Also in The Psychology of Moral Development (item 625).

637. Kohlberg, Lawrence. "Stages and Aging in Moral Development--Some Speculations." The Gerontologist, 13 (1973): 497-502.

After reviewing the cognitive-developmental stage concept and applying it to adulthood, an attempt is made to delineate a new stage 7, unique to advanced adulthood. This stage 7 involves the adoption of a religious and cosmic perspective and is related to Erikson's theory (item 552).

638. Kohlberg, Lawrence. "The Young Child as a Philosopher." The Psychology of Moral Development (item 625), Chapter 13.

Discusses the meaning of moral stages for understanding the young child (ages 3-8) and for communication between teacher and child.

639. Kohlberg, Lawrence, and Daniel Candee. "The Relations Between Moral Judgment and Moral Action." The Psychology of Moral Development (item 625), Chapter 4.

Reviews studies relating stages of moral reasoning to actual moral behavior. Argues that moral reasoning is a necessary but not sufficient condition for moral action. The importance of ego strength or will in moral behavior is discussed.

640. Kohlberg, Lawrence, and Anne Colby. "The Meaning and Measurement of Moral Development: The History of Stage Scoring and the Longitudinal Results." The Psychology of Moral Development (item 625), Chapter 8.

Reports the actual longitudinal findings of sequence in moral judgment. Responds to criticisms of the methodology of assessing stage of moral reasoning.

641. Kohlberg, Lawrence, and Donald Elfenbein. "The Development of Moral Judgments Concerning Capital Punishment." American Journal of Orthopsychiatry, 45 (1973): 614-640.

Fram data in a longitudinal study it was found that the most mature stages condemn the death penalty. Asserts that this provides a rational basis for arguing the immorality and unconstitutionality of the death penalty. Also in The Philosophy of Moral Development (item 624).

642. Kohlberg, Lawrence and Carol Gilligan. "The Adolescent as a Philosopher: The Discovery of the Self in a Postconventional World." Daedalus, 100 (1971): 1051-1086.

Discusses adolescence from the perspective of development in moral reasoning. Special attention is given to the issues of relativity, moral stages, and ego identity. Also in Adolescents' Development and Education (item 1512), Collected Papers on Moral Development and Moral Education (item 618), and The Psychology of Moral Development (item 625).

643   Kohlberg, L., and R. Kramer. "Continuities and Discontinuities in Childhood and Adult Moral Development." Human Development, 12 (1969): 93-120.

Explores the apparent phenomenon of a stage regression between stages 4 and 5 and explains it away as a transitional step in the developmental process. Also in The Psychology of Moral Development (item 625).

644. Kohlberg, Lawrence, and Richard Shulik. "The Aging Person as a Philosopher." The Psychology of Moral Development (item 625), Chapter 15.

Describes the two highest stages of moral development as an aspect of early adult development. Also discussed is a hypothetical stage of moral and metaphysical religious integration (stage 7).

645. Kohlberg, Lawrence, and Edward Zigler. "The Impact of Cognitive
      Maturity on the Development of Sex-Role Attitudes in the Years
      Four to Eight." Genetic Psychology Monographs, 75 (1967):
      91-165.

      Reports a set of studies designed to assess a cognitive-
      developmental interpretation of IQ-personality relationships.
      It was found that sex-role attitudes are to a considerable
      extent linked to rate of cognitive growth rather than to
      physiological or chronological development.

646. Kohlberg, Lawrence; Anne Colby; and Kelsey Kauffman. "An
      Introduction to Standard Issue Scoring." The Psychology of
      Moral Development (item 625), Chapter 11.

      Presents the logic of the stage-scoring manual and defines its
      basic unit, the criterion judgment, by issue, norm, element, and
      stage. See also items 703 and 807.

647. Kohlberg, Lawrence; Ann Higgins; and Clark Power. "Justice,
      Responsibility and Practical Moral Judgment." The Psychology
      of Moral Development (item 625), Chapter 5.

      Following Gilligan's (item 606) lead with reasoning on
      "real-life" moral dilemmas, the authors note that there appear
      to be levels of judgments of responsibility somewhat
      distinguishable from stages of judgments of justice; the former
      are tied to relationships of interpersonal caring and community.

648. Kohlberg, L.; R. La Crosse; and D. Ricks. "The Predictability
      of Adult Mental Health from Childhood Behavior." Handbook of
      Child Psychopathology. Edited by B. Wolman. New York:
      McGraw-Hill, 1971, pp. 1217-1284.

      Reviews an extensive corpus of literature on the
      predictability of adult mental health. Concludes that the
      school's mental health interest should focus on ego development.
      Enhancement of school learning and of social relationships is
      viewed as both a result and a cause of enhancement of ego
      development. Competence and ego maturity are seen as the best
      predictors of absence of mental illness.

649. Kohlberg, Lawrence; Clark Power; and Ann Higgins. "Exploring
      the Atmosphere of Institutions: A Bridge Between Moral
      Judgment and Moral Action." The Psychology of Moral
      Development (item 625), Chapter 6.

      Discusses research relating moral conduct to interviews about
      real rather than hypothetical situations. The importance of
      studying group and institutional norms is emphasized.

650. Kuhmerker, Lisa. "Dialog: Lawrence Kohlberg Talks to Lisa
     Kuhmerker about Moral Development and the Measurement of Moral
     Judgment." Evaluating Moral Development (item 1506), pp.
     87-99.

     Kohlberg discusses the evaluation of his thinking on the
     development of moral reasoning and reports reliability and
     validity data on the final version of the Moral Judgment
     Instrument Scoring Manual.

651. Kuhmerker, Lisa. "The Development and Scoring of Lawrence
     Kohlberg's Moral Judgment Instrument." Evaluating Moral
     Development (item 1506), pp. 75-85.

     Briefly discusses the evaluation of and vocabulary associated
     with the development of Kohlberg's Moral Judgment Instrument.

652. Kuhmerker, Lisa. "Developments in Kohlberg's Theory and Scoring
     of Moral Dilemmas." Occasional Paper No. 6. Philadelphia:
     Research for Better Schools, 1978. ED 157 815.

     Recounts the latest developments in the evaluation of the
     Kohlberg Moral Judgment Interview scoring process.

653. Kuhmerker, Lisa. "Growth Toward Principled Behavior: Lawrence
     Kohlberg's Studies of Moral Development." Journal of Moral
     Education, 2 (1973): 255-262.

     An adoring view of Kohlberg's theory and methodology.

654. Kuhmerker, Lisa. "A Report on Kohlberg's 1976 Scoring
     Workshop." Moral Education Forum, 1 (September 1976): 1-11.

     An account of the 1976 moral judgment scoring workshop held at
     Harvard University. Includes a dialog between author and
     Kohlberg.

655. Kuhn, Deanna, ed. Stage Theories of Cognitive and Moral
     Development: Criticisms and Application. Cambridge, MA:
     Harvard Educational Review, 1978.

     Contains reprints of eight articles on stage theories of
     cognitive development previously published in the Harvard
     Educational Review between 1969 and 1977. Included is
     Gilligan's "In a Different Voice" (item 606).

656. Lickona, T. "Moral Development and the Problem of Evil."
     Developmental Psychology. Edited by R.M. Liebert, R.W.
     Poulos, and G.D. Strauss. Englewood Cliffs, NJ:
     Prentice-Hall, 1977.

Attempts to draw the connection between low stage of moral reasoning and evil behavior.

657. Lickona, Thomas. "Research on Piaget's Theory of Moral Development." Moral Development and Behavior (item 519), pp. 219-240.

Presents the theoretical and research base for Piaget's conception of moral development.

658. Modgil, Sohan, and Celia Modgil, eds. Piagetian Research: Compilation and Commentary, Volume 6: The Cognitive-Developmental Approach to Morality. Windsor, England: N.F.E.R. Publishing Co., 1976.

An explication and review of research on the cognitive developmental approach to morality. Contains discussions of factors associated with Piaget's approach. Given equal attention is Kohlberg's extension of Piaget's schema. Contains 100 pages of annotated abstracts of research on the development of moral reasoning.

659. Ott, Helmut W. "Reasonable Universalism as an Approach to Moral Values and Some Implications for Moral Education." Ph.D. dissertation, University of Toronto, 1974. 37/05, p. 2808.

After dismissing value relativity he adopts a characterization of moral universalism based on the work of Piaget and Kohlberg. Moral development should be seen in the context of total human development--social, emotional, and rational.

660. Perry, W.G. Forms of Intellectual and Ethical Development in the College Years. New York: Holt, Rinehart and Winston, 1968.

Investigates changes in students' thinking patterns as they progress through college. Suggests that cognitive development proceeds through nine "positions," each with its own discernible set of qualities. Development proceeds from a black/white perception of absolute (dualism) to a realization that each person must make a personal commitment to particular ways of knowing and understanding.

661. Piaget, Jean. The Moral Judgment of the Child. New York: The Free Press, 1969.

Beginning with questions on and observations of the child's game of marbles, Piaget describes a developmental evaluation of children's moral reasoning. Two separate moralities are detected: moral constraint and moral autonomy. Under moral constraint (heteronomy) right is to obey the will of the adult. Moral autonomy emerges when the mind regards as necessary an

ideal that is independent of all external pressure. Piaget
compares his results with the fundamental theses of sociology
and psychology concerning the empirical nature of moral life.

662. Podd, Marvin H. "Ego Identity Status and Morality: The
     Relationship Between Two Developmental Constructs."
     Developmental Psychology, 6 (1972): 497-507.

     It was found that subjects who had achieved ego identity were
     more morally mature than those who had not. Motives, but not
     behavior on a moral conduct task, differed according to identity
     status and level of moral development.

663. Porter, Nancy. "Kohlberg and Moral Development." Journal of
     Moral Education, 1 (1972): 123-128.

     Kohlberg's stages of moral development are discussed and
     conjectures about a possible seventh stage are entertained.
     Problems of Kohlberg's stages in the motivation of moral
     behavior are discussed.

664. Reimer, Joseph. "A Structural Theory of Moral Development."
     Theory into Practice, 16 (1977): pp. 60-66.

     Flatly rejects social learning explanations of the learning of
     morality and then proceeds to offer cognitive-developmental
     theory as the most satisfactory interpretation of the
     acquisition of morality.

665. Rosen, Hugh. The Development of Sociomoral Knowledge: A
     Cognitive-Structural Approach. New York: Columbia University
     Press, 1980.

     A Piaget-Kohlberg model of the development of social moral
     knowledge is presented in an easy-to-understand manner.
     Comprehensive in scope, with chapters on critiques of the theory
     and strategies for implementation.

666. Selman, Robert. "The Relation of Role-Taking to the Development
     of Moral Judgment in Children." Child Development, 42 (1974):
     79-91.

     Finds that the development of the ability to understand the
     reciprocal nature of interpersonal relations is a necessary but
     not sufficient condition for the development of conventional
     moral thought.

667. Selman, Robert L. "Role-Taking Ability and the Development of
     Moral Judgment," Ph.D. dissertation, Boston University, 1969.
     30/05, p. 2154.

Explores the relationship between two aspects of social development role taking and moral reasoning. Finds that a greater ability to shift social perspective is related to higher levels of moral judgment in middle-childhood.

668.   Selman, Robert L. "Social-Cognitive Understanding: A Guide to Educational and Clinical Practice." Moral Development and Behavior (item 519), pp. 299-316.

Presents his research on the successive stages in the development of the ability to take the perspective of another (social role taking) and the relationship of these stages to stages of moral thought. Also discusses the implications of this approach for social intervention.

669.   Smith, Roger A. "Direct and Indirect Parent-Child Verbal Interaction and Young Children's Moral Judgments of Filmed and Intentional Single-Story Dilemmas." Ph.D. dissertation, Florida State University, 1977. 36/05, p. 2655.

Parents and children discussed filmed moral dilemmas. Flanders Interaction Analysis System was used to identify direct and indirect verbal interactions. Children made more mature judgments when discussing moral dilemmas with parents who used indirect parent-child interactions.

670.   Tapp, June L., and Lawrence Kohlberg. "Developing Senses of Law and Legal Justice." Journal of Social Issues, 27, 2 (1971): 65-91.

Presents a theory of legal development derived from cognitive developmental theory. Argues that development of legal orientation parallels reasoning in the moral domain. The movement is seen as from a preconventional law-obeying, to a conventional law-maintaining, to a postconventional law-making perspective. Cross-cultural data is presented to show the universal nature of this development.

671.   Turiel, Elliot. "The Development of Concepts of Social Structure." The Development of Social Understanding. Edited by J. Glick and K.A. Clarke-Stewart. New York: Gardner Press, 1978, pp. 25-107.

Argues that children form concepts of social organization that structure their thinking about such conventional issues as family patterns, forms of address, dress codes, and national order. The development of these concepts about these types of social-conventional issues forms an age-related sequence of seven levels. It is held that the societal domain forms a conceptual framework distinct from that of the moral domain. Social conventions form part of the individual's descriptive

understanding of systems of social interactions and therefore
are differentiated from moral prescriptions.

672. Turiel, Elliot. "The Development of Social Concepts: Mores,
Customs and Conventions." Moral Development: Current Theory
and Research (item 494), pp. 7-37.

Argues that moral judgment constitutes only one aspect of
social conceptions and that the development of social-
conventional reasoning involves different cognitive structures.
Extensive interview data is reported to support the claim for a
separate developmental sequence for social-conventional
reasoning.

673. Turiel, Elliot. "The Development of Social-Conventional and
Moral Concepts." Moral Development and Socialization (item
524), pp. 69-106.

Focuses on the development of concepts of social convention
and on the basis for distinguishing social convention from
morality. Argues that concepts of social convention are
structured by concepts of social organization. At each developmental level conventions are seen in relation to social
structure. Adherence to convention stems from the individual's
conceptualizations of systems of social interaction. The
picture put forth by many developmentalists of "less developed"
conformists and "more developed" reasoners is misleading, for
adherence to convention also follows a developmental framework.

674. Turiel, Elliot. "Developmental Processes in the Child's Moral
Reasoning." Trends and Issues in Developmental Psychology.
Edited by P. Mussen, J. Langer, and M. Covington. New York:
Holt, Rinehart and Winston, 1969, pp. 92-133.

Presents a thorough overview of developmental theory as
presented by Kohlberg.

675. Turiel, Elliot. "Distinct Conceptual and Developmental Domains:
Social Convention and Morality." Nebraska Symposium on
Motivation 1977. Edited by C.B. Keasey. Lincoln: University
of Nebraska Press, 1978, pp. 77-116.

Proposes a distinction between social convention and morality.
A body of data is presented that supports the distinctiveness of
the two domains. The role of interactions with the environment
in the development of social conventional thinking is discussed.

676. Turiel, Elliot. "Stage Transition in Moral Development."
      Second Handbook of Research on Teaching. Edited by R.M.
      Travers. Chicago: Rand McNally, 1973, pp. 732-758.

      A thorough and detailed presentation of the structural-
      developmental perspective of moral development.

677. Weiner, B.   "From Each According to His Ability: The Role of
      Effort in a Moral Society." Human Development. 16 (1973):
      53-60.

      Argues that Marx and Piaget have similar theories of social
      and personal development.   Too much attention has been focused
      on the intellectual side of man and not enough on his volitional
      side.   The moral aspects of achievement must be considered in
      turning toward the establishment of a moral society.

678. Ziv, A.; A. Shani; and S. Nebenhaus.   "Differences in Moral
      Judgment of Adolescents Educated in Israel and in the Soviet
      Union." Journal of Cross-Cultural Psychology, 6 (1975):
      108-121.

      Finds that Soviet-educated adolescents are significantly more
      realistically   oriented   in   their   moral   judgment   than
      Israeli-educated youth.   The differences are attributed to the
      different socialization processes.

Empirical Investigations in Cognitive Developmental Theory

679.   Abell, Phyllis K.   "Voluntary Sterilization and Moral Develop-
       ment of Women."   Ed.D. dissertation, Boston University, 1980.
       41/08, p. 3482.

       Women considering tubal ligations were interviewed. It was
       found that the women' perspectives on the operation, whether the
       focus was on themselves or others, were influenced by their
       level of moral development.

680.   Adkins, Gary A.   "Moral Judgment, Intelligence, Self-Concept and
       Social Behavior of Fourth Graders."   Ed.D. dissertation, West
       Virginia University, 1976.   37/04, p. 1970.

       Moral judgment, intelligence, and self-concept were not found
       to be measures of the same factor. Self-concept was the only
       variable that was a dependable predictor of social behavior.

681.   Ahlskog, Gary R.   "Moral Reasoning as an Ambiguous Construct in
       Moral Development Theory."   Ph.D. dissertation, Fordham
       University, 1977.   38/01, p. 164.

       Attempted to ascertain if subjects assessed at different
       stages of moral judgment also demonstrated differences in the
       reasoning process by which the decision was reached. Found that
       there were no significant differences in reasoning process
       (defined as consideration of moral payoff or moral penalty in a
       payoff matrix) by stage of moral development.

682.   Ahr, Paul R.   "Moral Development and Social Learning Modeling
       Effects on Children's Concepts of Intentionality."   Ph.D.
       dissertation, Catholic University of America, 1971.   32/04, p.
       2414.

       Finds that children having an objective or subjective view of
       morality can have that developmental view changed by exposure to
       adult models who consistently present the alternative view.
       Both groups changed--one upward, the other downward.   The
       implications for Piaget's theory of moral development are
       discussed.

683.   Anchor, Kenneth N.   "Levels of Moral Judgment and Education as
       Predictors of Maladaptive Aggression in an Experimental Social
       Conflict."   Ph.D. dissertation, University of Connecticut,
       1972.   33/06-B, p. 2800.

       Hypothesized that the lower one's level of moral reasoning and
       the more impoverished one's educational history, the more likely
       one would be to display maladaptive aggression in an

experimental situation. The hypothesized relations were confirmed in the study. Subjects were psychiatric patients and college students.

684. Arndt, A.W. "Maturity of Moral Reasoning about Hypothetical Dilemmas and Behavior in an Actual Situation." Ph.D. dissertation, University of California, Berkeley, 1975. 37/01-B, p. 435.

Finds that reasoning about an experienced cheating situation is about one-third of a stage lower than reasoning about hypothetical dilemmas.

685. Ashton, Patricia T. "Cross-Cultural Piagetian Research: An Experimental Perspective." Stage Theories of Cognitive and Moral Development (item 655), pp. 1-32.

Focuses on an analysis of empirical cross-cultural studies that have examined questions of generality, sequentiality, and universality of stage structures. The improvements needed in this type of research are pointed out. Also in Harvard Educational Review, 45 (1975): 475-506.

686. Bear, George G. "The Relationship of Moral Reasoning to Conduct Problems and Intelligence." Ph.D. dissertation, University of Virginia, 1979. 40/09, p. 4961.

Among sixth grade students conduct problems were found to decrease systematically in frequency and variability with increasing moral maturity. Children with higher intelligence were also found to be more morally advanced.

687. Benninga, Jacques S. "The Relation of Self Concept, Sex and Intelligence to Moral Judgment in Young Children." Ph.D. dissertation, George Peabody College for Teachers, 1976. 37/10, p. 6357.

Finds that they are not related.

688. Bischoff, Herbert G. "Adolescent Moral Judgment on Classical, Contextual and Practical Moral Dilemmas." Ph.D. dissertation, University of Oregon, 1977. 38/10, p. 6002.

No significant differences were found with regard to mean moral maturity scores across the three types of dilemmas. It was found that the higher the level of moral reasoning the less certain subjects were about what they would do in a situation.

689. Blatt, Moshe M., and Lawrence Kohlberg. "The Effects of Classroom Moral Discussion upon Children's Level of Moral Judgment." Journal of Moral Education, 4 (1975): 129-161.

A study which tests the hypothesis that discussion of moral delemmas will stimulate movement toward higher stages of moral reasoning. This paper reports results from a Jewish Sunday school and public junior and senior high schools. It was found that moral discussions did have a significant impact on the moral reasoning of children. Also in Collected Papers (item 618), Education and moral Development (item 1505, and Moral and Psychological Education (item 1521).

690. Blotner, Roberta, and David J. Bearson. "Developmental Consistencies in Children's Socio-Moral Knowledge: Justice Reasoning and Altruistic Behavior." Paper presented at the annual convention of the American Psychological Association, Montreal, 1980. ED 196 560.

Finds that with boys ages 4 to 11 different patterns of altruistic behavior emerge at different levels of social-cognitive maturity. Certain types of moral reasoning (within a practical altruistic context) were highly consistent with moral behavior.

691. Bresnitz, Shlomo, and Sol Kugelmass. "Intentionality in Moral Judgment: Developmental Stages." Child Development, 38 (1967): 469-479.

Finds that a cognitive principle underlying the use of intentionality in moral judgment emerges through four age-related stages.

692. Brooks-Walsh, Ira, and Edmund V. Sullivan. "The Relationship Between Moral Judgment, Causal Reasoning and General Reasoning." Journal of Moral Education, 2 (1973): 131-136.

Data indicates that increases in moral judgment are related to increased generality of cognitive functioning.

693. Brown, Patricia M. "The Congruence Between Moral Judgment and Selected Scales of the MMPI." Journal of Clinical Psychology, 32 (1976): 627- 630.

Investigates several hypothesized relationships between Kohlberg's three levels of moral judgment and personality processes measured by selected scales of the MMPI. It was found that Level I subjects did not, as predicted, score highest on the "psychopathic deviate" scale,but Level II subjects did, as predicted, score highest on the K or social-desirability scale.

694. Buck-Morss, Susan. "Socio-Economic Bias in Piaget's Theory and Its Implications for Cross-Cultural Studies." Human Development, 18 (1975): 35-48.

Argues that cross-cultural disparities in Piaget test performance may be due to "time lag," which is the result of particular social structures found in the industrialized West.

695. Buttner, E.J., and B. Seidenberg. "Manifestations of Moral Development in Concrete Situations." Social Behavior and Personality, 1 (1973): 64-70.

College-age students were asked to discuss a recently experienced personal moral conflict. Subjects experiencing political or ideological conflicts resolved them at a higher level than did subjects experiencing social or honesty conflicts.

696. Cagle, Bobby W. "The Comparison of Real-Life Moral Reasoning with Hypothetical Moral Reasoning of Children about Their Spontaneous Physically Aggressive Behaviors." Ed.D. dissertation, University of Tennessee, 1980. 41/02, p. 591.

Finds that preschool children predominantly use pragmatic moral justifications for their own spontaneous physical aggressions in both real-life and hypothetical situations.

697. Candee, Dan. "Structure and Choice in Moral Reasoning." Journal of Personality and Social Psychology, 34 (1976): 1293-1301.

Investigates the relationship between the structure of moral reasoning and specific moral choice. Subjects were asked to resolve dilemmas dealing with Watergate and MyLai. It was found that subjects at the higher stages consistently made choices that were consistent with human rights.

698. Cappadona, Dorothea L. "Perception of Moral Action Related to Risk and Moral Judgment Level." Ph.D. dissertation, Hofstra University, 1980. 41/12, p. 5068.

The perception of an act as moral was found to be a function of the interaction of the level of moral judgment and the degree of risk a particular situation posed to the satisfaction of a basic need (Maslow).

699. Carella, Stephen, et al. "Disciplinary Judgments and Disruptive Behavior by Individuals and Dyads Differing in Moral Reasoning." 1974. ED 158-171.

Finds that the level of moral judgment a prospective teacher has obtained influences judgmental behavior regarding disciplinary actions.

700. Carroll, James L. "Children's Judgments of Statements
     Exemplifying Different Moral Stages." Ph.D. dissertation,
     University of Minnesota, 1974. 35/06, p. 3507.

     Seventh, ninth, and eleventh grade students were asked to
     accept or reject lower-stage moral reasoning (stages 1, 2, and
     3). The rejection/acceptance rating scale showed clear
     developmental trends.

701. Choy, Catherine L. "The Relationship of Conceptual Tempo,
     Verbal Comprehension and Achievement Motivation to Level of
     Moral Development." Ph.D. dissertation, Marquette University,
     1974. 36/01, p. 184.

     No significant relationship was detected between mean reaction
     time, achievement motivation, and moral development. Verbal
     comprehension, however, did correlate significantly with moral
     development. The sample consisted of high school seniors.

702. Colby, Ann. "Logical Operational Limitations on the Development
     of Moral Judgment." Ph.D. dissertation, Columbia University,
     1973. 34/05-B, p. 2331.

     Hypothesized that Piaget's logical level of formal operations
     is a necessary but not sufficient condition for Kohlberg's stage
     5 and that intervention designed to stimulate moral development
     will be limited because stage 5 cannot occur in subjects who
     lack formal operations. The experimenter's hypotheses were
     confirmed.

703. Colby, Anne, et al. Standard Form Scoring Manual, Parts One,
     Two, Three and Four. Cambridge, MA: Center for Moral
     Education, June 1979.

     Consists of the latest, and supposedly last, of a long string
     of scoring manuals for the moral judgment interview of Lawrence
     Kohlberg. The manual reflects Kohlberg's latest revisions of
     the theory with stages 5A and 5B as the highest form of moral
     reasoning.

704. Craig, Robert P. "Education for Justice: Some Comments on
     Piaget." Contemporary Education, 47 (Winter 1976): 69-73.

     Presents Piaget's views on the development of moral reasoning
     and discusses ten specific implications for teachers.

705. Cruce-Mast, Ada L. "The Interrelationship of Critical Thinking,
     Empathy and Social Interest with Moral Judgment." Ph.D.
     dissertation, Southern Illinois University, 1975. 36/12, p.
     7945.

It was found that social interest did not contribute to moral decisions, but critical thinking and empathy did.

706. Daniels, Marion H. "Moral Judgment Development as a Function of Interpersonal Relationship Style: An Exploratory Study." Ph.D. dissertation, University of Iowa, 1978. 39/08, p. 4727.

It was found that moral reasoning did not vary as a function of preference for any of the six interpersonal relationship styles.

707. Davis, Glen R. "Moral Development and Impulse Control in Boys Ages 9 to 14 Diagnosed as Behavior Disorder, Psychoneurotic and Normal." Ph.D. dissertation, University of Michigan, 1980. 41/02, p. 592.

The behavior disorder group demonstrated significantly less moral maturity than the psychoneurotic and normal groups.

708. DeCaro, Patricia, and Greg Emerton. "A Cognitive-Developmental Investigation of Moral Reasoning in a Deaf Population." Paper presented at annual meeting of American Educational Research Association, Toronto, 1978. ED 154 572.

709. Decker, Celia A. "Young Children's Moral Judgments: An Examination of Piaget's Theory." Ph.D. dissertation, University of Arkansas, 1970. 31/03, p. 1133.

A study designed to investigate Piaget's claim that moral judgment is a single trait. A general factor was not detected.

Finds that deaf college-age students are largely at the preconventional level of moral reasoning.

710. DeMersseman, S.L. "A Developmental Investigation of Children's Moral Reasoning and Behavior in Hypothetical and Practical Situations." Ph.D. dissertation, University of California, Berkeley, 1976. 37/09-B, p. 4643.

Dilemmas in the social domain were constructed and no difference was found between children's reasoning in the social and moral domains. It was concluded that other findings showing different reasoning on practical and hypothetical dilemmas may be due to poor measurement techniques.

711. Durkin, D. "The Specificity of Children's Moral Judgments." Journal of Genetic Psychology, 98 (1961): 3-13.

Finds that children made significantly different kinds of judgments about four different kinds of behavior: aggressing against another, defaming character, physical aggression, and taking property.

712. Dworkin, Earl S. "The Effects of Imitation, Reinforcement, and
     Cognitive Information on the Moral Judgments of Children."
     Ph.D. dissertation, University of Rochester, 1968. 29/01-B,
     p. 365.

     Tested the effects of three different training procedures
     (imitation, imitation plus reinforcement, and cognitive
     information) on the moral judgments of young children. It was
     found that the treatment was more effective in producing an
     intentional orientation than were the other procedures.

713. Ecker, John F. "A Study of the Level of Moral Judgment in
     Adults as a Function of Their Advocacy of Certain Parental
     Discipline Practices." Ed.D. dissertation, Baylor University,
     1978. 39/05, p. 2827.

     Advocacy of power assertion and love withdrawal were found to
     correlate negatively with moral judgment. Advocacy of induction
     using reasoning was positively associated with moral reasoning.

714. Edwards, C.P. "Societal Complexity and Moral Development: A
     Kenyan Study." Ethos, 3 (1975): 505- 527.

     In a study of the moral reasoning of young adults in Kenya, it
     was found that among moral leaders whose frame of reference is
     the semitraditional rural village community, stage 3 represents
     the highest stage. In contrast, stage 4 modes are more fre-
     quently expressed by the new elite (college students).

715. Edwards, J.B. "Adolescent Pupils' Moral Judgments: Influence of
     Context." Journal of Moral Education, 9 (1979): 45-49.

     On Piaget-type tasks it was found that the context in which
     issues were presented was an important influence on level of
     moral reasoning used by subjects.

716. Eiferman, Deborah B. "Moral Judgment and Dogmatism in Adult
     College Students." Ph.D. dissertation, Fordham University,
     1979. 39/11, p. 6649.

     A slight negative correlation was found between level of moral
     judgment and dogmatism.

717. Eihl, John F. "Moral Judgments of Children in Need of Parents."
     Ed.D. dissertation, Indiana University, 1968. 29/10, p. 3415.

     Piaget's stages of moral judgment were confirmed. Children in
     restrictive social environments were found to lag behind other
     children in their moral development.

718. Eisenberg-Berg, Nancy. "The Relation of Political Attitudes to Constraint-Oriented and Prosocial Moral Reasoning." Developmental Psychology, 12 (1976), pp. 552-553.

     Prosocial moral reasoning, a form of reasoning ignored by Kohlberg, was found to correlate moderately with constraint-oriented moral reasoning and to exhibit similar developmental trends.

719. Elliott, Judith K. "Problem Solving in the Political Domain and Its Relation to Cognitive Development, Moral Reasoning and Political Attitudes." Ed.D. dissertation, Rutgers University, 1979. 40/07, p. 3887.

     No statistically significant results were found to support the hypothesis that subjects with higher stages of logical or moral reasoning and stronger political orientations would exhibit an increase in the amount of information used and the way it was used in evaluating opposing political perspectives.

720. Fay, Betty M. "The Relationships of Cognitive Moral Judgment, Generosity and Emphatic Behavior in 6 and 8 Year Old Children." Ph.D. dissertation, University of California at Los Angeles, 1970. 31/8, p. 3951.

     Found that measures of Piagetian cognitive moral judgment, generosity, and empathy are all positively interrelated.

721. Fedorko, Rose A. "Effects of Parent and Teacher Training on the Moral Development of Five, Six and Seven-Year-Olds." Ph.D. dissertation, The Catholic University of America, 1977. 38/11, p. 6495.

     No significant differences were observed in children's responses to Piagetian stories whether the children were trained by parents or teachers, or individually or in groups.

722. Fifis, Daniel F. "The Relation of Predictive Ability, Empathy, Intelligence, and Sex to Moral Judgment in Adolescents." Ph.D. dissertation, University of South Carolina, 1978. 39/12, p. 7161.

     Correlations between predictive ability, empathy, intelligence, sex, and moral judgment did not reach a statistically significant level.

723. Fodor, Eugene M. "Resistance to Social Influence among Adolescents as a Function of Level of Moral Development." Journal of Social Psychology, 85 (1971): 121-126.

Finds that adolescent boys most susceptible to shifting their position on a given moral issue were lower in moral reasoning than boys who resisted such a shift.

724. Fontana, A., and B. Noel, "Moral Reasoning at the University." Journal of Personality and Social Psychology, 27 (1973): 419-429.

Finds that administrators use law and order reasoning more than faculty and students. Also Rightists use law and order reasoning more than Leftists, and Leftists reason more egoistically than Rightists.

725. Freeman, Sue J. "Individual Differences in Moral Judgment by Children and Adolescents." Ph.D. dissertation, University of Wisconsin, 1974. 35/7, p. 4248.

Using familiar and remote theme dilemmas with 11, 14, and 17 year olds it was found that higher judgments were associated more with remote dilemmas, and same sex dilemmas elicited higher-stage reasoning than opposite sex dilemmas.

726. Friesen, Merle R. "Relationship Between Public Positions on Affirmative Action and Kohlberg's Levels of Moral Development." Ed.D. dissertation, Auburn University, 1976. 37/11, p. 7013.

Only very small differences were noted on stage of moral reasoning among individuals holding to a variety of positions on affirmative action.

727. Fulda, Trudi A., and Richard K. Jantz. "Moral Education Through Diagnostic-Prescriptive Teaching Methods." The Elementary School Journal, 74 (1975): 513-518.

Argues that teachers should diagnose children as either exhibiting a morality of constraint or a morality of cooperation. Once this is achieved, they should next ensure that the children be exposed to children at the next highest level. The behavior- thought distinction is blurred in this paper.

728. Garwood, S. Gary, Douglas Levine; and Linda Ewing. "Effect of Protagonist's Sex on Assessing Gender Differences in Moral Reasoning." New Orleans: Tulane University, 1979. ED 170 031.

Finds that altering the sex of the protagonist in the Rest Defining Issues Test has no significant impact on males' or females' moral reasoning.

729. Gash, H. "Moral Judgment: A Comparison of Two Theoretical
      Approaches." Journal of Genetic Psychology, 93 (1976): 91-111.

      Investigates the relationship between Kohlberg's stages and
      Hoffman's social learning moral orientations. Past conventional
      reasoning was found to be significantly associated with
      humanistic reasoning.

730. Gilligan, Carol, et al. "Moral Reasoning about Sexual Dilemmas:
      The Development of an Interview and Scoring System." In
      Technical Report of the Commission on Obscenity and
      Pornography, Vol. 1 (No. 5256-0010). Washington, DC:
      Superintendent of Documents, U.S. Government Printing Office,
      1971, pp. 141-174.

      Reports the development of moral dilemmas dealing with sexual
      issues and the field testing of a scoring process. One of the
      interesting findings was that high school juniors reason at a
      lower level about sexual dilemmas than they do about traditional
      Kohlbergian dilemmas.

731. Giraldo, M. "Moral Development and Its Relation to Role-Taking
      Ability and Interpersonal Behavior." Ph.D. dissertation,
      Catholic University of America, 1972. 33/03-B, p. 1285.

      With children ages 9 to 13 a positive relationship was found
      between role taking ability and moral maturity.

732. Gorsuch, R., and M. Barnes. "Stages of Ethical Reasoning and
      Moral Norms of Carib Youth." Journal of Cross-Cultural
      Psychology, 4 (1973): 283-301.

      No evidence was found for the position that stages might be a
      function of cultural norms. Boys in towns were found to be more
      advanced than rural youth, and younger boys were at a lower
      stage than the older youth.

733. Griffore, R.J., and D.D. Samuels. "Moral Judgment of Residents
      of a Maximum Security Correctional Facility." Journal of
      Psychology, 100 (1978): 3-7.

      Inmates at a maximum security correctional facility were found
      to possess the same general level of moral development as many
      nonincarcerated subjects.

734. Guttman, Joseph; Yaakov Bar-Zohar; and Klara Statter. "Locus of
      Control and Moral Judgment: A Cross-Cultural Study in Israel."
      Journal of Moral Education, 10 (1981): 186-191.

      Israeli adolescents of Eastern descent were found to be more
      externally oriented and to possess more realistic moral judgment

than adolescents of Western descent. Within groups no relationship between locus of control and moral judgment was found.

735. Hains, A.A., and D.J. Miller. "Moral and Cognitive Development in Delinquent Children and Adolescents." Journal of Genetic Psychology, 137 (1980): 21-35.

Finds that delinquents generally lag behind non-delinquents in moral and cognitive development.

736. Hales, Gary D. "Situation Specificity of Moral Judgments Manifested by a Student Population." Ph.D. dissertation, University of Texas at Austin, 1979. 40/06, p. 3198.

An objective test to assess moral judgment was developed, focusing on different, highly specific situations. It was found that moral dilemmas which juxtapose the same two moral issues but in different situations may result in significant differences in objectively scored moral judgment.

737. Hardeman, Annett. "Children's Moral Reasoning." Ph.D. dissertation, Columbia University, 1967. 28/05-B, p. 2126.

Using first grade children as subjects it was found that there exists parallel development in children's moral concepts and logical abilities. Ability to structure the world in terms of the principle of conservation and the ability to structure moral situations in a mature way are related. The implications for Piaget's theory are discussed.

738. Harris, Stephen; Paul Mussen; and Eldred Rutherford. "Some Cognitive, Behavioral, and Personality Correlates of Maturity of Moral Judgment." Journal of Genetic Psychology, 128 (1976): 123-135.

The findings of the research reported leave little doubt that levels of moral cognition are significantly related to aspects of overt moral behavior, particularly altruism and consideration for others. It is pointed out, however, that the findings give no real information about the mechanisms or processes underlying the associations discovered.

739. Harvan, Michael J. "Factors Affecting the Moral Reasoning and Moral Behavior of Fourth- and Sixth-Grade Children." Ph.D. dissertation, University of Akron, 1978. 39/04, p. 2144.

A battery of psychological tests were given in an attempt to identify relationships between these variables and moral behavior. No stable relationships were found between modes of moral judgment and moral behavior.

740. Hiett, Sharon L. "Moral Judgment of Disruptive and Non-
      disruptive Students and Their Teachers." Ph.D. dissertation,
      University of Florida, 1977. 38/07, p. 4047.

      Finds that disruptive students tend to reason predominantly at
      the preconventional level whereas those students not labeled as
      disruptive tend to reason at the conventional level.

741. Hilton, James M. "The Relationship Between the Level of Moral
      Judgment of High School Students and Their Levels of
      Interpersonal Trust, Socioeconomic Status and Intelligence."
      Ed.D. dissertation, University of Denver, 1978. 39/06, p.
      3375.

      Moral reasoning was found to be significantly correlated with
      intelligence and socioeconomic status but not with level of
      interpersonal trust.

742. Holland, M.F. "Effects of Moral Maturity and Essay Structure on
      Moral Persuasion." Journal of Personality, 44 (1976):
      449-466.

      Reports research findings that substantiate the general
      hypothesis that the persuasive effects of ethical essays are
      influenced by the relative structural disparity between
      information and recipient.

743. Holstein, Constance B. "Irreversible, Stepwise Sequence in the
      Development of Moral Judgment: A Longitudinal Study of Males
      and Females." Child Development, 47 (1976): 51-61.

      Finds developmental stage sequences for adolescents and adults
      over a three-year period only from level to level. Also,
      regression was found for higher stages. Implications for
      construct validity of Kohlberg's model of development are
      discussed.

744. Horrocks, Robert N. "The Relationship of Selected Prosocial
      Play Behaviors in Children to: Moral Reasoning, Youth Sports
      Participation, and Perception of Sportsmanship." Ed.D.
      dissertation, University of North Carolina at Greensboro,
      1979. 40/04, p. 1949.

      Scores for moral reasoning and perception of sportsmanship,
      but not scores for participation in youth sports, were related
      to prosocial play behavior scores. Subjects were fifth and
      sixth grade boys.

745. Hubers, Nancy H. "The Relationship of Language Performance to
      the Assessment of Moral Development by Two Different Methods
      in the Fifth Grade." Ed.D. dissertation, Northern Illinois
      University, 1977. 39/05, p. 2883.

Self-report scores of moral judgment were found to be higher than those assessed by the moral dilemma method. The higher language requirements in the moral dilemma task may possibly interfere with the subject's spontaneous production of a moral judgment and therefore depress the score.

746. Hurvitz, Liane. "The Influence of Child-Rearing Environments in Israel on First, Second and Third Grade Children's Level of Resistance to Temptation and Stages of Moral Judgment." Ed.D. dissertation, University of Southern California, 1977. 39/11, p. 6532.

The impact of communal peer-oriented (kibbutz) versus traditional family setting child rearing practices were assessed. Found that kibbutz reared children are higher in stage of moral reasoning. There was no difference between the groups on resistance to temptation.

747. Ismail, Mohamed A. "A Cross Cultural Study of Moral Judgments: The Relationship Between American and Saudi Arabian University Students on the Defining Issues Test." Ed.D. dissertation, Oklahoma State University, 1976. 37/09, p. 5702.

Finds that American students score more at stage 5 while Saudi students score more at stage 4. Also Saudi students who have been in the U.S. for two years of more score higher than new arrivals.

748. Jacobs, Mary K. "Women's Moral Reasoning and Behavior in Prisoner's Dilemma." Ph.D. dissertation, University of Toledo, 1975. 36/10, p. 6554.

Studied the impact of partner defection on women's cooperativeness and anxiety and the interaction of these factors with level of moral reasoning. When the partner defected, consistently principled women responded more cooperatively than conventional women.

749. Jantz, Richard K. "An Investigation of the Relationship Between Moral Development and Intellectual Development in Male Elementary School Students." Theory and Research in Social Education, 1 (October 1973): 1-25.

Using elementary-age school subjects it was found that a positive relationship exists between intellectual development and moral development, but those characteristics of the higher level of intellectual development are not necessarily the same as those reflecting a higher level of moral thinking.

750. Johnston, Mary A. "Relationships Between Moral Judgment and
     Moral Behavior: Studies of Fifth Grade Students in Dissimilar
     Settings." Ph.D. dissertation, University of Colorado, 1979.
     40/12, p. 6202.

     Positive but nonsignificant correlations between moral
     judgment and moral behavior were obtained regardless of the
     classroom environment (social constraint or reciprocity and
     cooperation).

751. Jones, James S. "Stability of Moral Reasoning Levels Across
     Moral Dilemmas Categorized by Topic Area and Student Strength
     of Feeling." Ed.D. dissertation, University of Illinois,
     1976. 37/10, p. 6431.

     The hypothesis that there would exist variability in subjects'
     moral reasoning across situations was not supported. Also there
     was no significant correlation between students' strength of
     feeling and students' level of reasoning on dilemmas.

752. Jordan, Valerie B., and Donna Waite. "Effects of Self-Oriented
     and Other-Oriented Questions on Moral Reasoning." Paper
     presented at the Annual Meeting of the American Educational
     Research Association, San Francisco, 1979. ED 181 367.

     Finds that boys' moral reasoning is higher on other-oriented
     dilemmas while girls were found to be consistent across both
     types of dilemma.

753. Jurkovic, G.J., and N.M. Prentice. "Dimensions of Moral
     Interaction and Moral Judgment in Delinquent and Nondelinquent
     Families." Journal of Consulting and Clinical Psychology, 42
     (1974): 256-262.

     Analyses of moral discussions between mothers and sons
     revealed significant differences between delinquent and
     nondelinquent families on a variety of interaction dimensions.
     The relationship of these dimensions to moral judgment and to
     delinquent behavior is discussed.

754. Kadivar, Parvin. "Relationships Between Moral Development and
     Selected Psychological Variables." Ph.D. dissertation,
     University of Missouri-Columbia, 1979. 40/09, p. 4967.

     Relationships between moral reasoning, self-concept, and
     parents' level of education for eighth grade students was
     determined. The results are not reported in the abstract.

755. Kane, M.H. "The Phenomenology and Psychodynamics of Moral
     Development." Ph.D. dissertation, University of Michigan,
     1975. 36/06-B, p. 3048.

Subjects were administered written Kohlberg questionnaires and interviewed to obtain information about life histories and subjective experiences related to moral development. A relationship was found between the variables and was interpreted in psychoanalytic terms. For example, stage 5 subjects were found to have experienced severe Oedipal conflicts within their families.

756. Keasey, C.T., and C.B. Keasey. "The Mediating Role of Cognitive Development in Moral Judgment." Child Development, 45 (1974): 291-298.

High correlations and systematic relationships were found between stages of cognitive development and moral development. Advances in cognitive development seem to be a prerequisite to advanced moral judgments. Subjects were sixth grade girls.

757. Kelly, James P. "Predicting Principled Morality of Franciscan Priests Using Age, Dogmatism, and Time of Training." Ph.D. dissertation, Fordham University, 1979. 40/02, p. 677.

On the Defining Issues Test, P-scores of priests were obtained which were the equivalent of juniors in high school.

758. Kishta, Mohammed A., and Eileen M. Mays. "The Relationship of Moral and Cognitive Development in Two Cultures and the Implications for Science Teaching." Paper presented at the annual meeting of the National Association for Research in Science Teaching, Toronto, 1978. ED 165 999.

Significant differences were found between students in Jordan and Iowa in the second and fifth grades on tests of cognitive and moral development.

759. Kohlberg, Lawrence, and Mordecai Nison. "Cultural Universality of the Stages: A Longitudinal Study in Turkey." The Psychology of Moral Development (item 625), Chapter 12.

Discusses the results of a ten-year longitudinal study in Turkey.

760. Krebs, Dennis L., and Alli Rosenwald. "Moral Reasoning and Moral Behavior in Conventional Adults." Merrill Palmer Quarterly, 23 (1977): 77-87.

Finds that subject's stage of moral reasoning is positively related to an incidence of everyday "moral" behavior--i.e., carrying out an agreed-upon contract.

761. Kruglanski, Arie W., and Yoel Yinon. "Evaluating an Immoral Act Under Threat versus Temptation: An Illustration of the Achievement Principle in Moral Judgment." Journal of Moral Education, 3 (1974): 167-175.

It was found that when an immoral act was committed in response to a threat it was judged less severely than when it was committed in response to a temptation. The magnitude of incentive had no effect on evaluation.

762. Kugelmas, S., and S. Bresnitz. "The Development of Intentionality in Moral Judgment in City and Kibbutz Adolescents." Journal of Genetic Psychology, 111 (1967): 103-111.

Finds with Kohlberg, and against Piaget, that there is no association between advances in intentionality and a measure of peer group's participation.

763. Kupfersmid, Joel H. "The Relationship Between Moral Maturity and Selected Characteristics of Mental Health among Young Adults." Ph.D. dissertation, Kent State University, 1975. 36/06, p. 3516.

No significant relationship was found between moral maturity and mental health. The only significant relationship found was between moral maturity and tolerance for ambiguity.

764. Kurdek, Lawrence A. "Developmental Relations among Children's Perspective Taking, Moral Judgment, and Parent-Rated Behaviors." Merrill Palmer Quarterly, 26 (1980): 103-121.

Synchronous correlations indicate that cognitive rather than perceptual perspective taking is related to moral judgment. The preponderance of causality indicated that moral judgment caused later developments in perspective taking.

765. Kurdek, Lawrence A. "Perspective Taking as the Cognitive Basis of Children's Moral Development: A Review of the Literature." Merrill-Palmer Quarterly, 24 (1978): 3-28.

Reviews the existing literature on perspective taking and moral development and finds that those two constructs have been conceived too globally. As a result the relationships between the two constructs have not been adequately assessed.

766. LaVoie, Joseph C. "Cognitive Determinants of Resistance to Deviation in Seven-, Nine- and Eleven-Year-Old Children of Low and High Maturity of Moral Judgment." Developmental Psychology, 10 (1974): 393-403.

The influence of sex, age, rationale focus, and rationale orientation was investigated within a standard punishment paradigm. The data suggests that level of moral judgment influences moral behavior. The results were discussed from a social learning as well as a cognitive developmental framework.

767. Lee, Charlotte L. "The Concomitant Development of Cognitive and Moral Modes of Thought: A Test of Selected Deductions from Piaget's Theory." Ph.D. dissertation, Ohio State University, 1968. 29/05-B, p. 1836.

Findings support Piaget's hypothesis of sequential stages in both cognitive and moral judgment.

768. Lee, Lee C. "Children's Understanding of Morals." Values, Feelings and Morals.   Edited   by   Hearn   D.   Dwain Washington, D.C.: Washington, D.C.: American Association of Elementary-Kindergarten-Nursery Educators, 1974. pp. 19-38.

Reviews the Piagetian conception of the development of moral judgment and then reports the results of research designed to test the assumption that changes in cognitive structures are related directly to comparable changes in moral judgments.

769. Leford, Dennis C. "The Assessment of Moral Reasoning, Sex, Class Status and Group Norms as Predictors of College Student Moral Behavior." Ph.D. dissertation, Case Western Reserve University, 1979. 40/05, p. 2501.

Sex was found to be the best predictor of moral behavior; males were found to be less moral. The findings suggested that moral behavior is situationally specific and that a trait theory is not a productive avenue of study.

770. LeFurgy, William G., and Gerald W. Woloshin. "Immediate and Long-Term Effects of Experimentally Induced Social Influence in the Modification of Adolescents' Moral Judgments." Journal of Personality and Social Psychology,   12   (1969): 104-110.

Morally realistic subjects (heteronomous) showed immediate and long-term shifts in judgmental styles due to social influence. Morally relativistic subjects (autonomous) showed short-term susceptibility to social influence, but this susceptibility diminished over time.

771. Leming, James S. "Adolescent Moral Judgment and Deliberation on Classical and Practical Moral Dilemmas." Ph.D. dissertation, University of Wisconsin, 1973. 34/10, p. 6452.

It was found that when adolescents reason about what they would do in a personally relevant situation they reason at a mean lower stage than when they reason about what someone else should do in a hypothetical situation (e.g., Heinz).

772. Leming, James S. "Intrapersonal Variations in Stage of Moral Reasoning among Adolescents as a Function of Situational Context." Journal of Youth and Adolescence, 7 (1978): 405-416.

Stage of moral reasoning associated with deliberation on practical moral dilemmas was found to be significantly lower than moral judgment on hypothetical moral dilemmas. See also item 771.

773. Levine, Charles. "Role-Taking Standpoint and Adolescent Usage of Kohlberg's Conventional Stages of Moral Reasoning." Journal of Personality and Social Psychology, 34 (1976): 41-46.

Subjects were presented with dilemmas concerning varied protagonists and issues. It was found that in reasoning about best friends or mothers, as opposed to strangers, stage 3 reasoning increases and stage 4 reasoning decreases.

774. Lickona, Thomas. "Piaget Misunderstood: A Critique of the Criticisms of His Theory of Moral Development." Merrill-Palmer Quarterly, 15 (1969): 337-50.

Presents eight criticisms of Piaget's theory of moral development and attempts to clarify his position on the particular issues raised.

775. Lieberman, Marcus. "Estimation of a Moral Judgment Level Using Items Whose Alternative Form a Gradual Scale." Ph.D. dissertation, University of Chicago, 1971. NR

776. Lieberman, Marcus. "Psychometric Analysis of Developmental Stage Data." Paper presented at Annual Meeting of American Educational Research Association, Montreal, 1973. ED 092 572.

Using complex statistical analysis, Lieberman concludes that for different dilemmas certain stages of reasoning are more easily attained than for others, and when particular moral issues are analyzed across situations, an "entry" issue for various stages is indicated corresponding to Kohlberg's theory.

777. Liebert, Diane E. "Children's Moral Judgments and Moral Expectations." Ph.D. dissertation, Hofstra University, 1978, 39/01, p. 196.

It was found that children's moral expectations (what they would do) display a greater degree of harm-avoidance than their moral judgments (what they should do).

778. Lockwood, Alan L. "Stage of Moral Development and Students'
     Reasoning on Public Policy Issues." Journal of Moral
     Education, 5 (1975): 51-61.

     It was hypothesized that the same type of reasoning will be
     common to subjects' discussion of moral dilemmas and public
     policy issues. The hypothesis was confirmed.

779. Lockwood, Alan L. "Stages of Moral Development in Students'
     Analysis of Public Value Controversy." Ph.D. dissertation,
     Harvard University, 1970.

     Finds consistency of stage of moral reasoning from Kohlbergian
     dilemmas to public policy dilemmas.

780. Lucas, L.F., and R.N. Tsujimoto. "Self-Actualization and Moral
     Judgment." Psychological Reports, 43 (1978): 838.

     Only weak support was found for the claim that emotional
     development is positively associated with moral judgment.

781. Lunn, Mary J. "Piaget's Theory of Moral Judgment Applied to
     First Grade Basal Readers." Ph.D. dissertation, Case Western
     Reserve University, 1970. 31/01, p. 307.

     Piaget's "Morality of Constraint" accounted for 76% of the
     judgments and behaviors of characters in first grade basal
     readers.

782. Lydiat, M. "Development of Moral Judgments in Children."
     Journal of Moral Education, 3 (1973): 367-377.

     Tests of moral judgment fashioned after Piaget and
     administered to youth ages 7-12 confirm developmental trends in
     moral reasoning.

783. McCullough, George D. "Moral Development Profile Variability:
     Its Relationship to Choice of Preferred Stage of Moral
     Reasoning and to Rokeach's Open-Closed Belief System." Ph.D.
     dissertation, University of Toronto, 1969. 32/03, p. 1340.

     The pattern of preferred choice in dilemmas was found to be
     unrelated to profile variability. It was dependent upon the
     dilemma's situation. Only at stage five was Rokeach's
     open-closed belief system related to stage. Stage 5 subjects
     had a consistently more open belief system.

784. McGee, Dorendia L. "Consistency of Moral Judgments on
     Ego-Involving Moral Dilemmas." Ph.D. dissertation, University
     of Oklahoma, 1979. 40/04, p. 1966.

Within a high moral development group, students who were supportive or critical of the Equal Rights Amendment made moral decisions concerning that issue at a higher level than students who were disinterested in the issue.

785. McGeorge, Colin. "Some Correlates of Principled Moral Thinking in Young Adults." Journal of Moral Education, 5 (1976): 265-273.

Using students from a New Zealand teacher's college McGeorge found that there were no significant correlates between principled thinking and such experiences as marriage, living away from home, vacation work, and church activity.

786. McGeorge, Collin. "Situational Variation in Level of Moral Judgment." The British Journal of Educational Psychology, 44 (1974): 116-122.

Significant variation from situation to situation was detected in the responses of 12-year-old boys and university students to Kohlberg dilemmas. Two factors were offered to account for the variation: one involving concepts of social rules and the other involving role-taking ability.

787. McNamee, S.M. "Moral Behavior, Moral Development and Needs in Students and Political Activists with Special Reference to the Law and Order Stage of Moral Development." Ph.D. dissertation, Case Western Reserve University, 1972. 33/04-B, 1800.

Investigates the relationship between moral development, moral behavior, and personality needs. Found that as level of moral development increased, an increasing percentage of subjects was willing to assist someone in need.

788. Mahaney, Edward J., and Beth Stephens. "Two Year Gains in Moral Judgment by Retarded and Non-retarded Persons." American Journal of Mental Deficiency, 79 (1974): 134-141.

Although moral development was found to be, in some cases, soporific, sporadic, and interspersed with regression, the data allows one to conclude that development in moral judgment does occur and continues to occur in retarded persons as they approach late adolescence. The article is followed by a discussion by Kohlberg (pp 142-144) and a reply by Stephens (pp. 145-146).

789. Malcolm, Daniel B. "The Relative Efficacy of Adult and Peer Models on Children's Moral Judgments." Ph.D. dissertation, Case Western Reserve University, 1970. 32/01, p. 246.

Fourth grade males were divided into two groups depending upon whether they functioned in a morally objective or morally subjective manner. Contrary to Piaget's findings, adults and peer models were more effective in producing changes in the objective group's moral judgments than in the subjective group's moral judgments.

790. Maqsud, M. "Locus of Control and Stages of Moral Reasoning." Psychological Reports, 46 (1980): 1243-1248.

Finds that among female secondary school students in Nigeria, stage 3 subjects are significantly more internal than students at stages 1, 2, and 4.

791. Maqsud, M. "Moral Reasoning of Nigerian and Pakistani Muslim Adolescents." Journal of Moral Education, 7 (1977): 40-49.

Both Piagetian and Kohlbergian means of assessing moral reasoning were used. The moral training of both sets of youth is discussed. It was found that the subjects' moral reasoning is greatly affected by their cultural values. Moral development appears to lag due to cultural preference for certain reasons for choices.

792. Maqsud, Muhammad. "Resolutions of Moral Dilemmas by Nigerian Secondary School Pupils." Journal of Moral Education, 9 (1979): 36-44.

Finds that Hausa Muslim adolescents resolve dilemmas in adult-approved directions. Day school pupils' moral reasoning is more advanced than that of boarding school pupils.

793. Masterson, M.R. "Structures of Thought and Patterns of Social Behavior: Stage of Ego and Moral Development and Their Relationship to Interpersonal Behavior." Ed.D. dissertation, Boston University, 1979, 41/05, p. 2019.

Students' stages of moral and ego development are related to behavior toward classmates and the teacher, and to who influences whom in classrooms.

794. Mays, Eileen M. "An Investigation of the Relationship of Moral and Cognitive Modes of Thought in Second and Fifth Grade Children." Ph.D. dissertation, University of Iowa, 1974. 36/01, p. 192.

Using Piaget-type tasks, levels of cognitive development were assessed. No significant differences were observed between relationships of cognitive and moral judgment task performances.

795. Medinnus, G.R.   "Moral Development in Childhood: Lying."
     Psychological Studies of Human Development.   Edited by R.G.
     Kuhlen and G.G. Thompson. New York: Appleton-Century-Crofts,
     1963, pp. 426-431.

     Confirms Piagetian concepts of development of thinking with
     respect to lying.

796. Melvin, Arthur I. "Cross-Cultural Moral Values." Morality
     Examined (item 1528), pp. 41-55.

     Through an analysis of various approaches to determining
     values, mostly taken from American authors, Melvin somehow
     arrives at seven basic values that he claims are cross-cultural.

797. Miller, Kenneth L. "The Relationship of Stages of Development
     in Children's Moral and Religious Thinking." Ed.D.
     dissertation, 1976. 37/02, p. 787.

     A significant correlation was found between Kohlberg's stages
     of moral reasoning and Goldman's test of religious thinking
     among Bible class students aged 8-18.

798. Modgil, Sohan.   Piagetian Research: A Handbook of Recent
     Studies. Windsor, Berks, England: NFER Publishing Co., 1974.

     Chapter ten, contributed by Celia Scaplehorn, is entitled
     "Piaget's Cognitive-Developmental Approach to Morality." It
     Consists of an integrated review of the range of recent studies,
     followed by abstracts of those studies. Part of the chapter
     deals with Kohlberg's extension of Piaget's schema. The chapter
     contains a wide range of studies which corroborate Piaget's
     theory. A comprehensive bibliography of over 1,500 citations is
     provided.

799. Musgrave, P.W. "Some Adolescent Moral Attitudes in Three
     Societies." Journal of Moral Education, 9 (1980): 192-203.

     A replication of Eppel's early 1960s study was conducted. It
     was found that adolescents today have the same general moral
     orientation as adolescents of nearly 20 years ago.

800. Olejnik, A.B., and A.A. LaRue. "Affect and Moral Reasoning."
     Social Behavior and Personality, 8, 1 (1980): 75-79.

     Finds that when temporary mood states are induced, Pscores on
     the Rest Defining Issues Test are higher in the positive affect
     condition than in either the negative or neutral mood
     conditions.

801. Parikh, Bindu S. "Moral Judgment Development and Its Relation to Family Environmental Factors in Indian and American Urban Upper Middle Class Families." Ed.D. dissertation, Boston University, 1975. 36/05, p. 3160.

A cross-cultural comparison of Indian and American moral development as it relates to family factors. The abstract is uninformative.

802. Pealting, John H. "Research on Adult Moral Development: Where Is It?" Religious Education, 72 (1977): 212-224.

Finds in developmental data on adults that moral development reverses itself and then proceeds--slowly--to recapture the developmental sequence.

803. Phillips, D.C., and Mavis E. Kelly. "Hierarchical Theories of Development in Education and Psychology." Harvard Educational Review, 45 (1975): 351-375.

Argues that the underlying assumptions of hierarchical theories of development have not been adequately explored. Questions are raised regarding the claim for invariance of the stages and the contribution that earlier stages make to latter stages. It is unclear whether the theories are conceptually or empirically grounded.

804. Preston, Charles F. "The Development of Moral Judgment in Young People." Ph.D. dissertation, University of Toronto, 1962. 24/07, p. 2999.

Describes the construction and evaluation of an objective test to assess Piaget's stages of moral judgment.

805. Reeves, John M. "The Modification of Age-Specific Expectations of Piaget's Theory of Intentionality in Moral Judgments of Four-to-Seven-Year Old Children in Relation to Use of Puppets in a Social (Imitative) Learning Paradigm." Ph.D. dissertation, University of Southern California, 1972. 32/12, p. 6815.

Film using puppets was shown to be effective in promoting moral development, but Piaget's age-specific expectations for this growth were brought into question by the data.

806. Register, M.C. "Moral Compatibility in Married Couples: A Study of Marital Satisfaction as Related to Stage of Moral Development of Spouses." Ph.D. dissertation, Georgia State University, 1976. 36/08-B, p. 4176.

Compared two sets of stage-paired married couples. On only one measure of compatibility were some stage pairs found to be more satisfied.

807. Rest, James R. Development in Judging Moral Issues. Minneapolis: University of Missesota Press, 1979.

As noted by Rest in the preface "the journal articles, dissertations, and manuscripts that report findings on the Defining Issues Test now form a stack over ten feet high." This book condenses and interprets those findings. In a foreward Lawrence Kohlberg compares the Harvard moral judgment interview technique with the Defining Issues Test. The references section is exhaustive and an appendix contains the Defining Issues Test.

808. Rest, James. "Moral Dilemmas of Young Adults." Minneapolis: University of Minnesota, 1980. ED 196 764.

Describes moral dilemmas that young adults formulate spontaneously and examines the relationship between these dilemmas and the subjects' environment and moral reasoning scores.

809. Rest, James. "Patterns of Preference and Comprehension in Moral Judgment." Journal of Personality, 41 (1973): pp. 86-109.

Finds that insofar as subjects comprehend various stages of thinking they tend to prefer the highest comprehended. Subjects can comprehend all stages below and about half could comprehend one stage higher than their current level of moral reasoning.

810. Rest, James; Elliot Turiel; and Lawrence Kohlberg. "Relations Between Level of Moral Judgment and Preference and Comprehension of the Moral Judgment of Others." Journal of Personality, 37 (1969), pp. 225-252.

Found that children understand all stages below and in some cases one stage above their current level of moral reasoning. Also found that they prefer stages above their own current stage to stages below.

811. Rorvik, Harold. "Content and Form in Kohlberg's Theory of Moral Development." Scandinavian Journal of Educational Research, 24 (1980): 105-119.

Reports on an empirical investigation into the claim that form and content in moral reasoning are distinct. Teachers, when studying pupils' answers from Kohlberg dilemmas, grade norm content and motivation for choice of norm. Argues that this invalidates Kohlberg's claim that form alone is being assessed in moral reasoning.

812. Rosebrough, Thomas R. "Children's Social Values Related to Age, Sex and Piagetian Level of Moral Judgment." Ph.D. dissertation, Ohio State University, 1976. 37/05, p. 2622.

Although fourth grade children make significantly more intentional judgments than second grade children, there is no concomitant increase in cooperation or sharing.

813. Rosenn, M.M. "The Relation of Moral Reasoning to Prosocial Behavior: A Developmental Perspective." Ph.D. dissertation, University of California, Berkeley, 1976. 38/02-B, p. 967.

The association between moral reasoning and prosocial behavior among second grade children was found to be slight.

814. Ross, Bernice L. "Interrelationships of Five Cognitive Constructs: Moral Development, Locus of Control, Creativity, Field Dependence-Field Independence, and Intelligence in a Sample of 167 Community College Students." Ph.D. dissertation, University of Southern California, 1977. 38/08, p. 4696.

Finds that moral development appears to tap a cognitive ability independent of the other cognitive variables in the study.

815. Rothman, Golda R. "The Influence of Moral Reasoning on Behavioral Choices." Child Development, 47 (1976): 397-406.

It was found that the presentation of higher stage reasoning had more of an effect on behavioral choice of stage 4 subjects than off stage 3 subjects.

816. Rubin, K.H., and K.T. Trotter. "Kohlberg's Moral Judgment Scale--Some Methodological Considerations." Developmental Psychology, 13 (1977): 535-536.

Low test-retest reliability is found for Kohlberg dilemmas presented to third and fifth grade students.

817. Sawyer, John C. "A Factor Analytic Study of the Dimensional Structure Within Stages of Moral Development and That Structure's Relationship to Specific Personality Traits." Ed.D. dissertation, University of Massachusetts, 1977. 38/04, p. 2009.

34 female subjects between the ages of 17 and 27 responded to Kohlberg's moral dilemmas and a battery of psychological tests. One overall initial factor was identified that indicated that all the moral issues measured are basic constructs. There was no relationship between personality measures and any moral issues dimension.

818. Schwarz, D.A. "The Relationships Among Sexual Behavior, Moral
      Reasoning, and Sex Guilt in Late Adolescence." Ph.D.
      dissertation, Columbia University, 1975. 36/12-B, p. 6400.

      Found that stages 3, 4, and 5 of sexual moral judgment showed
      a curvilinear relationship with sexual behavior such that
      advanced level of sexual experience related to an advanced level
      of sexual moral judgment. General moral judgment, however,
      showed no such relationship.

819. Selman, Robert, and William Damon. "The Necessity (but
      Insufficiency) of Social Perspective Taking for Conceptions of
      Justice at Three Early Levels." Moral Development: Current
      Theory and Research (item 494), pp. 57-73.

      Argue that social perspective taking is structurally different
      from moral reasoning and given levels of perspective taking are
      a necessary but not sufficient basis for attaining the
      concomitant stage of justice reasoning.

820. Sica, Robert B. "A Proposed Synthesis for Festinger's Theory of
      Cognitive Dissonance with Kohlberg's Model of Moral
      Development: An Exploratory Study." Ph.D. dissertation,
      University of Southern California, 1978. 39/05, p. 2846.

      No significant correlation was found between anxiety level and
      ability to function at a high level of moral reasoning. It had
      been hypothesized that higher levels of moral reasoning would
      lead to lower states of anxiety and tension.

821. Siefring, John J. "Intelligence, Sex and Behavioral Correlates
      of Moral Reasoning of Public Junior High School Students."
      Ph.D. dissertation, Fordham University, 1981. 42/04, p. 1560.

      Finds a significant relationship between moral reasoning and
      level of intelligence. Also finds that social conformity and
      impulse control are related to moral reasoning.

822. Siegal, M. "Socialization and the Development of Adult
      Respect." British Journal of Psychology, 80 (1979): 83-86.

      Examines Piaget's claim that increasing solidarity and mutual
      respect among peers liberates the child from a unilateral
      respect for adult-imposed constraints. In children ages 5 to 11
      no evidence was found that they think lying to a friend is worse
      than lying to an adult.

823. Singh, Balwant. "A Study of the Relationship among Moral
      Judgment, Self-Concept and Reading Achievement of Fifth-Grade
      Students." Ph.D. dissertation, University of Southern
      Mississippi, 1977. 38/10, p. 5915.

Indicates that there exists significant relationships between moral judgment and reading achievement (r = .58), self-concept and reading achievement (r = .34), moral judgment and self-concept (r = .58), and moral judgment and IQ (r = .64).

824. Smith, Alexander F. "Developmental Issues and Themes in the Discipline Setting--Suggestions for Educational Practice (A Study of the Moral Development of College Students in Disciplinary Trouble)." Ph.D. dissertation, Ohio State University, 1978. 39/02, p. 714.

Disciplinary subjects took the Defining Issues Test and their responses to judgments they made about the disciplinary process were compared with their moral reasoning. A high degree of association was found between their actual reasoning and their moral judgment level.

825. Smith, Marion E. "Moral Reasoning: Its Relation to Logical Thinking and Role Taking." Journal of Moral Education, 8 (1978): 41-49.

Relations between the development of logical thinking, role-taking, and moral reasoning were investigated with children aged 8 to 14 years. Positive correlation was found among the three areas.

826. Solomon, Marilyn. "The Relation of Reading Achievement to One Aspect of 'Realism' in Seven- to Twelve-Year Old Boys: A Study of the Incidence of 'Moral Realism' (as Conceived by Piaget) in a Sample Population of Retarded Readers and Successful Readers." Ph.D. dissertation, New York University, 1967. 28/04, p. 1314.

Piaget's stage theory is upheld, and significant stage differences are found in both groups of boys.

827. Stein, Joan L. "Adolescents' Reasoning about Moral and Sex Dilemmas: A Longitudinal Study." Ph.D. dissertation, Harvard University, 1974. 34/11-B, p. 5664.

Found that sexual moral dilemmas could be stage scored according to Kohlbergian methods, but about half of the subjects reasoned differently on the two sets of dilemmas with respect to major stage usage.

828. Stephens, Beth, and Katherine Simpkins. "The Reasoning, Moral Judgment, and Moral Conduct of the Congenitally Blind. Final Report." Philadelphia: Temple University, 1974. ED 116 377.

Only in the area of Piagetian reasoning did blind subjects lag behind sighted subjects. No significant differences were found in moral judgment and moral conduct.

829. Sullivan, Arthur P. "Scaling Five Stages of Moral Development."
     Ph.D. dissertation, Fordham University, 1978. 39/03, p. 1447.

     Investigated the existence of a preference pattern for higher
     stages among 1,105 subjects. The ordinal scaling of the stages
     which resulted exactly matched Kohlberg's predicted 1-2-3-4-5.

830. Sullivan, E.V., G. McCullough; and M. Stager. "A Developmental
     Study of the Relationship Between Conceptual, Ego and Moral
     Development." Child Development, 41 (1970): 399-411.

     Age developmental trends on all three measures (Conceptual
     Level, Moral Development, and Ego Development Tests) were
     consistent with stage formulations of all three theorists.
     Sample used 12, 14, and 17 year olds.

831. Sullivan, Frank L. "Logical Thinking and Moral Judgment in
     Young Adults." Ed.D. dissertation, Boston University, 1974.
     35/03, p. 1515.

     Examined whether development in logical and moral thinking was
     parallel and synchronized. An r of .62 was found between
     logical and moral thought.

832. Sumprer, Gerald F., and Eliot J. Buttner. "Moral Reasoning in
     Hypothetical and Actual Situations." Social Behavior and
     Personality, 6 (1978): 205- 209.

     No differences were found in the moral reasoning of college
     students between reasoning about hypothetical situations and
     about situations they thought would influence them. Rest's
     Defining Issues Test was used.

833. Taheri, B.J., and F.K. Willits. "Rurality and the Normative
     Order in a Developing Country." Rural Sociology, 40 (1975):
     251-267.

     Finds that as rurality declines e.g., in (Iran) the emphasis
     on the effect of an improper act declines and the importance of
     the actors' motives increases.

834. Thua, Nguyen P. "Moral Development: Institutional and Cultural
     Perspectives." Ph.D. dissertation, University of Illinois,
     1975. 36/01, p. 197.

     Using Vietnamese and American adolescents, Thua attempted to
     ascertain whether sociocultural factors and school systems play
     an important role in the formation of moral beliefs, judgments,
     feelings, and attitudes. The family is perceived as the most
     important factor.

835. Timm, Joan T. "The Relationship Between Moral Responses of
     Elementary School Children and Teachers' Ratings of Moral
     Conduct." Paper presented at the Biennial Southeastern
     Conference on Human Development, Alexandria, VA, 1980. ED 186
     118.

     No significant correlations were found between children's
     stages of moral reasoning and the teachers' overall rankings of
     children's moral conduct.

836. Toner, J. Ignatius, and C. Richard Potts. "The Effect of
     Modeled Rationales on Moral Behavior, Moral Choice, and Level
     of Moral Judgment in Children." Paper presented at the
     biennial Southeastern Conference on Human Development,
     Atlanta, 1978. ED 165 884.

     Finds that models using realistic reasoning to justify
     deviance have a significant impact on subjects' choices and
     actions. Models using autonomous reasoning have a lesser
     impact. Subjects were aged 5 to 7.

837. Turiel, Elliot. "Conflict and Transition in Adolescent Moral
     Development." Child Development, 45 (1974): 14-29.

     A detailed analysis of stage transition in adolescents' moral
     judgment is presented. Transition is viewed as involving a
     phase of conflict and disequilibrium. Relationships between
     regression and progression are discussed.

838. Turiel, Elliot. "An Experimental Test of the Sequentiality of
     Developmental Stages in the Child's Moral Judgments." Ph.D.
     dissertation, Yale University, 1965. 26/07, p. 4067.

     In a test of Kohlberg's theory it was found that exposure to
     +1 reasoning is more effective than -1 or +2 exposure.

839. Turiel, E., and G. Rothman. "The Influence of Reasoning and
     Behavioral Choices at Different Stages of Moral Development."
     Child Development, 43 (1972): 741-754.

     Reasoning presented at a stage above the subjects' reasoning
     level led to a shift in choice only for stage 4 subjects. Stage
     2 and 3 subjects were not influenced in their choices by +1
     reasoning.

840. Turiel, E.; C.P. Edwards; and L. Kohlberg. "Moral Development
     in Turkish Children, Adolescents, and Young Adults."
     Journal of Cross-Cultural Psychology, 9 (1978): 75-86.

     Finds that the stage sequence of moral development for rural
     and city youth is the same as that reported previously for other
     Western and non-Western samples.

841. Urbach, Nelly M. "Some Situational Effects on Moral Judgment Measured by a Multiple-Choice Test." Ph.D. dissertation, University of Maryland, 1976. 37/06, p. 3530.

     After presenting fourth and sixth grade boys with stories involving either honesty or altruism, it was found that subjects were not consistent in stage selection, on an objective test, across situation. Stage 1 was selected more in honesty situations, and stage 3 more in altruism situations.

842. Voloshen, Gail K. "Effects of Locus of Control, Field Independence-Dependence, and Their Congruence-Incongruence on Moral Judgment Maturity." Ph.D. dissertation, Claremont Graduate School, 1979. 39/12, p. 7255.

     For male subjects only, moral maturity was related to an internal locus of control. For female subjects only, moral maturity was correlated with IQ. Contrary to expectation, Field Independence/Internal Locus of Control subjects, males only, exhibited the highest moral judgment level.

843. Weiger, Myra L. "Moral Judgment in Children: Their Responses to Children's Literature Examined Against Piaget's Stages of Moral Development." Ed.D. dissertation, Rutgers University, 1977. 38/07, p. 4065.

     Investigates the development of children's moral judgment in their responses to moral issues in selected pieces of children's literature. The pattern across grade levels was found to be developmental.

844. Weiner, Bernard, and Nancy Peter. "A Cognitive- Developmental Analysis of Achievement and Moral Judgments." Developmental Psychology, 9 (1973): 290-309.

     Found that intent, ability, and outcome are used systematically in both achievement and moral appraisal. Highly significant age trends for the sample (4-18) were also detected. In both the achievement and moral conditions subjective intent replaced objective outcome as the main determinant of judgment.

845. Weinreich, Helen. "Some Consequences of Replicating Kohlberg's Original Moral Development Study on a British Sample." Journal of Moral Education, 7 (1977): 32-39.

     Kohlberg's original study using boys aged 10, 13, and 15 was replicated using 90 school boys in Sussex. Progression through the stages as a function of age was confirmed. Theoretical and methodological problems associated with Kohlberg's method are discussed.

846. Weiss, Jacqueline. "Self-Actualization and Moral Maturity: The
      Relationship Between Degrees of Self-Actualization and Levels
      of Moral Maturity in Selected Undergraduate College Students."
      Ed.D. dissertation, University of Southern California, 1980.
      40/09, p. 4974.

      A strong positive relation was found between self-actualiza-
      tion and moral maturity.

847. Weiss, Richard J. "The Relation of Adolescents' Understanding
      of Moral Thought to Their Moral Reasoning and Decision
      Making."   Ph.D. dissertation, University of California,
      Berkeley, 1980. 41/07, p. 3020.

      Attempts to demonstrate that adolescents' level of moral
      reasoning and the consistency of their decision making are
      related to their understanding of moral thought. It was found
      that subjects who changed their decision between dilemmas most
      likely were those who had the least understanding of what is
      involved in moral thought. Individuals apparently use their
      understanding of moral thought to guide their moral reasoning
      and decision making.

848. Werner, Sonia S. "Affect and Moral Judgment in Older Children."
      Ph.D. dissertation, Iowa State University, 1979.   40/11, p.
      5721.

      Investigates the influence of situationally induced affect on
      moral judgment in older children.   It was found that
      situationally induced affect did not have an impact on
      children's evaluation of advice statements representing
      differing levels of moral judgment.

849. White, C.B. "Moral Development in Bahamian School Children: A
      Cross-Cultural Examination of Kohlberg's Stages of Moral
      Reasoning." Developmental Psychology, 11 (1975): 535-536.

      Age-related developmental trends in moral reasoning were
      identified.   The   findings   were   consistent   with   other
      cross-cultural findings of moral development.

850. Womack, Milton O. "Utilization of Two Nonverbal Cues by
      Children Giving Moral Judgment Responses."   Ed.D.
      dissertation, University of Houston, 1970. 31/08, p. 3893.

      Finds that experimenters, through nonverbal cues, can
      influence children's responses to Piagetian stories.

851. Yussen, Steven R. "Characteristics of Moral Dilemmas Written by
      Adolescents." Developmental Psychology, 13 (1977): 162-163.

      Discusses   the   similarities   and   differences   between
      Kohlberg-created moral dilemmas and the moral dilemmas written
      by adolescents. Most often, adolescent moral dilemmas focused
      on social relationships and dealt with issues other than civil
      rights, life, and death.

852. Yussen, Steven R. "Moral Reasoning from the Perspective of
      Others." Child Development, 47 (1976): 551-555.

      Subjects (grades 9, 10, 12) were asked to respond to a moral
      reasoning questionnaire from the perspective of self, average
      policeman, and average philosopher. Results showed that across
      roles and with increasing age there was a tendency to choose
      principled moral issues to resolve dilemmas.

853. Ziv, A.; Green, D.; and Guttman, J. "Moral Judgment: Differences
      Between City Kibbutz and Israeli-Arab Preadolescents on a
      Realistic-Relativistic Dimension." Journal of Cross-Cultural
      Psychology, 9 (1978): 215-226.

      City children were found to be more relativistic (Piaget) than
      Kibbutz children and Israeli Arabs, who were similar in their
      scores. The results were attributed to differences in the
      socialization pattern in the three subcultures.

854. Zosimovskii, A.V. "Age-Related Characteristics in the Moral
      Development of Children." Soviet Education, 17 (November
      1974): 5-21.

      A scheme of classification of moral development according to
      age is presented.

Critiques of Cognitive Developmental Theory

855. Alston, William P. "Comments on Kohlberg's 'From Is to Ought.'"
     Cognitive Development and Epistemology. Edited by T. Mischel.
     New York: Academic Press, 1971, pp. 269-284.

     Argues that Kohlberg has failed to show that stage 6 is a
     superior way to resolve conflict. This is so because his
     criterion of "moral" as the end result of moral reasoning is
     arbitrary. He also criticizes Kohlberg for his oversimplifica-
     tion of the concept of virtues and his slighting of habit and
     affect in moral life.

856. Aron, Israela Ettenberg. "Moral Education: The Formalist Tradi-
     tion and the Deweyan Alternative." Moral Development, Moral
     Education and Kohlberg (item 1514), pp. 401-426.

     Discusses the contributions of the formalist tradition in
     moral philosophy (Hare, Frankena, Peters, Rawls) and the
     difficulties that arise when the formalist approach is used as
     the entire basis for a theory of moral education. Concludes by
     discussing Dewey's philosophical assumptions and showing how his
     ideas on practical deliberation provide a more adequate
     framework for values education.

857. Aron, Israela E. "Moral Philosophy and Moral Education: A
     Critique of Kohlberg's Theory." School Review, 85 (1977):
     197-217.

     Questions whether Kohlberg has adequately justified his theory
     on philosophical grounds and whether he has adequate evidence
     for his claims that his moral education programs are anything
     other than indoctrination.

858. Atherton, Thomas. "A Critique of Lawrence Kohlberg's Theories
     of Moral Development and Moral Education." Ph.D. dissertation,
     Boston University, 1979. 40/ 05, p. 2727.

     Criticizes Kohlberg's theory of moral development on the
     grounds that it is ethnocentric and commits the naturalistic
     fallacy. Argues that his educational proposals have the
     potential for indoctrination.

859. Baier, Kurt. "Moral Development." The Monist, 58 (1974):
     601-615.

Argues that Kohlberg is really offering two very different models of moral development: one dealing with a premoral phase (stages 1-3) and the other as the development of practical reasoning capable of explaining and justifying the overriding portion of the peculiar mode of reasoning called moral reasoning.

860. Bailey, Charles. "The Notion of Development and Moral Education." The Domain of Moral Education (item 30), pp. 205-219.

Contains a general discussion of the notion of development and the problems inherent when development is looked at in moral terms.

861. Beck, Clive. "Rationalism in Kohlberg's Morality and Moral Education." Philosophy of Education 1978 (item 1499), pp. 105-111.

Argues that Kohlberg's rationalist, principled, universalist approach is untenable. A more adequate approach would have a greater awareness of the complexity of moral life.

862. Bereiter, Carl. "Educational Implications of Kohlberg's Cognitive Developmental View." Interchange, 1 (1970): 25-32.

In a critical view of Kohlbergian theory Bereiter argues that Kohlberg's conclusion that specific instruction cannot contribute significantly to cognitive development is a "category error"--an attempt to set into opposition two concepts that are not of the same type.

863. Bergling, Kurt. Moral Development: The Validity of Kohlberg's Theory. Stockholm Studies in Educational Psychology 23. Stockholm, Sweden: Almquist & Wiksell International, 1981.

Examines the validity of Kohlberg's theory of moral development through a hypothetic-deductive research strategy. The theory is synthesized into two postulates from which four hypotheses are deducted; empirical evidence is cited to examine each hypothesis.

864. Berkowitz, Marvin L. "A Critical Appraisal of the Educational and Psychological Perspectives on Moral Discussion." Journal of Educational Thought, 15 (1981): 20-33.

Presents a critical review of the research on the +1 convention in developmental theory. Suggests that student skills and student interaction are the key ingredients in stimulating moral development.

865. Berkowitz, Marvin W. "A Critical Appraisal of the 'Plus One'
      Convention in Moral Education." Phi Delta Kappan, 62 (1981):
      488-489.

      Rejects the notion that successful moral education requires a
      discussion leader one stage above the majority of the class.
      Discusses the results of research where leaderless peer
      discussion groups experienced nearly as much moral development
      as teacher-led groups.

866. Berkowitz, Marvin W. "Moral Peers to the Rescue! A Critical
      Appraisal of the 'Plus 1' Convention in Moral Education."
      Milwaukee, WI: Marquette University, 1980. ED 193 138.

      Argues that students reacting to other students' reasoning is
      more effective in stimulating moral development.

867. Bolt, Daniel J., and Edmund V. Sullivan. "Kohlberg's
      Cognitive-Developmental Theory in Educational Settings: Some
      Possible Abuses." Journal of Moral Education, 6 (1977):
      198-205.

      The danger of using moral stages to "type" certain personality
      characteristics is discussed.

868. Braun, Claude M., and Jacinthe Baribeau. "Subjective Idealism
      in Kohlberg's Theory of Moral Development: A Critical
      Analysis." Human Development, 21 (1978): 289-301.

      Analyzes the epistemological and logical foundations of
      Kohlberg's theory of moral development. Kohlberg's under-
      standing of dialectics is criticized and an attempt is made to
      introduce a dialectical materialist outlook. Kohlberg's theory
      is shown to be based on a subjective idealist orientation.

869. Broughton, John. "The Cognitive Developmental Approach to
      Morality: A Reply to Kurtines and Greif." Journal of Moral
      Education, 7 (1978): 81-96.

      Broughton, a doctoral student of Kohlberg, responds point by
      point to Kurtines and Greif's analysis (item 895) of the
      weaknesses of the cognitive-developmental approach of Kohlberg.
      In the process of responding Broughton cites 112 sources in what
      is a careful defense.

870. Bunzl, Martin. "The Moral Development of Moral Philosophers."
      Journal of Moral Education, 7 (1977): 3-8.

      Attacks Kohlberg's theory on the basis that if psychology and
      philosophy are one in his theory then the capstone of his theory
      (Rawls's theory of justice) must be wrong because it is a purely
      philosophical notion.

871. Carter, Robert E. "What Is Lawrence Kohlberg Doing?" Journal
      of Moral Education, 9 (1980): 88-102.

      Claims that Kohlberg, instead of attempting to establish a
      "best" morality, should be limiting himself to his sequential
      typology of development from egoism to universalism--an
      achievement in itself.

872. Codd, John A. "Some Conceptual Problems in the Cognitive-
      Developmental Approach to Morality." Journal of Moral
      Education, 6 (1977): 147-157.

      Argues that Kohlberg's theory provides no satisfactory
      criteria for defining the moral domain; that its basic moral
      position is inconsistent; that the ultimate justification for
      the principle of justice is not established; and that the claim
      to logical necessity for the stage-sequence is not substanti-
      ated.

873. Conroy, Anne R., and John K. Burton. "The Trouble with Kohlberg:
      A Critique." Educational Forum, 45 (November 1980): 43-55.

      Presents a wide-ranging critique of Kohlberg focusing on
      methodological problems in testing moral development,
      philosophical concerns, and problems certain to be encountered
      in attempting to implement Kohlbergian programs in local
      communities.

874. Craig, Robert P. "Form, Content and Justice in Moral
      Reasoning." Educational Theory, 26 (1976): 154-157.

      Critiques the formalism of Kohlberg and Hare by showing that
      formal characteristics in moral reasoning cannot be separated
      from substantive characteristics.

875. Craig, Robert. "Lawrence Kohlberg and Moral Development: Some
      Reflections." Educational Theory, 24 (1974): 121-129.

      Presents an overview of the key aspects of Kohlberg's theory.
      The major criticisms leveled against Kohlberg are reviewed and
      their accuracy assessed.

876. Crittenden, Brian. "The Limitations of Morality as Justice in
      Kohlberg's Theory." The Domain of Moral Education (item 30),
      pp. 251-266.

      Suggests that Kohlberg's focus is too narrow. Morality cannot
      be equated with justice, nor can justice necessarily be given
      primacy in morality.

877. DeJardins, Joseph R. "A Philosophical Analysis of Lawrence
      Kohlberg's Theory of Moral Development." Ph.D. dissertation,
      University of Notre Dame, 1980. 41/06, p. 2638.

      Examines Kohlberg's theory from the perspective of practical
      reason, i.e., the claim that all men have reason to be moral.
      Concludes that in at least one sense Kohlberg's theory does
      support such a claim.

878. Diller, Ann. "Law, Morality and Educational Uses of Kohlberg's
      Scheme." Philosophy of Education 1980 (item 1509), pp.
      186-189.

      In responding to Freiberg (item 687) argues that Kohlberg's
      latest revision of stage descriptions has redefined the
      conventional level in nonlegal terminology.

879. Diorio, Joseph A. "Cognitive Universalism and Cultural
      Relativity in Moral Education." Educational Philosophy and
      Theory, 8 (April 1976): 33-53.

      Presents a critique of Kohlberg's work which focuses on the
      argument that Kohlberg's formalist principles closely correspond
      to the moral outlook of one particular cultural orientation. An
      interesting comparison of Kohlberg's and the Buddhist's moral
      views is presented.

880. Dykstra, Craig. "Moral Virtue or Social Reasoning." Religious
      Education, 75 (1980): 115-128.

      Presents a mild critique of Kohlberg that focuses on three
      claims made by Kohlberg: virtue is one (justice); a person's
      morality can be judged by looking at his/her judgments about
      situations; and there is one structure of morality (cognitive).

881. Feldman, Ray E. "The Promotion of Moral Development in Prisons
      and Schools." Moral Development and Politics (item 1531), pp.
      286-328.

      Reports the results of an evaluation of Kohlberg's just
      community prison programs and just community school programs.
      The results are highly critical of the programs. Argues that in
      these programs there is little talk of justice. These programs
      are simply another way of keeping order and exist only because
      people prefer the informal setting. The critique is well
      conceived, well documented, and essential reading for those
      interested in evaluating just community programs.

882. Fishkin, James. "Relativism, Liberalism, and Moral
      Development." Moral Development and Politics (item 1531), pp.
      85-106.

Regards Kohlberg's typology of stages as flawed because it fails to satisfactorily integrate a relativistic morality. Fishkin argues that relativistic behavior can be seen as consistent and coherent; however, once the viability of the more modest, liberal alternative to developmental theory is admitted, the relativistic arguments can be rejected.

883. Freiberg, Jo Ann. "Morality and the Law: Where Does Kohlberg Stand?" Philosophy of Education 1980 (item 1509), pp. 178-185.

Attempts to show that Kohlberg has tacitly assumed a particular philosophy of law and has therefore built into his stage 4 a content base. By doing so he has ruled out alternative interpretations of stage 4 reasoning.

884. Giarelli, J. "Lawrence Kohlberg and G.E. Moore on the Naturalistic Fallacy." Educational Theory, 26 (1976): 348-354.

Compares Kohlberg and G.E. Moore and finds that Kohlberg neither committed the naturalistic fallacy nor got away with it.

885. Gibbs, John C. "Kohlberg's Moral Stage Theory: A Piagetian Revision." Human Development, 22 (1979): 89-112.

Presents a reconceptualization of Kohlbergian theory in light of criticisms that the highest stages are elitist, ethnocentric and excessively abstract. The proposed revision describes moral development in adulthood as existential rather than Piagetian, and restricts moral judgment in the standard stage sense to childhood and adolescence.

886. Gibbs, John C. "Kohlberg's Stages of Moral Judgment: A Constructive Critique." Harvard Educational Review, 47 (1977): 43-61.

Distinguishes between naturalistic and existential themes in modern psychology and argues that the higher stages (5 and 6) appear to be existential or reflective extensions of the lower stages. Higher stages are not theories in action, but rather are detached reflections on one's theories in action.

887. Grover, S. "An Examination of Kohlberg's Cognitive-Developmental Model of Morality." Journal of Genetic Psychology, 136 (1980): 137-144.

Argues that people come to choose the good and act on it by not only abiding by the universal principle of justice. Courage is often required in moral decisions and knowledge of ethical principles is insufficient to account for it.

888. Hamm, Cornel M. "The Content of Moral Education, or In Defense
      of the Bag of Virtues." School Review, 85 (1977): 218-228.

      Argues, against Kohlberg, that there is in fact a content to
      morality, that this content is properly conceived of as virtues,
      and that virtues can be taught. A list of virtues that are
      beyond reasonable dispute is presented.

889. Jones, Herbert T. "Kohlberg and the Deweyan Tradition." Ed.D.
      dissertation, Rutgers University, 1981. 42/01, p. 129.

      Examines the extent to which Kohlberg's work is supported by
      Deweyan views on morality and moral education. Argues that
      Kohlberg may not have fully grasped the full force of Dewey's
      contextualism.

890. Kincaid, M. Evelyn. "A Philosophical Analysis of Lawrence
      Kohlberg's Developmental Stages of Moral Reasoning." Ph.D.
      dissertation, University of Florida, 1977. 38/07, p. 4016.

      Criticizes Kohlberg's theory by pointing out the difficulties
      of simultaneously holding a Deweyan position on epistemology and
      a Rawlsian theory of justice. Argues that Kohlberg and Dewey
      are not nearly as close as Kohlberg would have us believe.

891. Kohlberg, Lawrence. "Reply to Bereiter's Statement on
      Kohlberg's Cognitive-Developmental View." Interchange, 1
      (1970): 40-48.

      Kohlberg responds to Bereiter (item 862) and argues that he
      has misunderstood his concept of instructional reorganization as
      natural and inevitable. Kohlberg's response is followed by a
      reply by Bereiter.

892. Kohlberg, Lawrence. "A Response to Critics of the Theory." The
      Psychology of Moral Development (item 625), Chapter 7.

      Summarizes and responds to criticisms of the theory.

893. Krahn, John H. "A Comparison of Kohlberg's and Piaget's Type 1
      Morality." Religious Education, 66 (1971): 373-375.

      Casts doubt on Kohlberg's description of Type 1 morality and
      argues that Piaget's description of early morality based on
      respect for adult authority and conformity to rules is more
      accurate.

894. Kuhn, Deanna. "Inducing Development Experimentally: Comments on
      a Research Paradigm." Developmental Psychology, 10 (1974):
      590-600.

Critiques studies designed to produce developmental changes in Piagetian tasks, i.e., induce conservation in nonconserving subjects. Four major difficulties with the studies are noted, and suggestions for improving the research are presented.

895. Kurtines, William, and Esther B. Greif. "The Development of Moral Thought: Review of Evaluation of Kohlberg's Approach." Psychological Bulletin, 81 (1974): 453-470.

Examines and evaluates the research base supporting Kohlberg's theory concerning the development of moral thought. Serious questions are posed concerning the reliability and validity of assessment procedures of Kohlberg. Also noted is the absence of direct evidence for the basic assumptions of the theory. Concludes that the empirical utility of the model has yet to be demonstrated.

896. Lange, Deborah. "Kohlberg's Social Value Theory: An Ethical Analysis." Philosophy of Education 1977 (item 1527), pp. 89-99.

Argues that there is no clear notion of what values are operative at each stage and how these values can be identified within the context of a student's response. Students and teachers are asked to adjudicate moral conflict from principles containing key concepts that are vague and ambiguous.

897. Levine, C.G. "Stage Acquisition and Stage Use: An Appraisal of Stage Displacement Explanations of Variation in Moral Reasoning." Human Development, 22 (1979): 145-164.

Argues that the stage mixture perspective does not constitute a sufficient explanation for variation in stage usage. An alternative conceptualization of transformation--the nondisplacement perspective--is offered as an adequate explanation for varying stage use.

898. Locke, Don. "Cognitive Stages or Developmental Phases? A Critique of Kohlberg's Stage Structural Theory of Moral Reasoning." Journal of Moral Education, 8 (1979): 168-181.

Kohlberg's theory is criticized under the following headings: structural wholes, invariance, cultural universality, logical necessity, increasing cognitive adequacy, and increasing moral adequacy.

899. Locke, Don. "The Illusion of Stage Six." Journal of Moral Education, 9 (1980): 103-109.

900. Luizzi, Vincent. "How People Become Moral--Is Kohlberg Correct and Has He Told Us Enough?" Journal of Thought, 13 (1978): 322-330.

Challenges Kohlberg's wholesale rejection of the Aristotelian view that morality is acquired through habituation.

901. Mapel, Brenda M. "An Act-Theory Alternative to Rationalistic Moral Education." Philosophy of Education 1978 (item 1499), pp. 85-104.

Presents an ethical act-theory critique of Kohlberg's rule-theory account of moral development and argues for an alternative act-theory interpretation of cognitive moral development.

902. Margolis, Joseph. "Does Kohlberg Have a Valid Theory of Moral Education?" Growing Up with Philosophy (item 1507), pp. 240-255.

Shows that the internal structure of Kohlberg's thought is inconsistent and thus the practical consequences are not merely trivial, could well be pernicious. The history of philosophical inquiry shows that it is consistently dialectical and pluralistic. Kohlberg attempts to reduce all morality to the principle of justice and dispose of all ethical positions other than his own. Such an approach in ethics, if applied to education, could amount to indoctrination.

903. Maschette, Diane. "Moral Reasoning in the 'Real World.'" Theory into Practice, 16 (1977): 124-128.

Presents a theoretical exploration of how the reasoning one uses in hypothetical dilemmas is related to the reasoning one uses in real moral dilemmas, and of the factors to be considered in addition to reasoning in accounting for moral reasoning.

904. Meacham, John A. "A Dialectical Approach to Moral Judgment and Self-Esteem." Human Development, 18 (1975): 159-170.

Argues that moral development (from a dialectical perspective) must be conceptualized within a cultural and historical context. The reciprocal significance of individual moral development for changes in the family and society should be recognized.

905. Morelli, Elizabeth A. "The Sixth Stage of Moral Development." Journal of Moral Education, 7 (1978): 97-108.

Subjects Kohlberg's sixth stage to a dialectical critique and finds unresolved conflicts within this stage. Points to the need for a further moral stage of development.

906. Morgan, Kathryn P. "Philosophical Problems in Cog-
      nitive-Developmental Theory: A Critique of the Work of
      Lawrence Kohlberg." Philosophy of Education 1973: Proceedings
      of the Philosophy of Education Society. Edwardsville:
      Southern Illinois University Press, 1973, pp. 104-117.

      Argues that Kohlberg equates moral principle and value.
      Claims that Kohlberg and other developmentalists need to learn
      the language of philosophy and pay attention to its
      distinctions.

907. Mosher, Ralph. "Who Is the Fairest of Them All?" Adolescents'
      Development and Education (item 1512), pp. 61-65.

      Reviews Kohlbergian theory and offers five problems associated
      with the theory.

908. Munsey, Brenda. "Cognitive-Developmental Theory of Moral
      Development: Metaethical Issues." Moral Development, Moral
      Education and Kohlberg (item 1514), pp. 161-181.

      Criticizes Kohlberg's formalistic interpretation of moral
      development and defends an alternative pragmatic interpretation
      which holds that as an individual encounters exceptions to the
      rules his/her present structure of norms would be subtly modi-
      fied in ways that will make the norms a more adequate summary of
      his/her particular moral experience. Argues that psychology's
      attempt to explain the development of moral judgment would be
      better served if guided by a normative act theory (rather than
      rule theory) conception of sound moral judgment.

909. Murphy, J., and C. Gilligan. "Moral Development in Late
      Adolescence and Adulthood: A Critique and Reconstruction of
      Kohlberg's Theory." Human Development, 23 (1980): 77-104.

      The persistence in late adolescence of a relativistic
      regression in moral development requires a revision in
      Kohlbergian theory. Based on a new revision of the scoring
      manual, the regressors are seen as progressors when evaluated
      against a standard of commitment in relativism instead of
      against absolute principles of justice.

910. Nicolayev, Jennie, and D.C. Phillips. "On Assessing Kohlberg's
      Stage of Moral Development." The Domain of Moral Education
      (item 30), pp. 231-250.

      Examines whether or not the Kohlbergian research program is a
      progressive one, i.e., have its activities been content
      increasing? Finds that its claims for logical necessity,
      assertion of invariance, and even the stage assumption all lack
      solid evidence. Also published under a different title in
      Educational Theory, 28 (1978): 286-301.

911. O'Connor, Robert W. and Victor L. Worsfold. "Kohlberg's
     Developmental Stages as Ethical Theory: Some Doubts."
     Philosophy of Education 1973: Proceedings of the Philosophy of
     Education Society. Edwardsville: Southern Illinois University
     Press, 1973, pp. 118-125.

     Argues that Kohlberg asks us to accept substantive moral
     principles (of saving a life) without advancing the sort of
     metaethical argument which must be used to warrant such
     principles.

912. Olmsted, Richard. "Was Dewey at Stage 6? Reflections in the
     Ethical Theory of Lawrence Kohlberg." Philosophy of Education
     1977 (item 1527), pp. 156-162.

     Argues that Kohlberg's claim that stages 5 and 6 exhaust
     morality is unwarranted.

913. Paton, James W. "An Analysis of Cognitive Moral Development
     Theory in Relationship to Moral Education Strategy Making
     Procedures." Ph.D. dissertation, Kent State University, 1980.
     41/06, p. 2074.

     Presents an analysis of Kohlberg's theory focusing on the
     form-content distinction intervention techniques, the
     relationship to social learning theory and possible negative
     effects of disequilibrium.

914. Peters, R.S. "Moral Development: A Plea for Pluralism."
     Psychology and Ethical Development (item 311), pp. 303-335.

     After reviewing Kohlberg's theory Peters argues that virtues
     and habits do have a place in moral development. Many virtues
     are not tied down to specific situations and habit is not
     incompatible with intellegence and reasoning. Kohlberg is
     criticized for taking an overly narrow view of moral develop-
     ment. Originally appeared in T. Mischel, Ed. Cognitive
     Development and Epistemology. NY: Academic Press, 1971.

915. Peters, Richard. "The Place of Kohlberg's Theory in Moral
     Education." Journal of Moral Education, 7 (1978): 147-157.

     Kohlberg is criticized for his general neglect of the
     affective side of moral development. How his work might be
     supplemental by a concern for others is presented. The
     importance of the content of morality is reaffirmed.

916. Peters, Richard. "Virtues and Habits in Moral Education." The
     Domain of Moral Education (item 30), pp. 267-287.

An abridged version of "Moral Development: A Plea for Pluralism (item 914). Contains a spirited defense of the role of virtues, traits and habits in morality.

917. Peters, Richard S. "Why Doesn't Lawrence Kohlberg Do His Homework?" Moral Education ... It Comes with the Territory (item 1519), pp. 288-290.

Lists the main omissions of Kohlberg's work: holding that Kantian morality is the only acceptable morality, not taking "good-boy" morality seriously enough, paying scant attention to affective development, and not considering how ego-development occurs.

918. Philbert, P.J. "Lawrence Kohlberg's Use of Virtue in His Theory of Moral Development." International Philosophical Quarterly, 15 (1975): 455-497.

Argues that the acquisition of virtue by repeated acts has been conceived in too superficial a manner by both Kohlberg and his critics.

919. Puka, Bill. "Kohlbergian Forms and Deweyon Acts: A Response." Moral Development, Moral Education and Kohlberg (item 1514), pp. 429-454.

Defends Kohlbergian views on moral education. Shows how the critics have misinterpreted Kohlberg and urges the continued use of Deweyan ideas to inform Kohlbergian theory and practice.

920. Puka, Bill. "A Kohlbergian Reply." The Domain of Moral Education (item 30), pp. 288-301.

Replies to critics of Kohlberg's works.

921. Puka, Bill. "Moral Education and Its Cure." Reflections on Values Education (item 1510), pp. 47-87.

Presents an analysis and critique of Kohlberg's view of moral education. A major problem found with Kohlberg's views is that it does not pay adequate attention to unconscious influences on peoples choices and behavior. The focus for Puka is on a total personality development, which he feels if allowed to develop naturally will be good and moral.

922. Reid, Herbert G. and Ernest J. Yanarella. "The Tyranny of the Categorical: On Kohlberg and the Politics of Moral Development." Moral Development and Politics (item 1531), pp. 107-132.

Confronts Kohlberg's theories as a species of liberal ideology. Arguing from a modern critical theory perspective, it is concluded that Kohlberg's theory cannot be regarded as universal because it is an ideological reflection of the Anglo-American liberal tradition.

923. Rest, James. "Developmental Psychology as a Guide to Value Education: A Review of 'Kohlbergian' Programs." Moral Education ... It Comes with the Territory (item 1519), pp. 252-274.

Analyzes the fundamental ideas of Kohlberg and how these ideas have been extended into practice. Rest concludes that developmental psychology guides the educational programs in global programmatic ways, but not in day-by-day planning or analysis. Also in Review of Educational Research. 44(1974).

924. Roberts, David B. "Foundations and Implications for Adult Moral Education in Lawrence Kohlberg's Theory of Moral Development and Walter G. Muelder's Conception of Moral Laws." Ph.D. dissertation, Boston University, 1977. 38/04, 2020.

A rather critical view of Kohlberg's work coupled with a perspective on adult moral education based on Muelder's conception of moral laws.

925. Rosen, Bernard. "Moral Dilemmas and Their Treatment." Moral Development, Moral Education and Kohlberg (item 1514), pp. 232-265.

Examines the nature of moral dilemmas as a certain logical form derived from philosophical analyses of logic. In Rosen's analysis the problem of a dilemma involves knowing which of two competing antecedents or negations of consequents is true. He compares act and rule theory treatments of dilemmas and shows how the methodology of act theories, moral negotiation, fits in a most natural way the structure of moral dilemmas.

926. Rubin, K.H., and Trotter, K.T. "Kohlberg's Moral Judgment Scale: Some Methodological Considerations." Developmental Psychology, 13 (1977): 535-536.

Children in grades three and five were administered the moral judgment scale and then two weeks later half were given an objective scale of moral judgment and the other half readministered the moral judgment interview scale. The results raised serious questions concerning the psychometric properties of the Kohlberg moral judgment scale.

927. Schleifer, M. "Moral Education and Indoctrination." Ethics, 86
      (1976): 154-163.

      Kohlberg is lauded for his emphasis on developing general
      cognitive abilities but criticized for eschewing the nonrational
      in moral education. Kohlberg's more recent writings (item 410)
      negate much of the criticism in this article.

928. Schmitt, Rudolf. "The Stages of Moral Development--A Basis for
      an Educational Concept?" International Review of Education,
      26 (1980): 207-216.

      Argues that the longitudinal evidence does not support
      Kohlberg's claims, that the stages are not differentiated
      structurally, but rather according to content on the basis of
      implicit moral concepts, and that the dominance of a certain
      ethical philosophy influences the development of moral judgment.
      A new arrangement of stage sequence is presented organized
      around ethical principles and educational climate.

929. Schwartz, Edward. "Traditional Values, Moral Education, and
      Social Change." Moral Development and Politics (item 1531),
      pp. 221-236.

      Is concerned whether moral development theories can give
      adequate instruction concerning the behavioral attributes of
      high stages. Argues that alternative visions of the good life
      and justice compete in a society--an abstract conception of
      justice does not offer a clear way to choose. Concludes that
      the content of an argument must be examined, not merely the
      structures of authority it represents.

930. Shawver, David J. "Character and Ethics: An Epistemological
      Inquiry with Particular Reference to Lawrence Kohlberg's
      Cognitive Theory of Moral Development." Ph.D. dissertation,
      McGill University, 1979. 40/09, p. 5087.

      Kohlberg's claim that he is operating in the traditions of
      Piaget and Rawls is challenged it is claimed that they are
      incompatible traditions.

931. Sichel, Betty A. "Can Kohlberg Respond to Critics?"
      Educational Theory, 26 (1976): 337-347.

      Indicates how in two areas (habits and reason, and passion and
      norm) Kohlberg's theory may be expanded to include the
      conceptualization necessary for any viable theory of moral
      development. It is stressed, however, that Kohlberg has made no
      such movement in that direction.

932. Sichel, Betty A.   "A Critical Study of Kohlberg's Theory of the
      Development of Moral Judgments." Philosophy of Education 1976
      (item 1529), pp. 209-220.

      Focuses on four dimensions of Kohlberg's theory which are of
      special interest to philosophers and which have not been
      adequately examined: The relationship between moral judgment and
      moral behavior, differences between logical judgments and moral
      judgments, the inception of moral reasoning and moral
      justification and moral judgments.

933. Sichel, Betty A.   "The Relation Between Moral Judgment and Moral
      Behavior in Kohlberg's Theory of the Development of Moral
      Judgments."   Educational Philosophy and Theory, 8 (April
      1976): 55-67.

      Argues that there are empirical and logical reasons to reject
      Kohlbergs conceptualization of the relationship between moral
      judgment and moral behavior.

934. Siegal, Michael.   "Kohlberg Versus Piaget: To What Extent Has
      One Theory Eclipsed the Other?" Merrill-Palmer Quarterly, 26
      (1980): 285-297.

      Based on an examination of research it is concluded that
      Kohlberg's theory is but a modest improvement over Piaget's.
      Kohlberg's evidence appears to be weakest when it strays from
      Piaget's formulation-stages 1, 5 and 6.

935. Siegal, M.   "Spontaneous Development of Moral Concepts." Human
      Development, 18 (1975): 370-383.

      Four types of non-spontaneous solutions to moral problems are
      suggested and it is argued that spontaneous, rational
      development of moral concepts can only occur when one perceives
      the pseudo-rigorousness of these non-spontaneous solutions.
      Moral conceptual development requires more than one moral
      virtue: that of courage as well as justice.

936. Simpson, Elizabeth Leonie.   "Moral Development Research: A Case
      Study of Scientific Cultural Bias." Human Development, 17
      (1974): 81-106.

      Analyzes Kohlberg's claims for the cross-cultural universality
      of the stages and finds that the definitions of stages and the
      assumptions underlying them are ethnocentric and
      culturally-biased. Also in Moral and Psychological Education
      (item 1521).

937. Stanton, Michael. "Pupils' Assessments of Social Action: A
      Cross-Cultural Study." Educational Review, 27 (1975):
      126-137.

      Argues that because of substantial differences in ratings of
      forms of positive and negative behavior among a cross-cultural
      sample there does not appear to be a basis for postualating
      universal stages of moral judgment.

938. Straughan, Roger R. "Hypothetical Moral Situations." Journal
      of Moral Education, 4 (1975): 183-189.

      Drawing on the logical distinctions between different types of
      moral conflict, it is argued that any approach to moral
      education based on hypothetical moral dilemmas must have serious
      limitations.

939. Sullivan, Edmund V. Kohlberg's Structuralism: A Critical
      Appraisal, Monograph Series 115. Toronto: Ontario Institute
      for Studies in Education, 1977.

      Criticizes Kohlberg from a post-critical perspective arguing
      that what is said to constitute disinterested and abstract
      fairness is in fact defined by the dominant group in the
      society. Moral education needs to be viewed from a much broader
      perspective.

940. Sullivan, Edmund V. "Structuralism per se When Applied to Moral
      Ideology." Readings in Moral Education (item 1522), pp.
      272-286.

      Criticizes Kohlberg for not giving convincing attention to the
      notion of moral commitment--the fusion of thaught and action.
      Discusses moral blindness--where moral reasons become rationali-
      zations. An excerpt from item 755.

941. Sullivan, Edmund V. "A Study of Kohlberg's Structural Theory of
      Moral Development: A Critique of Liberal Social Science
      Ideology." Human Development, 20 (1977): 352-76.

      Kohlberg's stage theory is characterized as a species of
      liberal ideology.

942. Trainer, F.E. "A Critical Analysis of Kohlberg's Contribution
      to the Study of Moral Thought." Journal for the Theory of
      Social Behavior, 7 (1977): 41-63.

      Presents a wide ranging critique of Kohlbergian theory
      touching on questions of whether the stages are discoveries of
      speculative constructions, whether high stages are somehow
      better, difficulties within the account of stage 6 thought, and
      the phenomena of adolescent regression.

943. Wilson,   John.   "Philosophical   Difficulties   and   Moral
      Development." Moral Development, Moral Education and Kohlberg
      (item 1514), pp. 214-231.

      Offers a sympathetic but critical view of what he sees as
      Kohlberg's interesting data built too quickly into theory. He
      argues that Kohlberg's theory is not content free, contains
      ambiguity in interview language, especially with regard to
      differences between causes and reasons, and is unclear with re-
      spect to what exactly is a "stage."

944. Wilson, Richard W.   "Some Comments on Stage Theories of Moral
      Development." Journal of Moral Education, 5 (1976): 241-248.

      Based on studies of variations in moral responses of Chinese
      and American children it is concluded that developmental theory
      has ignored the type and extent of manipulation of affect.
      There is a crucial need for the development of internalized com-
      mitments to various types of behavior.

945. Wonderly, D.M. and J.H. Kupfersmid. "Promoting Postconventional
      Morality: The Adequacy of Kohlberg's Aim." Adolescence, 15
      (1980): 609-631. NR

The Family in the Moralization Process

946. Barclay, James R. "Values in Adolescent Males and Father-Son Relations." Personnel and Guidance Journal, 58 (1970): 627-629.

Discusses the role of the father in the transmission to sons of socially responsible values. Four special factors in value transmission between father and son are described: model of masculine behavior, the communicator, the moral model (non-absolutist), and the fallible reinforcing agent.

947. Baumrind, Diana. "Current Patterns of Parental Authority." Developmental Psychology, 4, 1, Part 2 (1971): 1-103.

In this major study of child rearing practices, the effects of authoritative parental control on boys and girls was noted. Also reported are the effects of permissive and nonconforming behavior of parents in social responsibility. This is one of the more extensive studies available on the relationship between patterns of parental authority and social responsibility of children.

948. Borstelmann, L.J. "Changing Concepts of Childrearing, 1920's-1950's: Parental Research, Parental Guidance, Social Issues." Paper presented at Biennial Southeastern Conference on Human Development, Nashville, 1976. ED 127 010.

949. Bronfenbrenner, Urie. "The Split Level Family," Readings in Values Clarification (item 1504), pp. 249-264.

Documents the changing nature of the American family--its gradual loss of influence over the development of young people alongside the simultaneous gain in influence by television and by the peer group. Argues that socially constructive activities can be found that involve adults in the lives of children in a significant way. This sort of program offers some hope for reversing adult-child segregation and resulting loss of ability to socialize into positive social roles.

950. Erickson, V. Lois. "Sex Role Assignment in Family and School Systems: An Issue of Justice." Development of Moral Reasoning (item 1495), pp. 195-208.

Discusses sex-role stereotyping of females in the family as an issue of justice. She traces the limiting growth patterns of such stereotyping and argues for the need to redefine our conceptions of maleness and femaleness. She concludes with several suggestions for transcending sex-role stereotypes.

951. Finn, Edward J. "The Effect of Parental Influence and Peer Influence on the Moral Judgment of Suburban Ninth Grade Students." Ph.D. dissertation, St. John's University, 1978. 40/05, p. 2477.

Subjects were told their Defining Issues Tests would be either kept confidential, sent home, or seen by their peers. There was a significant treatment effect, with students under parental influence increasing their scores more than controls, and students under peer influence increasing less than controls.

952. Haan, N.; J. Langer; and L. Kohlberg. "Family Patterns of Moral Reasoning." Child Development, 47 (1976): 1204-1206.

Investigates intrafamilial patterns of moral reasoning. Husbands' and wives' patterns of moral reasoning were modestly related, but siblings' patterns were not. Parents' and sons' moral reasoning did show positive relationships, but this disappeared with age.

953. Hoffman, M.L. "Childrearing Practices and Moral Development: Generalization from Empirical Research." Child Development, 34 (1963): 295-318.

Pulls together research from a variety of sources in an effort to understand the relationship between childrearing practices and moral development. Concludes that behavioral generality and dynamic consistency increase with age. Psychological discipline was found to contribute to both guilt and resistance to temptation.

954. Hoffman, Martin. "The Role of the Parent in the Child's Moral Growth." Religious Education, 57 (July-August 1962): S18-S33.

Looks at the acquisition of values from the viewpoint of the effects of parental influences.

955. Hoffman, M.L., and H. Saltzstein. "Parent Discipline and the Child's Moral Development." Journal of Personality and Social Psychology, 5 (1967): 45-57.

With seventh grade children it was found that advanced development along various moral dimensions was associated with the infrequent use of power assertion and frequent use of induction. Love withdrawal related infrequently to moral development.

956. Holstein, Constance B.   "Parental Consensus and Interaction in Relation to the Child's Moral Judgment." Ph.D. dissertation, University of California, Berkeley, 1969. 31/04, p. 1888.

Child's level of moral judgment was found to be positively related to mother's (not father's) level of moral judgment, amount of time spent discussing moral dilemmas in families, and parental encouragement of child participation in moral decision making.

957. Hower, John T.   "Parent Behavior and Moral Education." Development of Moral Reasoning (item 1495), pp. 158-168.

Analyzes, along acceptance-rejection and firm-lax continuums, the impact of different styles of parenting on the moralization of children. Moral character, defined in terms of conformity, empathy, and autonomy, is the result of a strong relationship between parent and child. The proper parenting behaviors for the development of moral character are discussed.

958. Hower, John T., and Keith J. Edwards.   "The Effects of Parent-Child Relationships on the Development of Moral Character." Paper presented at the annual meeting of the American Educational Research Association, San Francisco, 1976. ED 128 728.

Uses Hogan's dimensional model of moral character and the concepts of parental acceptance and parental control to study the interrelationships between family relationships and moral character.

959. Karrby, Gunni. "A Report on Some Studies of the Influence of Family Background upon Moral Development." Journal of Moral Education, 2 (1973): 263-268.

Reports the results of a series of studies by the author that suggest that greater emphasis should be placed on the social learning process in child rearing and education.

960. Kobett, Lorraine A.   "The Relationship Between Home Background School Achievement and Adolescent Values." Ph.D. dissertation, Claremont Graduate School, 1978. 39/06, p. 3377.

Adolescent values were found to be unrelated to school achievement. Parents' values and age of student were found to be related to his/her values.

961. Lydiat, M. "Parental Attitudes and the Moral Development of Children," _Journal of Moral Education_,3 (1971): 271-281.

Inconclusive results are achieved on the Parental Attitude Research Instrument. Possible reasons for the results are discussed.

962. Morvell, J. "Moral Socialization in a Multi-Racial Community." _Journal of Moral Education_, 3 (1974): 249-257.

Found that the family had the greatest influence on children with the school some way behind. Differences in parent/school emphases are rated.

963. Mullis, Ronald L. "Relationships Between Parental Behaviors and Children's Moral Reasoning." Ph.D. dissertation, Iowa State University, 1978. 39/10, p. 5929.

No significant relationships were found to exist between parental behaviors and moral intentionality levels of their children.

964. Nevius, John R. "The Relationship of Child Rearing Practices to the Acquisition of Moral Judgments in Ten Year Old Boys." Ph.D. dissertation, University of Southern California, 1972. 33/04, p. 1524.

The acquisition of stage of moral reasoning and child rearing practices of parents were found to be unrelated.

965. Olejnik, Anthony E. "Moral Development: How Adults Reason with Children." Paper presented at the annual meeting of the Midwestern Psychological Association, Chicago, 1979. ED 179 830.

Found that principled individuals preferred to use induction in talking with children while conventional individuals tended to use power assertion.

966. Pembroke, Eileen. "Parent Education as a Means of Fostering Moral Development in Beginning Primary Age Children." Ph.D. dissertation, Loyola University of Chicago, 1980. 41/03, p. 994.

A lack of significant change in children's self-concept and level of social reasoning was attributed to the parent education intervention's inability to change parents' attitudes.

967. Peterson, Gail B.; Larry Peterson; and Richard Hey. "Family
     Structure and Moral Education." Development of Moral
     Reasoning (item 1495), pp. 147-157.

     Discusses research into ways that the family structure can be
     used to facilitate the moral development of children.

968. Saltzstein, Herbert D. "Social Influence and Moral Development:
     A Perspective on the Role of Parents and Peers." Moral
     Development and Behavior (item 519), pp. 253-265.

     Discusses the research on discipline, specifically regarding
     the relationship between parental discipline and different kinds
     of moral orientations. Parallels are drawn between Kelman's
     social influence processes and Kohlberg's stages of moral
     development.

969. Santrock, J.W. "Father Absence, Perceived Maternal Behavior and
     Moral Development in Boys." Child Development, 46 (1975):
     753-757.

     Few differences were found between father-absent and
     father-present boys; however, father-absent boys were reported
     by their teachers to be less morally advanced than
     father-present boys.

970. Schneider, Barry H. "An Elaboration of the Relationship Between
     Parental Behavior and Children's Moral Development." Ph.D.
     dissertation, University of Toronto, 1977. 39/07, p. 4152.

     A perceived parenting style consisting of high demand,
     enforced by punishment, but in an affectionate context, was
     found to be associated with moral behavior ratings. Moral
     reasoning did not relate materially to any parenting style.

971. Stroup, Atlee L. "Family Stability: Climate for Moral
     Development." Educational Horizons, 56 (Winter 1977-78):
     71-76.

     The role of the family in moral development is analyzed from
     a sociological perspective. Recent problem areas and their
     impact on the family are discussed.

972. Sugarman, Barry. "Altruistic Attitudes in School: Validation
     Data for Two Questionnaires and Some Preliminary Findings."
     Journal of Moral Education, 2 (1973): 145-155.

     Home background is found to be most strongly associated with
     questionnaire altruism. Differences were detected between
     age-sex groups and schools.

973. Vergote, Antoine. "The Dynamics of the Family and Its
      Significance for Moral and Religious Development." Toward
      Moral and Religious Maturity (item 403), pp. 89-114.

      Explores what psychological conditions are necessary for the
      formation of the moral and religious personality. Knowing one's
      structure of reasoning is not nearly as important as knowing how
      spontaneous moral judgment comes about. A process of
      identification with parental figures is seen as the dominant
      factor. The perspective taken is psychoanalytic, with the
      formation of the ego-ideal seen as the crucial variable.

974. Westerhold, Ruth E. "The Effects of a Parent Training
      Experience on the Moral Character of Children." Ph.D.
      dissertation, Southern Illinois University, 1978. 39/04, p.
      2074.

      A training program based on emotional acceptance, providing
      example and explanation and discipline, was developed and field
      tested. The results indicated that the program had no major
      impact on the development of moral character.

975. Whiting, John W. "Socialization Process and Personality."
      Psychological Anthropology. Edited by Francis L.K. Heu.
      Homewood, IL: Dorsey, 1961, pp. 355-399.

      Reviews cross-cultural studies of child rearing practices.
      Evidence is offered to support the hypothesis that personality
      and values are determined by the maintenance systems and child
      training practices of the culture.

976. Windmiller, Myra. "Introduction, Part II: The Role of Parents
      in Moral Development and Socialization." Moral Development
      and Socialization (item 524), pp. 13-33.

      Reviews the role of the parent in moralization from
      developmental, social learning, and psychoanalytic perspectives.
      Similarities and differences between the three interpretations
      are discussed.

977. Abel, Louise W. "Social and Moral Values Presented in Children's Textbooks." Ph.D. dissertation, University of California at Berkeley, 1966. 27/03, p. 695.

Compares McGuffey's Reader with today's textbooks as with regard to social and moral values presented. Found that today's texts contain more social and moral values, but without the religious emphasis.

978. Abercrombie, Charlotte M. "A Content Analysis of Reading Textbooks in Terms of Moral Value." Ed.D. dissertation, Columbia University, 1974. 36/03, p. 1262.

The greatest amount of attention was given to helpfulness. Very little attention was given to self-reliance, honesty, or courage. In Kohlberg's stages the most frequent emphasis was at stage 3.

979. Abrams, Macy L. and James A. Saxon. "VIDAC: A Computer Program for Value Identification and Classification." Ph.D. dissertation, United States International University, 1969. 31/05, p. 2491.

A content analysis program is developed to interpret the value emphasis of written content.

980. Anyon, Jean. "Ideology and United States History Textbooks." Harvard Education Review, 49 (1979): 361-386.

Examines the content of 17 widely used secondary-school U.S. history texts. The content of the textbooks was found to reflect an ideology that serves the ruling class to the exclusion of others.

981. Apple, Michael W., and Nancy R. King. "What Do Schools Teach?" Humanistic Education. Edited by Richard H. Weller. Berkeley, CA: McCutchan, 1977, pp. 29-47.

Focuses on the hidden curriculum through an in-depth study of the early phases of a kindergarten class. The authors conclude that children learn to distinguish between work and play and to develop attitudes toward work. The long-range social ramifications of the hidden curriculum are discussed. Indicates how the hidden curriculum serves the interests of the conservative elements in society.

982. Bailey, John R. "Implicit Moral Education in Secondary Schools." Journal of Moral Education, 8 (1978): 32-40.

Heads and pupils are found to have differing perceptions of the areas of school life that implicitly relate to moral education. Heads claim to have few rules, but pupils still want more freedom.

983. Baker, James H. "A Comparison of Moral Development of Ninth and Twelfth Graders in Three Schools of Different Types." Ed.D. dissertation, University of Northern Colorado, 1976. 34/04, p. 1954.

Compares students attending public, non-denominational and denominational high schools. Found that in ninth grade the students were not significantly different but by twelfth grade the students in the denominational school had shown significant growth compared to public school students.

984. Biber, Barbara, and Patricia Minuchin. "The Impact of School Philosophy and Practice on Child Development." The Unstudied Curriculum (item 1516), pp. 27-52.

Compares the psychological impact on children of modern (experimental and progressive) schools and traditional schools. Found that children in modern schools are likely to be more aware of and focused on their current experiences. They also were found to be less traditional and more open in their role conceptions and attitudes.

985. Blanchard, Lois J. "The Values of the School: A Study of Student and Staff Perceptions of the Goals of the School and the Hidden Curriculum." Ph.D. dissertation, Wayne State University, 1977. 38/05, p. 2514.

Students rated hidden curriculum items on questionnaire as more important than stated goals of the schools. Teachers rated the items in the reverse order.

986. Bond, David J. "An Analysis of Valuation Strategies in Social Science Education Materials." Ph.D. dissertation, University of California, Berkeley, 1971. ED 055 948.

Finds that the axiological basis of valuation strategies in social studies texts is inconsistent, at times contradictory, and seldom based on the best available knowledge regarding the theory of valuation.

987. Boocock, S.S. "The School as a Social Environment for Learning."
      Sociology of Education, 46 (1973): 15-50.

      Reviews the picture of the school as a social environment
      presented in the work of Durkheim, Weber, Waller, and Jackson.
      Research is presented on the impact on children of structural
      features in schools. Reforms in school social structures are
      discussed, and a research agenda directed toward a new theory of
      the school as social environment for learning is presented.

988. Bothwell, H. Roger. "Moral Development of Seventh-Day Adventist
      High School Seniors versus Other Parochial Public High School
      Seniors." Ed.D. dissertation, Drake University, 1979. 40/11,
      p. 5728.

      On the Defining Issues Test, that Adventist parochially
      educated boarding high school seniors exhibit no difference in
      moral development from Adventist day school seniors, public high
      school seniors, Mormon high school seniors, and Catholic high
      school seniors.

989. Bowles, S., and H. Gintis. Schooling in Capitalist America.
      New York: Basic Books, 1976.

      Discusses the relationship between the structure of the
      American economic system and the organization of the public
      school system. Presents the correspondence theory that the
      social relationships in the workplace are the same as those in
      schools: capital and profit make schools what they are.
      Students need to be subordinated to authority, alienated from
      work, cut off from community and one another. Although this
      work does not discuss moral education per se, the implications
      are clear.

990. Burbules, Nicholas C. "The Hidden Curriculum and the Latent
      Functions of Schooling: Two Overlapping Perspectives, 2. Who
      Hides the Hidden Curriculum?" Philosophy of Education 1980
      (item 1509), pp. 281-291.

      In a response to Phillips (item 1064), urges caution in
      judging the intentions of those involved in schooling and the
      hidden curriculum. The hidden curriculum should be evaluated in
      terms of the intentions of school personnel.

991. Card, Alva M. "An Analysis of Values Contained in Secondary
      Literature Books on the State-Adopted List in Oklahoma."
      Ph.D. dissertation, University of Oklahoma, 1979. 40/04, p.
      2043.

      Found that many values are present in literature, with love
      the most frequently occurring and temperance and thrift the
      least frequently occurring.

992. Carlson, Ruth K. "Ten Values of Children's Literature." Paper
     presented at International Reading Association Conference,
     Kansas City, 1969. ED 033 826.

     Children's literature is discussed in terms of 10 values it
     may bring to children; representative books for each of the
     values are cited. Includes a bibliography on the subject.

993. Chandler, Richard E. "An Assessment of the Potential of
     Selected Text Materials for Moral Development." Ed.D.
     dissertation, University of Georgia, 1977. 38/03, p. 1195.

     Assesses the potential of three social studies textbooks to
     stimulate students' moral development. Finds, using a content
     analysis manual, that commonly used texts contain about 6% moral
     content while "Man: A Course of Study" contained 11% moral
     content.

994. Coleman, James. The Adolescent Society. Glencoe, IL: Free
     Press, 1961.

     Presents an account of the social world of the adolescent.
     The major influences on adolescents are found to be the "dating
     and rating" game, the stress upon appearance, and, for boys,
     athletics and the sacrifice of scholastic performance for social
     popularity. Teachers, administrators, and the norms of the
     school are perceived as relatively unimportant.

995. Constant, Ann P. "An Examination of Values Contained in
     Representative American Literature Anthologies." Ed.D.
     dissertation, University of Virginia, 1979. 40/09, p. 4870.

     The study incorporates tri-level, value-centered literacy
     analyses of 125 selections taken from two representative high
     school literature anthologies. The results are not reported in
     the abstract.

996. Couturier, Lance C. "An Evaluation of Group Homes for
     Delinquent Male Adolescents: The Relationships of Various
     Program Variables to the Youths' Academic and Talented
     Achievements, School Attendance, Ego Development, Moral
     Development, and Group Home Behavior." Ph.D. dissertation,
     Temple University, 1980. 41/04, p. 161.

     Examines the relationship between program features of 35 group
     homes and characteristics of 150 male residents. None of the
     program features is found to be related to moral development;
     however, significant relationship is found for other features.

997. Covington, Martin V., and Richard G. Beery. Self-Worth and
     School Learning. New York: Holt, Rinehart and Winston, 1976.

Explores the relationship between the school's achievement orientation and students' feelings of self-worth. Concludes that schools have a significant but negative impact on many children's sense of self-worth.

998. Crockenberg, S., and B. Bryant. "Socialization: The 'Implicit Curriculum' of Learning Environments." Journal of Research and Development in Education, 12, 1 (1978): 69-78.

Concludes on the basis of a research program with 8- to 11-year-old children that how a teacher structures the learning environment and how he/she relates to children influence the affective and interpersonal development of children.

999. Croghan, Penelope P. "Moral Universe As Portrayed in Third Grade Readers." Ph.D. dissertation, Northwestern University, 1979. 40/06, p. 3553.

Third grade readers were analyzed to discover the role models and moral values presented. The results are not reported in the abstract.

1000. Cusick, Philip. Inside High School: The Student's World. New York: Holt, Rinehart and Winston, 1973.

On the basis of extensive interviews and time spent with students, concludes that the effect of the hidden curriculum on students is often overdrawn. It was found, for example, that students can do well in school even if they give only minimal compliance to the system. Students' group activity with peers appears to be the real area in which life in schools is lived.

1001. Cusick, Philip. "An Rx for Our High Schools." Character, 2 (May 1981): 1-5.

Argues that current arrangements in schools lead to a fragmentation of social life. Schools should group students and teachers more closely into smaller ongoing entities.

1002. DeCharms, R., and Moeller, G.H. "Values Expressed in American Children's Reading: 1800-1950." Journal of Abnormal and Social Psychology, 64 (1962): 136-142.

Attempts to plot the incidence of achievement and affiliation imagery and moral teaching in a sample of children's readers from 1800 to the present. Finds that achievement imagery increased from 1800 to 1900 but declined thereafter. A steady decline in the amount of moral preaching is identified and there is a tentative indication of an increase in affiliation imagery.

1003. Dhard, Hargopal. "A Value Analysis of Saskatchewan Social Studies Textbooks." Ed.D. dissertation, University of Montana, 1967. 28/08, p. 2888.

Using Laswell's value framework, finds that power and wealth receive more emphasis than any other values.

1004. Dilling, H.J., and Marilyn Wideman. "Value Education in the Classroom: A Study of Teacher Attitudes and Classroom Strategies." Moral Education Forum, 4 (Winter 1979): 24-25.

Through observation in 78 classrooms without values education programs, assessed the values transmitted through teacher behavior. The values observed and rated most frequently were obedience to authority, affection, and cooperation.

1005. Dreeben, Robert. On What Is Learned in School. Reading, MA: Addison-Wesley, 1968.

Shows the relationship between school structure and learning outcomes, and the relevance of those outcomes to the surrounding institutions. Argues that the dispositions and norms necessary to survival in a technological-industrial society cannot be instilled in the warm, nurturant environment of the family. The schools play a necessary and important role in teaching the norms of independence, achievement, universalism, and specificity.

1006. Dreeben, Robert. "Schooling and Authority: Comments on the Unstudied Curriculum." The Unstudied Curriculum (item 1516), pp. 85-103.

Argues that the structural arrangements of schools provide reasonably enduring and systematic experiences from which students can infer that acting impersonally, distinguishing between persons and positions, and recognizing different principles of legitimacy and authority are appropriately associated with particular social situations.

1007. Dreeben, Robert. "The Unwritten Curriculum and Its Relation to Values." Curriculum Studies, 8 (1976): 111-124.

Argues that while it is relatively clear that there is a relationship between schooling and the acquisition of certain values, we have not yet identified the connections between school experiences and values. Concludes that teachers and administrators should treat social arrangements and instruction as part of the curriculum with a view to exercising more control over that dimension of the educational process.

1008. Duggans, James H. "Certain Social Values in Tenth Grade Literature Anthologies: A Content Analysis." Ph.D.

dissertation, University of California, Berkeley, 1970. 31/10, p. 5030.

Finds that main characters in literature are always aided by outside forces and agencies and that a unitary, determinate notion of the universe is featured.

1009. Feinberg, Walter. "A Critical Analysis of the Social and Economic Limits to the Humanizing of Education." Humanistic Education. Edited by Richard H. Weller. Berkeley, CA: McCutchan 1977, pp. 247-254.

His analysis suggests that schools are as humane as they can be within the society they serve and that an expansion of the humaneness of schools is unlikely without a similar change in society.

1010. Fitzgerald, Frances. America Revised: History Schoolbooks in the Twentieth Century. Boston: Atlantic-Little, Brown, 1979.

Consists of three essays: the first describes the changes in textbooks from the 1830s to the 1970s, the second examines the portrayal of minorities since 1830, and the third treats concepts of intellectual history apparent in the texts. Contains useful insights into the social values that were to be fostered through the study of U.S. history.

1011. Forbes, William M. "An Analysis of the Value Orientation Toward the Protestant Ethic of Elementary Social Studies Textbooks." Ph.D. dissertation, Syracuse University, 1971. 32/08, p. 4239.

Elementary social studies textbooks published in the 1960s were found to contain significantly fewer statements reflecting a Protestant Ethic value orientation than texts published in the 1940s.

1012. Friedenberg, Edgar Z. "Curriculum as Educational Process: The Middle Class Against Itself." The Unstudied Curriculum (item 1516), pp. 16-26.

Argues that the socialization occurring in schools has a definite lower-middle-class flavor. It is surprising to Friedenberg that the middle class continues to put up with schools that socialize children into a style of life it is trying to escape. The current impact of this oppressive socialization seems to be to alienate many youth.

1013. Gerety, Maryclaire A. "A Study of the Relationship Between the Moral Judgment of the Teacher and the Moral Atmosphere in the Classroom." Ed.D. dissertation, Boston University, 1980. 41/05, p. 1952.

Examines the question: "What does moral atmosphere mean in a single classroom?" No significant correlation was detected between teachers' scores on the Defining Issues Test and the Classroom Environment Scale, but based on interviews it was found that classroom moral atmosphere was directly related to teacher level of moral reasoning.

1014. Getzels, Jacob. "The Acquisition of Values in School and Society." The High School in a New Era. Edited by Francis S. Chase and Harold A. Anderson. Chicago: University of Chicago Press, 1958, pp. 146-161.

Presents America's traditional values and discusses the changes and stresses to which they are subject. Reports the results of a study that showed that children leave school with the values they brought to school. Argues that since students acquire their values largely through the process of identification, consideration should be given to the roles that teachers and other school personalities communicate to children.

1015. Giroux, Henry A. "Developing Educational Programs: Overcoming the Hidden Curriculum." The Clearing House, 52 (1978): 148-151.

Argues that the hidden curriculum, based on power and perpetuation of the status quo, has a harmful psychological and intellectual effect on students. Suggestions for changing the structural properties of the classroom and school are presented.

1016. Giroux, Henry A., and Anthony N. Penna. "Social Education in the Classroom: The Dynamics of the Hidden Curriculum." Theory and Research in Social Education, 7 (Spring 1979): 21-42.

Argues that the hidden curriculum must be eliminated or neutralized if social studies educators are to reach their goals of solidarity, individual growth, and dedication to social action.

1017. Gordon, David. "The Immorality of the Hidden Curriculum." Journal of Moral Education, 10 (1980): 3-8.

Argues that since learning associated with the hidden curriculum is likely to be unconscious, it violates basic rights of children. The potential for "raising the hidden curriculum to consciousness" is discussed. Claims that this is essential for the moral education of pupils.

1018. Grady, Laura A. "A Comparison of Selected Social Values in Students Attending Catholic Schools with Those of Students Attending Public Schools." Ed.D. dissertation, Indiana University, 1979. 40/07, p. 3721.

Found that type of school attended (Catholic, public, or weekly religious instruction classes) is not an indicator of attitudes toward altruism, independence, and trustworthiness of others among high school students.

1019. Graney, Marshall. "Role Models in Children's Readers." School Review, 85 (1977): 247-263.

Compares role models in McGuffey Readers with role models presented in contemporary children's books and finds that a peer-oriented, other-directed personality is currently presented as compared with earlier models where adult and inner-directed models were presented.

1020. Guldin, Robert M. "An Analysis of Approaches to Value Oriented Content Material in Selected Fifth Grade Social Studies Textbooks and Corresponding Teacher's Guides." Ed.D. dissertation, Temple University, 1975. 36/06, p. 3354.

Concludes that a general lack of value-oriented material exists in social studies textbooks.

1021. Hardin, Joyce F. "A Study of the Relationship of Moral Development to School Setting, Comparing Students in a Church Related School with Students in a Public School." Ed.D. dissertation, Oklahoma State University, 1978. 39/12, p. 7134.

No significant differences were found between level of moral development of junior high school students in a public school and junior high school students in a private church school.

1022. Heers, J. Jean. "An Exploratory Analysis of School Adaptability and Principled Moral Development." Ph.D. dissertation, University of Minnesota, 1979. 40/09, p. 4827.

No significant differences between normative means and open school students' means (after one year) were detected on the Rest Defining Issues Test. Apparently, differences in school organization and administration are not accompanied by differences in the principled moral development of high school students.

1023. Henry, Jules. On Education. New York: Vintage Books, 1972.

Presents a powerful picture of the competitiveness and interpersonal hostility encouraged by contemporary schooling procedures. The result is that children learn to dislike other children and to resent their successes.

1024.   Ho, Edward H. "A Study of the Implications of the Piagetian
        Theory of Moral Development for Seventh-Day Adventist Schools:
        Based on a Comparison of Selected Schools in Hong Kong,
        Michigan and Indiana." Ed.D. dissertation, Andrews
        University, 1978. 39/12, p. 7300.

        No differences in response to Piagetian stories were found
        between children in the United States and Hong Kong and between
        Seventh-Day Adventist youth and non-Seventh-Day Adventist youth.

1025.   Hobson, Stanley P. "A Value Analysis of Selected Elementary
        Reading Textbooks." Ph.D. dissertation, East Texas State
        University, 1967. 27/12, p. 4040.

        Assesses the extent to which Laswell's system of values are
        present in third grade reading texts. Finds that rectitude,
        well-being, and skill receive the major emphasis.

1026.   Hoge, John D. "An Analysis of the Values Content of Florida
        State Adopted Elementary Social Studies Textbooks and the
        Curriculum Guidelines of the National Council for the Social
        Studies." Ph.D. dissertation, Florida State University, 1978.
        39/03, p. 1465.

        Analyzes elementary social studies textbooks in terms of 67
        instrumental and terminal values derived in part from the work
        of Rokeach.

1027.   Holt, John. "The Values We Teach in School." Readings in
        Values Clarification (item 1504), pp. 31-37.

        An interview with John Holt in which he discusses his views on
        the values taught in schools--mostly negative--and the values
        that should be fostered--mostly humanistic.

1028.   Hornsby-Smith, Michael, and Margaret Petit. "Social, Moral and
        Religious Attitudes of Secondary School Students." Journal of
        Moral Education, 4 (1975): 261-272.

        Surveys Catholic and public school students. Some differences
        are detected, but there are also large areas of commonality of
        social, moral, and religious attitudes.

1029.   Horowitz, Ronald S. "Student Values in a High School with an
        Alternative Option." Ed.D. dissertation, Temple University,
        1978. 39/02, p. 802.

        Alternative school students strive for more enduring and
        permanent contact with peers and focus more on their internal
        life than do conventional students.

1030. Jackson, Philip W. "The Consequences of Schooling." The
       Unstudied Curriculum (item 1516), pp. 1-15.

       Focuses on the relationship between what occurs in school and
       what Jackson calls the secondary consequences of schooling, that
       is, those changes which cannot be described as the memory of a
       specific event or isolated happening. Most importantly he
       focuses on the student's appraisals of himself and of the world
       in general. He argues that mechanistic, technological views of
       the schooling process are inadequate for understanding the
       secondary consequences of schooling.

1031. Jackson, Philip. Life in Classrooms. New York: Holt, Rinehart
       and Winston, 1968.

       Summarizes the three central characteristics of schools as the
       crowds (learning to live and be treated as a member of a crowd),
       the power (learning to live in a world in which there is
       impersonal authority and in which a relative stranger gives
       orders and wields power), and the praise (learning to live in
       such a way as to enhance the likelihood of praise and reduce the
       likelihood of punishment). The net effect of school
       organization is seen as negative in the development of a sense
       of humaneness in students.

1032. Jelinek, James. Principles and Values in School and Society:
       Fourth Yearbook of the Arizona ASCD. Tempe Arizona
       Association for Supervision and Curriculum, 1976. ED 118 513.

       70 principles are identified and listed. Principles are
       defined as solutions to problems. 797 values present in
       individuals, schools, and society are also listed. The 70
       principles and 797 values are then used to analyze a host of
       problems associated with schooling. The problem of the learning
       of human values is discussed.

1033. Jensen, Larry, and Mark Zelig. "Analyzing Value Content in
       Television Programs." Logan Utah State University, 1979. ED
       179 201.

       College students rated television programs using a scale
       developed by the authors. Significant differences were found
       between programs.

1034. Kelly, Joseph T. "Values and Valuing in Recent Social Studies
       Textbooks." Ed.D. dissertation, University of California,
       Berkeley, 1970. 31/12, p. 6470.

       Found that no social studies textbook was completely adequate
       in terms of a fully-developed and systematic approach to values.
       There is seldom a step-by-step analysis consistently applied.

1035. Killeen, Catherine D. "The Relationship Between Cognitive
       Levels of Thinking and Levels of Moral Judgment as Compared in
       Adolescents 12-18 in Catholic and Public Schools." Ed.D.
       dissertation, Rutgers University, 1977. 38/11, p. 6621.

       Principled moral judgment and abstract religious thinking are
       both contingent upon the attainment of formal thinking.
       Catholic school adolescents scored higher in principled moral
       reasoning than public school adolescents.

1036. Kingsbury, Mary E. "Socialization for Work and Leisure:
       Cultural Values Reflected in Children's Literature." Ph.D.
       dissertation, University of Oregon, 1973. 34/06, p. 2924.

       Found through content analysis procedures that leisure is
       increasingly emphasized, but work is cited 2.7 times as often.
       Concludes that neither work nor the significance of leisure in
       our society is accurately reflected in children's books.

1037. Kohlberg, Lawrence. "The Moral Atmosphere of the School." The
       Unstudied Curriculum (item 1516), pp. 104-127.

       Argues that the only way to think of the hidden curriculum is
       as moral education: the perceived nature of the hidden
       curriculum rests on a prior perspective that is both a social
       theory and a mode of valuing. Presents two views of the hidden
       curriculum: as social constraint (Durkheim) and as freedom (A.S.
       Neill). In conclusion, presents the conception that the moral
       atmosphere of schools is consistent with a developmental
       conception of moral education. Also in Moral Education ... It
       Comes With the Territory (item 1519), Collected Papers (item
       618), Readings in Moral Education (item 1522), and Education and
       Moral Development (item 1505).

1038. Kohlberg, Lawrence, and Phillip Whitten. "Understanding the
       Hidden Curriculum." Learning, 1 (December 1972): 10-14.

       Presents Kohlberg's stages of moral development and analyzes
       the values implicit in the school's hidden curriculum.

1039. Krebs, Richard L. "Girls--More Moral Than Boys or Just
       Sneakier?" Paper presented at the American Psychological
       Association Convention, San Francisco, 1968. ED 030 125.

       Finds that teachers do in fact rate girls as more moral than
       boys, but that this rating is not borne out in the level of
       moral reasoning exemplified by these students.

1040. Krogh, Suzanne F. "Altruism as a Component of Moral Development
       in Montessori and Traditional Preschools." Ph.D.
       dissertation, University of Oregon, 1979. 40/09, p. 4960.

Montessori five year olds and traditional five year olds do not essentially differ in altruistic behavior or positive justice reasoning.

1041. Kuhmerker, Lisa. "The School Assembly as Creative Pace-setter for Moral Development," Values Concepts and Techniques (item 1491), pp. 177-188.

Finds that in British schools, which require daily school assemblies, assemblies contribute to the overall psychological development of children by focusing on feelings and creativity.

1042. Lemmond, Lewis E. "A Value Analysis of Social Studies Textbooks." Ph.D. dissertation, East Texas State College, 1964. 26/02, p. 798.

Fifth grade social studies textbooks were analyzed. It was found that wealth and power received the greatest emphasis using Laswell's framework of eight social values.

1043. Lortie, D. Schoolteacher: A Sociological Study. Chicago: University of Chicago Press, 1975.

In a sociological study of teachers based on extensive interviews, it was found that about half stressed moral outcomes in their teaching, but the focus of the outcomes was on compliance and obedience.

1044. Loubser, Jan J. "The Contribution of Schools to Moral Development: A Working Paper in the Theory of Action." Moral Education: Interdisciplinary Approaches (item 1492), pp. 147-179.

Examines the structural characteristics of the school and compares them to those of the family. Because the school does not provide care as the parents do, and does not intrinsically value the child, it is only a weak extension of the family. Age and sex differentiation tends to alienate children from potential human bonds and "universalistic norms." Also in Interchange, 1 (1970): 99-117.

1045. Lowery, Heath W. "An Exploratory Study of the American Middle-Class Moral and Ethical Values Found in the John Newbery Medal Books." Ed.D. dissertation, The University of the Pacific, 1966. 27/06, p. 1712.

Found that most books contained some middle-class values, but mostly only in moderate intensity. Books were not found to be charged with didactic teachings in any traditional manner.

1046. Lystad, Mary. From Dr. Mather to Dr. Seuss: 200 Years of
       American Books for Children. Boston: G.K. Hall & Co., 1980.

       Arguing from the premise that literature reflects social
       values, ecamines how children's books of the past 200 years have
       portrayed society and children's perceptions of society. Her
       arguments are based on a random sample of 1,000 children's
       books. Society's conception of children is also discussed.

1047. McCarthy, Michael J., and Joseph A. Sarthory. "The Ethical
       Dimension of Educational Leadership: The Administrator as a
       Moral Agent." Journal of Thought, 13 (1978): 8-13.

       Argues that morality is at the heart of an administrators
       work, especially with respect to instituting or not instituting
       change.

1048. McCormick, Donald C. "Teaching of Implicit Values in a Primary
       School." Ph.D. dissertation, University of California,
       Berkeley, 1973. NR.

1049. Madison, John P. "An Analysis of Values and Social Action in
       Multi-Racial Children's Literature." Ph.D. dissertation,
       University of Illinois, 1972. 34/02, p. 516.

       Analyzes the value content and social actions presented in 32
       books published between 1960 and 1971 which included as
       characters children between the ages of 10 and 15.

1050. Martin, Jane R. "What Should We Do with a Hidden Curriculum
       When We Find One?" Curriculum Inquiry, 6 (1976): 135-151.

       Argues that consciousness raising regarding the nature of the
       hidden curriculum can be a form of self-defense against the
       onslaught of unasked for learning states.

1051. Maul, June P. "A Study of the Moral Atmosphere in and the
       Development of Moral Reasoning in a School with Intensive
       Education." Ed.D. dissertation, Rutgers University, 1979.
       40/02, p. 761.

       It was found that moral/social reasoning was significantly
       dependent upon the number of years a student had been exposed to
       a particular school's environment. The alternative school's
       environment was perceived by students as involving fairness and
       a sense of community.

1052. Mays, Annabelle M. "The Concept of Moral Atmosphere in
       Educational Settings." Ph.D. dissertation, University of
       Toronto, 1979. 40/12, p. 6247.

Develops a conceptual and operational definition of "moral atmosphere" as it applies to classrooms. Using "hidden curriculum" literature and Kohlberg "issues" the Moral Atmosphere Questionnaire was developed. The role of program structure in moral atmosphere is addressed.

1053.   Meyer, John.   "The Effects of Education as an Institution." American Journal of Sociology, 83 (1977): 54-76.

Explores the institutional effects of education as a legitimation system. Education is seen as creating and expanding elites and redefining the rights and obligations of members.

1054.   Minuchin, Patricia, et al.   The Psychological Impact of School Experience. New York: Basic Books, 1969.

A study of the effects of traditional and "modern" types of education in urban schools. Useful regarding the effects on moral development of authoritarian and open approaches. The results are far from conclusive.

1055.   Moore, Meredith E.   "The Differential Effect of a Church-Related College Environment and a State College or University Environment on the Moral Development of Self-Described Religious Students." Ed.D. dissertation, University of Virginia, 1979. 40/09, p. 4901.

It was hypothesized that the heterogeneous environment of state institutions would be more conducive to moral development than the homogeneous environment of conservative church-related institutions. Religious students (seniors) attending state institutions scored higher in moral development than seniors at church-related schools, but incoming freshmen at these institutions also scored higher than those selecting church-related institutions.

1056.   Morris, Floy E.   "Changes in Values in High-Risk Adolescents after One Year in an Alternative School Setting." Ph.D. dissertation, University of Alabama, 1978. 40/01, p. 111.

One year in an alternative school setting was found to have a significant impact on two of six subscales of Gordon's Survey of Personal Values: Goal Orientation and Practical Mindedness.

1057.   Mortensen, Earl L.   "A Value Content Analysis of Certain Textbooks for Their Implications for Moral Education." Ph.D. dissertation, University of California, Berkeley, 1973. NR.

1058.   Nelson, William L.   "A Comparison of the Value Development of Children in an Open School and a Traditional School." Ed.D. dissertation, Lehigh University, 1975. 36/05, p. 2616.

The open school environment was found to be more conducive to stage growth of the students than the traditional school environment.

1059. Nordstrom, Carl; Edgar Z. Friedenberg; and Hilary A. Gold. Society's Children: A Study of Resentment in the Secondary School. New York: Random House, 1968.

Resentment--a lasting mental attitude caused by the systematic repression of certain emotions and affects which, as such, are normal components of human nature--is seen as a major result of the repressive and freedom-denying environment of schools. This repression is seen as leading to the constant tendency to indulge in certain kinds of value delusions and value judgments. The emotions and affects primarily concerned are revenge, hatred, malace, envy, the impulse to detract, and spite. An empirical study to assess the extent of resentment is reported.

1060. O'Gorman, Teresa P. "An Investigation of Moral Judgment and Religious Knowledge Scores of Catholic High School Boys from Catholic and Public Schools." Ph.D. dissertation, Boston College, 1979. 40/03, p. 1365.

High scores on moral judgment were found to be significantly associated with high scores on religious knowledge. Catholic-educated youth showed a higher level of relationship than did public school youth.

1061. Overly, Norman L., ed. The Unstudied Curriculum: Its Impact on Children. Washington, D.C.: Association for Supervision and Curriculum Development, 1970.

Contains a collection of papers on the impact on children of the hidden curriculum.

1062. Ozman, Howard A., and Joseph C. Johnson. "Value Implications in Children's Reading Materials." Charlottesville: University of Virginia, 1967. ED 033 020.

Reports the results of a research study on the value implications in children's reading material. Analyzes value themes in five series of local readers, classifies the value themes according to dominance, categorizes these themes in terms of major educational philosophy, and factor analyzes the value themes.

1063. Petty, Michael F. "Socialization to Values in English Public Schools and Its Effects on Performance in Two Careers." Ph.D. dissertation, University of Wisconsin, 1975. 36/10, p. 6378.

Childhood educational socialization into the norms and values of the school was not found to explain adult performance in careers that stress those same norms.

1064. Phillips, D.C. "The Hidden Curriculum and the Latent Functions of Schooling Two Overlapping Perspectives: 1. Why the Hidden Curriculum is Hidden." Philosophy of Education 1980 (item 1509), pp. 274-280.

Argues that in light of the multitude of unintended consequences of every social practice, one should be judicious in selecting some subset of those consequences as the "real" explanation for the practice. The hidden curriculum is analyzed in terms of latent and manifest functions.

1065. Plimpton, Richard A. "The Relationship of Organizational Climate to Levels of Student Moral Judgment." Ph.D. dissertation, The University of Toledo, 1979. 40/04, p. 1798.

It was hypothesized that students attending schools with a more open climate would reason at higher levels than students in more traditional settings. Results indicated no significant difference in students' moral reasoning by type of school.

1066. Proctor, Derrick. "Students' Perception of the High School Environment as Related to Moral Development." Ph.D. dissertation, Purdue University, 1975. 36/10-B, p. 5236.

Finds that students who perceive the school environment as authoritarian have lower mean moral maturity scores than students who do not so perceive the school environment.

1067. Proctor, Derrick L., and J. Kent Davis. "Perception of the High School Environment as Related to Moral Reasoning." Paper presented at the Annual Meeting of the American Psychological Association, Chicago, 1957. ED 119 071.

Finds that those students who perceive the school environment as totalitarian tend to be lower in mean level of moral reasoning.

1068. Purpel, David, and Kevin Ryan. "It Comes With the Territory: The Inevitability of Moral Education in the Schools," Moral Education ... It Comes With the Territory (item 1519), pp. 44-54.

The schools are inevitably involved in moral education through the visible curriculum and the hidden curriculum, classroom culture, formal school activities, student culture, and school culture.

1069. Rihn, Bernard A. "Kohlberg Level of Moral Reasoning of
      Protagonists in Newbery Award Winning Fiction." Reading
      Research Quarterly, 15 (1980): 377-398.

      Finds that post-1949 books contain dilemmas that are resolved
      at higher levels of moral reasoning than those in books
      published before 1949. Male authors include dilemmas that are
      resolved at higher stages than those of female authors. Male
      protagonists resolve dilemmas at a higher level than do female
      protagonists.

1070. Rihn, Bernard A. "Kohlberg Level of Moral Reasoning of
      Protagonists in Newbery Award Winning Fiction." Ph.D.
      dissertation, Stanford University, 1978. 38/12, p. 7141.

      An analysis of the moral content of Newbery Award-winning
      books reveals that books written since 1949 contain dilemmas
      which are resolved at a higher level than those in pre-1949
      books. Male authors wrote books with higher stage concerns than
      women authors.

1071. Rosenthal, Robert. "Teacher Expectation and Pupil Learning."
      The Unstudied Curriculum (item 1516), pp. 53-84.

      Finds that a teacher's expectations regarding a learner's
      academic abilities have a significant impact on student
      achievement. Although this study does not deal directly with
      moral values, it does ask whether a teacher's expectations
      regarding moral learning might not likewise be a significant
      factor in the student's learning.

1072. Rudder, M., et al. 15,000 Hours of Secondary Schools and Their
      Effects on Children. Cambridge, MA: Harvard University Press,
      1979.

      In attempting to account for those variables that make a
      school good it was found that the "ethos" of the school was the
      most significant variable. The "ethos" was found to depend
      almost entirely upon the staff-teachers' having high
      expectations of students, praising students when they progress
      toward those goals, and correcting students when they are wrong.

1073. Russo, Charles W. "Moral Development Content Analysis and the
      Moral/Value Dimensions of Television Drama: A Methodological
      Inquiry." Ed.D. dissertation, The University of North
      Carolina at Greensboro, 1980. 41/04, p. 1576.

      Three television programs were analyzed. It was found that
      there are rich moral/value dimensions in television shows and
      that the coding schema (using Kohlberg stages) is a useful
      methodology.

1074. Ryals, Kelvin, and Dennis Foster. "Classroom Climate and Value
      Teaching." Education, 95 (1974): 354-359.

      Explores the dimensions of classroom climate that would
      affectively facilitate the learning of values. Concludes that
      the classroom should be characterized by openness. 13
      classroom-management assumptions are presented.

1075. Ryder, Mary S. "Personal Values and Values Identified in
      Newbery Medal Award Books by Students and Children's
      Librarians." Ed.D. dissertation, University of Denver, 1978.
      39/04, p. 2186.

      Students and children's librarians identify quite different
      values in the Newbery books.

1076. Scharf, Peter. "Developmentalists' Approach to Alternative
      Schooling." Paper presented at the Annual Meeting of the
      American Educational Research Association, San Francisco,
      1976. ED 124 491.

      Finds that students attending a democratic school accept the
      atmosphere of the school much more than do students attending
      traditional or laissez-faire schools.

1077. Sergiovanni, Thomas J. "The Odyssey of Organizational Theory
      and Implications for Humanizing Education." Humanistic
      Education, Edited by Richard H. Weller. Berkeley, CA:
      McCuthan, 1977, pp. 197-231.

      Charts the evolution of organizational thought and analyzes
      the impact of these schools of thought on the structure and
      operation of schools. With regard to humanistic values the
      evolution is seen as not too glorious.

1078. Shaver, James P. "Reflective Thinking, Values and Social
      Studies Textbooks." The School Review, 73 (1965): 226-257.

      Analyzes textbooks in use in the schools to see what they
      contribute to reflective thinking and value-formation. Finds
      great deficiencies in both areas.

1079. Shuch, Sheldon. "Effects of Exposure to an Open Education
      Environment on Locus of Control and Moral Development." Ph.D.
      dissertation, Fordham University, 1980. 40/12, p. 6138.

      It was found that open education does not seem to enhance
      moral development or the development of an internal locus of
      control.

1080. Sicoli, M.L. "A Comparative Study of the Moral Judgments of Adolescents Attending an Alternative and a Traditional High School." Paper presented at the annual meeting of the American Educational Research Association, Boston, 1980. ED 194 602.

It was found that significantly more stage 4 usage was present in students attending the traditional high school than was present in students attending the alternative school.

1081. Silver, Michael. "School and Society: Barriers to Values Education." Values Concepts and Techniques (item 1491), pp. 64-71.

Points out the obstacles posed to values education by the inimical values in the hidden curriculum. Argues that the schools must undergo change if values education is to be implemented effectively.

1082. Spence, Larry D. "Moral Judgment and Bureaucracy." Moral Development and Politics (item 1531), pp. 137-171.

Discusses some of the ways institutional settings impede the manifestation of mature moral behavior. Argues that modern bureaucracies foster environments that are inimical to the expression of mature moral behavior.

1083. Stanton, Michael. "Assessment of Behavior and Categories of Judgment." Journal of Moral Education, 3 (1974): 151-158.

Teachers and college students rated various forms of positive and negative behavior for children, adolescents, and adults. There were some considerable differences in ratings between male and female teachers. Suggests that assessments of moral judgments need to take the categories of judgment.

1084. Sugarman, Barry. "Moral Education and the Social Structure of the School." Journal of Curriculum Studies, 1 (1968): 47-67.

Discusses the consequences of formal school structure on the moral development of pupils. Presents a model of independent variables (schooling factors) and dependent variables (conceptions of moral behavior) which, it is argued, is in need of testing, but no evidence for the hypothesized relationships is offered.

1085. Thrower, Joan S. "The Effects of Orphanage and Foster Care on Development of Moral Judgment." Ph.D. dissertation, Harvard University, 1971.

In institutionalized orphanage children ranging in age from 10 to 18, both moral and role taking stages were found to be depressed well below levels achieved by control groups.

1086. Vallance, Elizabeth. "Hiding the Hidden Curriculum." Curriculum Theory Network, 4 (1973-74): 1-6.

Suggests that the hidden curriculum was not always hidden. It went underground in the late 19th century when the justification for schooling was changed from shaping citizens to promoting the child's welfare.

1087. Warshaw, Rhonda. "Moral Reasoning of Children in Fourth and Sixth Grades in Two Different Educational Environments." Ph.D. dissertation, Fordham University, 1978. 39/03, p. 1450.

It was hypothesized that children in open classrooms would achieve higher levels of moral judgment than children in traditional classrooms. This hypothesis was not borne out by data using sixth grade students.

1088. Willis, Paul. Learning to Labour. Fransborough, England: Saxon House, 1977.

An examination of the socialization of working-class children in England. Specifically, Willis is concerned because working-class youth always end up in working-class jobs. Racism, sexism, and the glorification of violence permeate the culture of Willis' boys. If anything, then, the awkward autocracy of the hidden curriculum is a step toward democracy. The fallacy that the hidden curriculum turns innocent working-class democrats into cynical authoritarians is exposed.

1089. Wolf, Lois C. "Children's Literature and the Development of Empathy in Young Children." Journal of Moral Education, 5 (1975): 45-49.

Attempts to distinguish four stages in the development of empathy during the preschool years. Discusses how four children's books are used to elicit different developmental empathetic responses from children.

1090. Wood, Terry L. "A Comparison of Values Found in Pre-School and Primary-Aged Children's Books and Values Held by Adults." Ph.D. dissertation, Michigan State University, 1976. 37/09, p. 5593.

Examines the commonly held belief that the values stressed in children's books are the same as those held by society. Finds that values held by adults and those stressed in children's books are quite different as measured by the Rokeach Value Survey.

1091. Wynne, Edward. "Facts about the Character of Young Americans."
       Character, 1 (November 1979): 1-7.

       Presents data about the character of contemporary youth, and
       offers an interpretation and prescription. The declining
       character of youth is seen as the result of ten faults of
       current educational systems. Educational institutions should be
       examined to see if the attitudes and values they implicitly
       transmit are consistent with social continuity.

1092. Wynne, Edward A. Looking at Schools. Lexington, MA:
       Heath/Lexington, 1980.

       An ethnographic analysis of two Chicago public schools
       focusing on the contribution such schools make to the character
       development of youth. Concludes that in isolated cases the
       schools are working effectively in this regard, but overall, the
       story is one of missed opportunity. Presents suggestions for
       improving the school's role in character formation.

1093. Yeazell, Mary F. "A Qualitative Analysis of the Value Content
       of Selected Literature for Ninth-grade English." Ed.D.
       dissertation, University of Illinois, 1966. 27/11, p. 3788.

       Using White's Value Analysis Categories it was found that in
       137 short stories drawn from anthologies, white middle-class
       values were stressed, and moral and ethical questions were
       generally ignored.

1094. Young, James L. "The Relationship of Principal's Level of Moral
       Development and School Organizational Climate." Ed.D.
       dissertation, College of William and Mary, 1978. 39/08, p.
       4653.

       It was found that level of moral development of the principal
       and openness of the school climate were significantly related.

Society in the Moralization Process

1095. Bronfenbrenner, Urie. "On Making Human Beings Human."
      Character, 2 (December 1980): 1-7.

      Presents four propositions relating to the environmental
      conditions essential for human development. Shifts in our
      current human ecosystem which undermine these principles are
      noted, and constructive activities for compensating for these
      shifts are presented. The idea of a curriculum for caring is
      presented. Suggestions for changing communities and society are
      also presented.

1096. Bryan, J.H., and T. Schwartz. "Effects of Film Material upon
      Children's Behavior." Psychological Bulletin, 75 (1971):
      50-59.

      Reviews research experiments concerned with film influences
      upon aggression, phobic and altruistic responses, as well as
      their impact on social judgments and communications.

1097. Candee, Daniel. "The Moral Psychology of Watergate and Its
      Aftermath." Moral Development and Politics (item 1531), pp.
      172-189.

      Discusses the moral behavior of some of the actors in the
      Watergate crisis and analyzes the effect of that crisis on the
      moral development of the American people generally.
      Demonstrates how the Watergate actors felt that their behavior
      was modified by the conditions under which they acted.

1098. Coates, B.; H.E. Pusser; and I. Goodman. "The Influence of
      'Sesame Street' and 'Mister Rogers Neighborhood' on Children's
      Social Behavior in the Preschool." Child Development, 47
      (1976): 138-144.

      Finds that watching "Mister Rogers" significantly increased
      the giving of positive reinforcement to, and social contacts
      with, other children and with adults in the preschool. "Sesame
      Street" had the same effect for students whose baseline scores
      were low.

1099. Cole, Edward H., and Patricia A. Moseley. "Moral Reasoning: A
      Values Process. Adolescent Values and Watergate. Notes."
      Paper presented at the Annual Meeting of the National Council
      for the Social Studies, Atlanta, 1975. ED 115 564.

      Finds that all secondary school students disapproved of the
      Watergate break-in. Older students and higher S.E.S. students
      disapproved more strongly.

1100. Coleman, James. "Youth in Man-Made Environments." Character, 1
       (April 1980): 4-8.

       Argues that in contemporary society we are failing to bring up
       children to be happy and productive adults. In an urban,
       industrialized society character formation can be facilitated by
       the construction of a living environment and the reconstruction
       of community.

1101. Comstock, George.   "Television Entertainment: Taking   It
       Seriously." Character, 1 (October 1980): 1-8.

       Discusses research on the impact of television on the young.
       Three principles are found to apply: vicarious experience can
       have an impact similar to direct experience, behavioral
       effectiveness can be improved by watching others perform, and
       the inclination to behave in a specific way can be altered by
       watching others engage in comparable behavior. Television's
       beneficial and negative effects are noted.

1102. Eppel, E.M. "The Adolescent and Changing Moral Standards,"
       Moral Education in a Changing Society, (item 1515), pp.
       112-137.

       Reports the results of a survey to assess the contemporary
       (early 1960s) climate of opinion in England on the morality of
       young people.   The survey taps both adults and teens.
       Intergenerational differences are noted, and implications for
       character education are discussed.

1103. Eron, L.D., et al. "Does Television Violence Cause Aggression?"
       American Psychologist, 27 (1972): 253-263.

       Reports the results of a large-scale study of aggressive
       behavior in third grade school children. It was found that
       aggressive children preferred aggressive television programs.
       From a 10-year follow-up study it was concluded that there is
       a probable causal relatonship between watching violent
       television programs in early, formative years and later
       aggression.

1104. Friedrich, L.K., and A.H. Stein. "Aggressive and Prosocial
       Television Programs and the Natural Behavior of Preschool
       Children." Monographs of the Society for Research in Child
       Development, 38 (1973): 4, Serial No. 151.

Preschool children were shown either aggressive ("Batman" and "Superman") or prosocial ("Mister Rogers' Neighborhood") programs. Children who saw the aggressive programs showed a decline in tolerance of delay and rule obedience. Aggressive children became more aggressive. Lower S.E.S. students who viewed the prosocial programs demonstrated increased prosocial behavior.

1105. Hardaway, F. "The Language of Popular Culture: Daytime Television as a Transmitter of Values." College English, 40 (1979): 517-521.

Judging from a month's watching of daytime television there are three predominant clusters of values marketed to morning viewers: love and sex, money and materialism, and shame and guilt. Argues that by teaching students to watch daytime television from a critical perspective, teachers can sharpen the analytic skills of their students.

1106. Huston-Stein, A., and J.C. Wright. "Children and Television: Effects of the Medium, Its Content and Form." Journal of Research and Development in Education, 13, 1 (1979): 20-31.

Following a summary of the shifting emphases of research on television's impact on children's lives--from which it is concluded that no dramatic effects have been demonstrated--concludes that it is time to examine the effects more carefully.

1107. Hutsebaut, Dirk. "Reference Figures in Moral Development." Toward Moral and Religious Maturity (item 403), pp. 193-221.

Reports the results of an inquiry in which adolescents between 15 and 18 were asked what they considered good and bad and who they consider the important figures in such a judgment. Two clusters of referents were identified: people and social and legal norms.

1108. Keniston, Kenneth. "Youth and Violence: The Contexts of Moral Crisis," Moral Education: Five Lectures, (item 1524), pp. 109-131.

Attempts to identify the nature of and reasons for our current moral crisis. Describes the style of contemporary radical youth and argues that the issue of violence is to this generation what the issue of sex was to the Victorian world. Concludes with an analysis of how youth come to use violence in an attempt to stop it.

1109. Liebert, Robert M., and Rita Wicks Poulos. "Television as a Moral Teacher." Moral Development and Behavior (item 519), pp. 284-298.

Present a theoretical framework on the process of observational learning in order to interpret the impact of television on the moral standards of youth. They discuss the evidence for television's impact on aggression, willingness to break established rules, blunting sensitivity to violence, stereotypes, and reduction in cooperative behavior.

1110. Much, Nancy C., and Richard A. Shiveder. "Speaking of Rules: The Analysis of Culture in Breach." New Directions for Child Development, No. 2: Moral Development (item 1497), pp. 19-39.

From a study of five and six year olds the authors infer that various cultural control mechanisms (regulations, conventions, morals, truths, instructions) are differentiated and at work in regulating conduct. It was found that children were more apt to recognize breaches of morals than were adults.

1111. Murdock, Graham. "Differential Reactions to the Regulation of Emotional and Physical Expression among Third Year Pupils in Secondary Schools." Journal of Moral Education, 1 (1981): 53-60.

Finds that there are two major sources of expressive roles: the street culture and the pop media. These roles play a major part in structuring attitudes and values. Unless the school can adjust to meet the need for such expressive roles its influence will remain superficial.

1112. Murray, J.P.; E.A. Rubenstein and G.A. Comstock, eds. Television and Social Behavior. Vol. I: Media Content and Control. Vol. II. Television and Social Learning. Washington, DC: Government Printing Office, 1972. NR

1113. Rokeach, M. "Change and Stability of American Value Systems, 1968-1971." Public Opinion Quarterly, 38 (1974): 222-228.

Reports and discusses changes noted on the Rokeach Value Survey over the 1968-1971 time period.

1114. Rushton, J. Phillippe. "Effects of Prosocial Television and Film Material on the Behavior of Viewers." Advances in Experimental Psychology, Vol. 12. Edited by L. Berkowitz. New York: Academic Press, 1979.

Reviews 35 different studies that indicate that television and film programs can modify viewers' behavior in a prosocial direction.

1115. Sams, Janice. "Ghetto Child and Moral Development." Religious Education, 70 (1975): 636-648.

Argues that the conditions of life in the ghetto force a different--but not inferior--form of moral development on children. The ghetto child has to deal with two moralities: that of the ghetto and that of the society at large.

1116. Schochet, Gordon J. "From Household to Polity." Moral Development and Politics, (item 1531), pp. 206-215.

Addresses the consequences for democratic society of changes in the structure of authority in the household.

1117. Searle, Ann. "A Study of 'Admired People' among Adolescents in Relation to Aggression and Sex Differences." Journal of Moral Education, 1 (1971): 61-66.

Highly aggressive boys tend to choose powerful and active figures and are more likely to choose people they do not know. Boys who rate low in agression choose from among family and friends. Girls tend to choose pop figures and a substantial portion choose males.

1118. Spindler, G.D. "Education in a Transforming American Culture." Harvard Educational Review, 25 (1955): 145-53.

Argues that a major shift in American values is taking place from traditional values (puritan morality, work-success ethic, individualism, achievement orientation, and future time orienta- tion) to emergent values (sociability, relativistic moral attitude, consideration for others, hedonistic, present-time orientation, and conformity to the group). Much of the conflict over schools is seen as the result of a clash of these two value orientations.

1119. Stein, Aletha H. "Mass Media and Moral Development." Values, Feelings and Morals. Edited by H.D. Dwain. Washington D.C.: American Association of Elementary-Kindergarten-Nursery Educators, 1974, pp. 39-53.

Reviews the current moral and value content of mass commercial television (mostly white, male, and middle class), the effects of current television on moral behavior (mostly negative), and the potential for positive effects on children's moral develop- ment (promising).

1120. Stein, A.H. "Mass Media and Young Children's Development." Early Childhood Education, The Seventy-first Yearbook of the National Society for the Study of Education. Chicago: University of Chicago Press, 1972, pp. 181-202.

Summarizes existing research, focusing on the effects on moral behavior.

1121. Stein, Aletha H., and Lynette K. Friedrich. "The Impact of
       Television on Youth." Review of Child Development Research,
       Vol. 5. Edited by E. Mavis Hetherington, et al. Chicago:
       University of Chicago Press, 1975, pp. 183-256.

       An extensive review of research assessing the impact of
       television on youth. Sections of the review address children's
       personal and social values.

1122. Weibel, Kathryn P. "Life Styles and Ethical Values of Men and
       Women on Television, 1960-1974." Ph.D. dissertation, Michigan
       State University, 1975. 36/12, p. 8140.

       From an analysis of leading characters in popular prime time
       television series it is concluded that television portrays
       individuals as primarily conventional (stages 3 and 4) in their
       moral reasoning.

1123. Whiting, Beatrice B., and John W.M. Whiting. Children of Six
       Cultures: A Psycho-Cultural Analysis. Cambridge, MA: Harvard
       University Press, 1979.

       Six cultures were analyzed in 12 categories relating to the
       cultural and structural orientation of the community. One focus
       of the research was on the question of whether developmental
       trends exist regardless of social environment. Two independent
       cultural features--the complexity of the socio-economic system,
       and the composition of the household--were shown to be
       predictive of the social behavior of children. Children in
       complex cultures tended to be more dependent-dominant and less
       nurturant-responsible; where nuclear households existed children
       were more sociable-intimate and less authoritarian-aggressive.

1124. Wynne, Edward. "Socialization to Adulthood: Different Concepts,
       Different Policies." Interchange, 5, 1 (1974): 23-35.

       Analyzes a number of serious dysfunctions in the socialization
       arrangements around upper-middle-class children and adolescents.
       It is argued that too much attention has been paid to cognitive
       development and too little to affective development.
       Society-at-large should resume some of its traditional
       responsibilities for socialization.

1125. Wynne, Edward, ed. "Symposium on Television Entertainment."
       Character, 2 (November 1980): 1-9.

       Contains a series of responses to the Comstock article (item
       1101) by Charren and Hays, Gerbner, Irvine, Milavsky, Murray,
       and Stein. Comstock responds to the respondants.

1126. Adorno, T.W., et al. The Authoritarian Personality. New York: W.W. Norton, 1969.

In a massive and intricate study of the authoritarian personality and the nature of prejudice, it was found, consistent with psychoanalytic theory, that prejudice was a result of an individual's own insecurities. Includes the F scale, a paper and pencil questionnaire designed to assess the individual's authoritarianism.

1127. Agresta, Frank J. "An Analysis of the Value Profiles of Sixth Grade Pupils with High Intellectual Ability." Ph.D. dissertation, Kent State University, 1977, 38/12, p. 7265.

Pupils with high intellectual ability are more strongly socially oriented and less self-oriented than students of normal intellectual ability.

1128. Ajzen, I., and M. Fishbein. "Attitude-Behavior Relations: A Theoretical Analysis and Review of Empirical Research." Psychological Bulletin, 84 (1977): 888-918.

Reviews available literature and finds that strong attitude-behavior relations are obtained only where high correspondence between at least the target and action elements of the attitudinal and behavioral entities exists.

1129. Allen, Jerry L. "Persuasion Through Self-Confrontation: An Experimental Study of Value, Attitude, and Behavior Change Initiated by Interpersonal and Mass Media." Ph.D. dissertation, Southern Illinois University, 1979. 40/01, p. 24.

Replicates Rokeach's study where long-term changes in values were achieved with a single session of self-confrontation. Changes in attitude and behavior were not significant.

1130. Anchor, K.N., and H.J. Cross. "Maladaptive Aggression, Moral Perspective and the Socialization Process." Journal of Personality and Social Psychology, 30 (1974): 163-168.

A direct relationship between level of moral reasoning and maladaptive aggression was detected. The less developed the moral reasoning, the more likely the subjects were to aggress against another in the Prisoners Dilemma Game when there was no observable benefit from doing so.

1131. Bar-Tal, Daniel. Prosocial Behavior: Theory and Research. New
       York: Hemisphere Publishing Co., 1980. NR.

1132. Bem, Daryl J. Beliefs, Attitudes, and Human Affairs. Belmont,
       CA: Brooks/Cole, 1970.

       Discusses the cognitive, emotional, behavioral, and social
       foundations of beliefs and attitudes. The relationship between
       behavior and attitudes is discussed, as are the factors that
       contribute to attitude change.

1133. Bem, D.J., and A. Allen. "On Predicting Some of the People Some
       of the Time: The Search for Cross-Situational Consistencies
       in Behavior." Psychological Review, 81 (1974): 506-520.

       Reports on a study that shows that it is possible to identify
       those individuals who will be cross-situationally consistent and
       those who will not. Concludes that personality assessment must
       attend not only to situations but also to persons.

1134. Black, Lyn. "Differences in Attitudes to Lying in Children."
       Journal of Moral Education, 1 (1972): 135-140.

       Older children more often took motive into account and in
       general were less severe in their judgments.

1135. Blackingston, Frank H. "A Philosophical Analysis of 'Life
       Adjustment.'" Ph.D. dissertation, Michigan State University,
       1960. 21/11, p. 3485.

       Questions whether life adjustment contains any particular
       observable range and level of human activity. The history and
       literature of the area are reviewed. Decides that life
       adjustment is a preferred state, equivalent to the good life in
       both the relative and absolute senses.

1136. Blasi, Augusto. "Bridging Moral Cognition and Moral Action: A
       Critical Review of the Literature." Psychological Bulletin,
       88 (1980): 1-45.

       Two opposite views of the relations between moral cognition
       and moral action are described: the trait approach and the
       process approach. The available empirical literature which
       relates moral reasoning to moral behavior is reviewed. Overall,
       the studies seem to support the cognitive-developmental
       perspective. Suggestions for further research are offered.
       Contains an excellent bibliography on the subject.

1137. Boyce, William D., and Larry C. Jensen. Moral Reasoning: A
       Psychological-Philosophical Integration. Lincoln: University
       of Nebraska Press, 1980.

       Based on the recognition that the conceptual framework
       utilized by philosophers in discussing moral issues is adaptable
       to the examination of moral content in psychological research, a
       model is developed showing how philosophical insights can be
       used to examine the content of individuals' moral reasoning.

1138. Brackman, John; Terri Anderson; and Sara Armstrong. "The
       Developmental Relationship among Moral Judgment, Moral
       Conduct, and a Rationale for Appropriate Behavior." Paper
       presented at annual meeting of Western Psychological
       Association, San Francisco, 1978. ED 165 051.

       The relationships between moral reasoning and moral conduct
       were studied, using both Piaget's and Kohlberg's interviewing
       and scoring procedures. Some differences in results were
       obtained depending upon the assessment procedure used.

1139. Brito, Dyla T. "Effects of Intent, Outcomes, and Adult Power
       and Authority on Children's Moral Judgments." Ph.D. disserta-
       tion, University of California, Los Angeles, 1981. 42/01, p.
       136.

       Both age groups (5-6, 8-9) use intent and outcome information
       in their judgments. Older subjects use intent more in their
       judgments. High status power and authority are judged less
       severely than low status actors.

1140. Bryan, James H. "Why Children Help: A Review." Journal of
       Social Issues, 28, 3 (1972): 87-104.

       Studies of the impact of the social responsibility norm,
       experimenter demand characteristics and proprieties are reviewed
       for their influence on two areas of helping behavior in
       children. Emphasizes the importance of modeling in the learning
       of helping behavior.

1141. Bryan, James H. "You Will Be Well Advised to Watch What We Do
       Instead of What We Say." Moral Development: Current Theory
       and Research (item 494), pp. 95-111.

       Reviews the results of research on the effects of models on
       children's donation behavior. The puzzling minimal effect that
       hypocrisy (as preaching generosity but practicing greed) has on
       children's behavior is noted. Actions appear to speak much
       louder than words.

1142. Bryan, J.H., and London, P. "Altruistic Behavior by Children."
      Psychological Bulletin, 73 (1970): 200-211.

      In a review of the literature on altruistic behavior in
      children and adolescents the role of behavioral example,
      reinforcement, and personality characteristics is seen as
      salient.

1143. Burton, Roger V. "Generality of Honesty Reconsidered."
      Psychological Review, 70 (1963): 481-499.

      Reanalyzes the data of Hartshorne and May and finds that there
      is more generality in moral behavior (across situations) than
      was previously reported.

1144. Burton, Roger V. "Honesty and Dishonesty." Moral Development
      and Behavior (item 519), pp. 173-197.

      Reviews the empirical research on honesty, with the purpose of
      arriving at some conclusions about the factors that influence
      moral conduct and how these influences operate. Looks at
      research focusing on behavioral, judgmental, and affective
      factors. Reviews the generality-specificity issue for the
      behavioral realm. Concludes with directions needed for research
      to develop solid generalizations.

1145. Bushway, Ann, and William R. Nash. "School Cheating Behavior."
      Review of Educational Research, 47 (1977): 623-632.

      A brief review of the literature which focuses on
      characteristics of the cheaters, influence of situational
      factors, and reasons for cheating.

1146. Campagna, A.F., and S. Harter. "Moral Judgment in Sociopathic
      and Normal Children." Journal of Personality and Social
      Psychology, 31 (1975): 199-205.

      Finds that moral reasoning is higher for normal than for
      sociopathic children. This is attributed to relative lack of
      opportunities for role taking and identification in the families
      of sociopathic children.

1147. Campbell, Donald T. "On the Genetics of Altruism and the
      Counter-Hedonic Components in Human Culture." Journal of
      Social Issues, 28, 3 (1972): 21-37.

      Since genetic selection for altruism is unlikely Campbell
      concludes in favor of social evolution. Social institutions
      require cooperative rather than heroic genes for continuation.
      Heroic genes too frequently result in death.

1148. Candee, Dan. "The Moral Psychology of Watergate," Journal of
       Social Issues, 31, 2 (1975): 183-192.

       Shows that the Nixon team reasoned at stages 3 and 4. Of
       persons not involved in Watergate, those at stages 3 and 4
       agreed with the decisions of the participants but those at stage
       5 generally did not.

1149. Caring, Lillian C. "The Relation of Cognitive Style, Sex and
       Intelligence   to   Moral   Judgment   in   Children."   Ph.D.
       dissertation, New York University, 1970. 31/12-B, p. 7568.

       Studies   the   relation   between   cognitive   style, sex, and
       intelligence and moral judgments in children.   The major
       implication of the study is that of the variables, intelligence
       is the most closely related to moral judgment. The population
       studied was children ages 10- 12.

1150. Chandler, Michael J. "Egocentrism and Antisocial Behavior: The
       Assessment and Training of Social Perspective-Taking Skills."
       Developmental Psychology, 9 (1973): 326-332.

       Finds that increasing role taking behavior by adolescent
       delinquents results in significant reductions in delinquent
       behavior.

1151. Cohen, Ronald. "Altruism: Human, Cultural, or What?" Journal
       of Social Issues, 28, 3 (1972): 39-57.

       Argues that altruism has cultural survival value and that the
       high degree of empathy of modern man is the result of
       affect-oriented parent-child relations. Altruism is defined as
       a function of giving, of empathy, and of sympathy.

1152. Conroy, William J. "Human Values, Smoking Behavior, and Public
       Health Programs." Understanding Human Values (item 1520), pp.
       199-209.

       A form of value therapy is described in which health-related
       behavior modification can be brought about as a result of
       earlier changes in the values that underlie a particular
       behavior.

1153. Cook, Charles D.   "The Influence of Moral Reasoning on
       Physicians' Attitude Toward Treatment of the Critically Ill."
       Moral Education Forum, 4 (1979): 28-29.

       Resident physicians with higher levels of moral reasoning tend
       to be more sensitive to a negative family attitude and treat the
       patient less actively than those lower in moral reasoning.

1154. Cook, Stuart W., ed. "Review of Recent Research Bearing on
       Religious and Character Formation." Religious Education, 57
       (July-August 1962).

       A research supplement in which a variety of papers discuss the
       implications of psychological research for character formation.

1155. Davies, J. "Shaken with the Wind: The Effects of Group Pressure
       upon the Expression of Moral Belief." Journal of Moral
       Education, 1 (1971): 49-52.

       Students were asked questions about their moral beliefs under
       two conditions: alone and in a group where others have spoken
       first. It was found that the group has a significant impact on
       their verbal statements.

1156. Deigh, John G. "Guilt and Shame: Philosophical Investigations
       in Moral Psychology." Ph.D. dissertation, University of
       California, Los Angeles, 1979. 40/10, p. 5469.

       Proposes that guilt and shame differ as two species of the
       same genus; their chief difference is one of scope. Shame is an
       emotion related to our status as moral beings, while guilt
       presupposes a background of specific social practices and
       institutions.

1157. DePalma, David J. "The Effects of Social Class, Moral
       Orientation and Severity of Punishment on Children's Moral
       Responses to Transgression." Ph.D. dissertation, Michigan
       State University, 1972. 33/09-B, p. 4538.

       Finds with 8 year olds that subjects of high social class and
       flexible moral orientation may have a more highly internalized
       conscience and not need overt stimuli (punishment and self-
       criticism) to control their behavior. Imitation and past
       socialization experiences are important factors in children's
       responses to transgression.

1158. Dickstein, Ellen B. "Biological and Cognitive Bases of Moral
       Functioning." Human Development, 22 (1979): 37-59.

       Presents a theory of moral functioning based on three
       components underlying moral behavior: (1) genetically programmed
       social tendencies, (2) role taking, and (3) the making of
       ingroup-outgroup distinctions. Evidence to support the theory
       is presented.

1159. Duffy, Eugene J. "Attitudes to Lying in Children Aged 8/9 and
       11/12." Journal of Moral Education, 8 (1978): 52-54.

       Older children were found to be more morally mature in judging
       attitudes toward lying. Replication of Black (item 1093).

1160. Eisenberg-Berg, Nancy. "Relationship of Prosocial Moral
      Reasoning to Altruism, Political Liberalism, and
      Intelligence." Developmental Psychology, 15 (1979): 87-89.

      It was found that males' level of prosocial moral reasoning
      was related to intelligence and altruism. For females, moral
      judgment was related to liberal sociopolitical attitudes.

1161. Eisenberg-Berg, Nancy, and Elizabeth Geisheker. "Content of
      Preachings and Power of the Model/ Preacher: The Effect on
      Children's Generosity." Developmental Psychology, 15 (1979):
      168-175.

      Empathetic preachings were found to significantly enhance
      children's generosity. Persons with direct control over
      children and competent individuals also were effective in
      stimulating generosity.

1162. Eysenck, H.J. Crime and Personality. Boston: Houghton Mifflin,
      1964.

      Within an extensive analysis of the correlates of criminal
      behavior a small but positive correlation between moral
      knowledge and moral acts was detected.

1163. Feather, N.T. Values in Education and Society. New York: Free
      Press, 1975.

      Based on Rokeach's Value Survey this book reports data which
      relates the value construct to a wide range of personal, social,
      and cross-cultural variables.

1164. Festinger, Leon. "Behavioral Support for Opinion Change."
      Public Opinion Quarterly, 28 (1964): 404-417.

      Reviews evidence for and offers speculations on the apparent
      lack of relationship between opinion and behavior.

1165. Festinger, Leon. A Theory of Cognitive Dissonance. Evanston,
      IL: Row-Peterson, 1957.

      Festinger's theory postulates, among other things, that if an
      individual is induced to engage in behavior that is inconsistent
      with his beliefs or attitudes, he will experience the discomfort
      of "cognitive dissonance", which will motivate him to resolve
      that inconsistency.

1166. Fishbein, Martin, ed. <u>Readings in Attitude Theory and Measurement</u>. New York: John Wiley and Sons, 1967.

       An excellent collection of 52 papers on attitude measurement, attitude theory, and historical foundations of the study of attitudes. Many of the papers touch on the relationship between attitudes and behavior.

1167. Fishbein, M. "A Theory of Reasoned Action: Some Applications and Implications." <u>Nebraska Symposium on Motivation, 1979</u> (item 1245), pp. 65-116.

       Attempts to develop a theoretical framework from which it is possible to predict action. Within this framework, attitude is viewed in the context of belief, intention, and behavior sequence. According to the theory of reasoned action, any behavior can be predicted from intentions and can ultimately be explained by reference to a person's behavioral beliefs, outcome evaluations, normative beliefs, and motivations to comply. Data is supplied to support this formulation.

1168. Fishkin, James; Kenneth Keniston; and Catherine MacKennon. "Moral Reasoning and Political Ideology." <u>Journal of Personality and Social Psychology</u>, 27 (1973): 109-119.

       Finds that college students who reason at the conventional level are politically conservative while those students at the preconventional level favor radicalism and violence.

1169. Fodor, E.M. "Delinquency and Susceptibility to Social Influence among Adolescents as a Function of Level of Moral Development." <u>Journal of Social Psychology</u>, 86 (1972): 257-260.

       Finds that delinquents yield moral development scores at a lower stage than nondelinquents. Delinquents who were susceptible to social influence were found to be lower in moral reasoning than those who were not susceptible.

1170. Fodor, E.M. "Resistance to Temptation, Moral Development, and Perceptions of Parental Behavior among Adolescent Boys." <u>Journal of Social Psychology</u>, 88 (1972): 155-156.

       No significant relationship was found between cheating and level of moral development on a "ray gun" test where students could falsify their scores to win prizes. All subjects were at stages 1-4.

1171. Fraenkel, Jack R. "The Relationship Between Moral Thought and Moral Action: Implications for Social Studies Education." <u>Theory and Research in Social Education</u>, 9 (Summer 1981): 39-54.

Following a review of the literature on the relationship of moral thought and moral action, concludes that moral reasoning is only one of many factors influencing behavior.

1172. Froming, W.J., and R.G. Cooper. "Predicting Compliance Behavior from Moral Judgment Scales." Journal of Research in Personality, 11 (1977): 368-379.

Finds that compliance behavior can be interpreted in terms of the trend away from external standards and toward internal standards with higher levels of moral judgment.

1173. Gallagher, Michael. "A Comparison of Hogan's and Kohlberg's Theories of Moral Development." Ph.D. dissertation, Columbia University, 1975. 36/ 05-B, p. 2446.

Using college students as subjects, found that there was no relationship between Hogan's personality types and Kohlberg's stages of moral judgment.

1174. Gergen, K.J.; M.M. Gergen; and K. Meter. "Individual Orientations to Prosocial Behavior." Journal of Social Behavior, 28, 3 (1972): 105-130.

Reviews findings relating personality and demographic variables to prosocial behavior. Argues that the general search for correlates is shortsighted given the importance of situational factors.

1175. Goldiamond, I. "Moral Development: A Functional Analysis." Psychology Today, 2, 4 (1968): 31-34; 70.

From a social learning perspective argues that if we define behavioral relations with subtle consequences that define our use of terms such as morality or altruism, we may be able to begin to develop programs in which such behavioral relations are our objectives. Argues that moral behavior can be shaped through step-by-step reinforcement approximations.

1176. Gorman, Margaret. "Moral and Faith Development in Seventeen-Year-Old Students." Boston: Boston College, 1977. ED 151 643.

Finds that SES and IQ are highly correlated with faith (Fowler) and moral (Kohlberg) scores.

1177. Grim, Paul F.; Lawrence Kohlberg; and Sheldon White. "Some Relationships Between Conscience and Attentional Processes." Journal of Personality and Social Psychology, 8 (1968): 239-252.

With children in grades one and six it was found that there is a significant relationship between attention (nondistractability) and resistance to temptation. Concludes that ego-strength, not superego-strength, best accounts for moral behavior.

1178. Grube, J.W., et al. "Behavior Change Following Self-Confrontation: A Test of the Value-Mediation Hypothesis." Journal of Personality and Social Psychology, 35 (1977): 212-216.

In a test of Rokeach's theory of behavior change as a result of self-confrontation it was found that the changes observed are not primarily mediated through changes in value priorities. The changes were found to take place, in fact, as the result of inconsistencies between behaviors and self-conceptions that were revealed during the treatment session.

1179. Gutkin, D.C., and J. Suls. "The Relation Between the Ethics of Personal Conscience-Social Responsibility and Principled Moral Reasoning." Journal of Youth and Adolescence, 8 (1979): 433-441.

Finds a relationship between the "ethics of personal responsibility" of Hogan's Survey of Ethical Attitudes and principled moral reasoning on Rest's Defining Issues Test.

1180. Haan, Norma. Coping and Defending: Process of Self-Environment Organization. New York: Academic Press, 1977.

Presents a conception of the development of morality that runs counter to cognitive developmental theory. Morality is seen as consisting of constructed interpersonal understandings that involve persons in a network of interpersonal accountabilities related to independent situations of social living. Moral meanings are constructed out of interpersonal experiences of interdependency and negotiation.

1181. Haan, Norma. "Hypothetical and Actual Moral Reasoning in a Situation of Civil Disobedience." Journal of Personality and Social Psychology, 32 (1975): 255-270.

Found that two-thirds of the college students used a different stage of moral reasoning (46% higher and 20% lower) for reasoning about an actual social-protest situation that they were personally involved in than they did for hypothetical dilemmas.

1182. Haan, Norma. "Two Moralities in Action Contexts: Relationships to Thought, Ego Regulation, and Development." Journal of Personality and Social Psychology, 36 (1978): 286-305.

Using adolescent friendship groups it was found that in playing moral games participants used interpersonal moral reasoning more frequently than formal (Kohlbergian) moral reasoning. Interpersonal moral reasoning is reasoning designed to maintain old moral balances or achieve a new moral balance. Possible relationships between these two modes of reasoning is discussed.

1183. Haan, Norma; M. Brewster Smith; and Jeanne Block. "Moral Reasoning of Young Adults: Political-Social Behavior, Family Background, and Personality Correlates." Journal of Personality and Social Psychology, 10 (1968): 183-201.

Found that there was a strong relationship among college students between principled moral reasoning and political protest and social action. Subjects were students arrested during the Free Speech Movement protests in Berkeley in 1964.

1184. Haier, Richard J. "Moral Reasoning and Moral Character: Relationships Between the Kohlberg and the Hogan Models." Psychological Reports, 40 (1977): 215-226.

Empirical relationship between Kohlberg's stages of moral development and Hogan's model of moral character was examined. No relationships were detected between moral character and moral reasoning.

1185. Handel, Irving S. "The Relationship Between Jungian Typology and Cognitive Development." Ph.D. dissertation, Yeshiva University, 1980.

Investigates the relationship between the function and attitude types described by C.G. Jung and Kohlberg's typology of moral stages. The study indicated that introverts are at higher levels of moral development than extroverts.

1186. Handy, Rollo. Value Theory and the Behavioral Sciences. Springfield, IL: Charles C. Thomas, 1969.

Reviews various naturalistic interpretations of value. Proposes a need theory based on the work of Perry, Dewey, and Pepper. Need is defined as instability or a disturbed equilibrium in behavior-tension. Value is defined as that which satisfies that tension.

1187. Harris, S.; P. Mussen; and E. Rutherford. "Some Cognitive, Behavioral, and Personality Correlates of Maturity of Moral Judgment." Journal of Genetic Psychology, 128 (1976): 123-135.

With fifth grade boys, maturity of moral judgment was found to be significantly correlated with general cognitive ability, resistance to temptation, reputation for being concerned for the welfare of others, self-confidence, and security in social relationships with peers.

1188. Henshel, A.M. "The Relationship Between Values and Behavior: A Developmental Hypothesis." Child Development, 42 (1971): 1997-2007.

Finds that in a cheating situation older children (4th through 7th grades) show a stronger value/behavior relationship than younger children.

1189. Hetherington, M.E., and S.E. Feldman, "College Cheating as a Function of Subject and Situational Variables." Journal of Educational Psychology, 55 (1964): 212-218.

Four types of cheating were identified: individualistic-opportunistic, individualistic-planned, social-active, and social-passive. Both the tendency to cheat and the specific type of cheating were found to be related to demographic, personality, and intellectual characteristics.

1190. Hoffman, Martin L. "The Development of Altruistic Motivation." Moral Development: Current Theory and Research (item 494), pp. 137-151.

Argues that empathetic responses in interaction with cognitive development as represented by role-taking skills provides the basis for altruistic motives and actions.

1191. Hoffman, M.L. "Developmental Synthesis of Affect and Cognition and Its Implications for Altruistic Motivation." Developmental Psychology, 11 (1975): 607-622.

Presents an argument for the plausibility of an intrinsic altruistic motive based on inferences regarding human evaluation. A theoretical model for the development of such a motive is outlined. The model suggests that young children would experience empathetic distress even before acquiring the necessary cognitive skills and that certain experiences could enhance this naturally occurring motivation to help others in distress.

1192. Hogan, Robert. "Moral Conduct and Moral Character: A Psychological Perspective." Psychological Bulletin, 79 (1973): 217-232.

Presents Hogan's five-dimensional model of moral character. Each dimension is given a theoretical and operational definition; the developmental antecedents of each dimension are discussed; and the model's usefulness for explaining moral conduct is argued.

1193. Hogan, Robert. "The Structure of Moral Character and the Explanation of Moral Action." Journal of Youth and Adolescence, 4 (1975): 1-15.

Argues that since human behavior is rule-governed, differences in moral conduct can be explained in terms of differences in the manner in which people use, justify, and maintain rules. Moral behavior can be understood in terms of five dimensions: moral knowledge, style of moral judgment, socialization, empathy, and autonomy. Evidence is presented that indicates that this model works reasonably well in predicting behavior.

1195. Hornstein, H.A. Cruelty and Kindness: A New Look at Aggression and Altruism. Englewood Cliffs, NJ: Prentice-Hall, 1976.

Discusses a wide range of research on helping behavior and insensitivity to the plight of others. Concludes that there needs to be a greater emphasis on the we rather than the I in our society.

1195. Hornstein, Harvey A. "Promotive Tension: The Basis of Prosocial Behavior from a Lewinian Perspective." Journal of Social Issues, 28, 3 (1972): 191-218.

Altruism is examined from a Lewinian perspective: what conditions determine whether an individual develops tension systems coordinated to another's goal attainment?

1196. Huckaby, Loucine. "A Developmental Study of the Relationship of Negative Moral-social Behaviors to Empathy, to Positive Social Behaviors and to Cognitive Moral Judgment." Ph.D. dissertation, University of California, Los Angeles, 1974. 32/03, p. 1337.

Investigates the relationship of the negative moral-social behaviors of cheating, lying, lack of resistance to temptation, and aggression to the prosocial moral behaviors of generosity, cognitive moral judgment, and affective behaviors of empathy. It was found that negative moral-social behaviors decrease with age but are not inversely related to positive social behaviors of empathy, cognitive moral judgment, and generosity. A well-conceived and significant study.

1197. Hudgins, William, and Norman M. Prentice. "Moral Judgment in Delinquent and Nondelinquent Adolescents and Their Mothers." Journal of Abnormal Psychology, 82 (1973): 145-152.

Finds that nondelinquent adolescents demonstrate a higher
stage of moral reasoning than delinquent adolescents.
Similarly, the mothers of nondelinquents manifested higher
levels of moral reasoning than the mothers of delinquents.

1198. Huston, Ted L., and Chuck Korte. "The Responsive Bystander: Why
       He Helps." Moral Development and Behavior (item 519), pp.
       269-283.

       Examining the literature on bystander intervention the authors
       develop a profile of the Good Samaritan and propose strategies
       for enhancing bystander responsiveness.

1199. Insko, Chester A. Theories of Attitude Change. New York:
       Appleton-Century-Crofts, 1967.

       Following a brief discussion of the concept of attitude, 11
       theories of attitude change are discussed.

1200. Jensen, Larry C. What's Right? What's Wrong?: A Psychological
       Analysis of Moral Behavior. Washington, D.C.: Public Affairs
       Press, 1975.

       Reviews the psychological literature on resistance to
       temptation and the learning of prosocial behavior. Discusses
       such topics as the relationship of parental practices to moral
       action, antecedent determinants of the ability to defy grati-
       fication, guilt and shame, and the possibility of learning a
       rational morality. Presents a series of practical suggestions
       for teachers and parents interested in raising morally
       responsible children.

1201. Johnson, C.D., and J. Gormly. "Academic Cheating: The
       Contribution of Sex, Personality and Situational Variables."
       Developmental Psychology, 6 (1972): 320-325.

       Found with fifth graders that the previously reported
       relationship between academic ability and cheating is largely
       attributable to the obviousness of the measure used to assess
       cheating. Interactions between sex and cheating were noted in
       relation to personality and situational factors.

1202. Johnson, Kenneth L. "The Relationship Between the Components of
       Musicality and Ethical Values among High School Students."
       Ed.D. dissertation, Boston College, 1979. 40/04, p. 1942.

       There was no evidence to suggest that a statistically
       significant correlation exists between the measures of
       musicality (classical or popular) and the measures of moral and
       ethical values.

1203. Katz, Joseph.   "Altruism and Sympathy: Their History in
       Philosophy and Some Implications for Psychology." Journal of
       Social Issues, 28, 3 (1972): 59-69.

       Analyzes three major philosophical approaches that have tried
       to provide a rationale for the moral obligation of one person to
       help another person.   Argues that psychologists have not
       utilized many of the theoretical clarifications philosophers
       have already made.   The study of altruism could be greatly
       improved if they would.

1204. Kay, William. "The Self-concept as a Moral Control." Journal
       of Moral Education, 2 (1972): 63-67.

       Attempts to discover the primary sanctions governing the moral
       conduct of children.   The results indicate that both a child's
       self-concept and his subscription to the process of reciprocity
       are dominant as moral controls for all pupils for most of their
       school lives.

1205. Keasy, Charles B.   "Social Participation as a Factor in the
       Moral   Development   of   Preadolescents."   Developmental
       Psychology, 5 (1971): 216-220.

       Examines the hypothesis that higher stages will be positively
       associated with social participation. Teachers and peers rated
       subjects for leadership and popularity.   The hypothesis was
       confirmed.

1206. Kelman, Herbert C. "The Role of Action in Attitude Change."
       Nebraska Symposium on Motivation 1979 (item 1245), pp.
       117-194.

       Presents and defends the basic proposition that significant
       attitude change always occurs in the context of action that
       produces change in the environment and has real-life
       consequences for the actor. It is in the context of nontrivial
       public actions that significant attitude change is affected.
       The three central features of attitudes--they are functionally
       based, socially shared, and represent a range of commitment to
       the attitude object--are discussed. Data on the results of
       discrepant action on attitude change is cited.

1207. Kloss, Ellen T. "Psychological Effects of Immoral Actions: The
       Experimental Evidence."   Psychological Bulletin, 85 (1978):
       756-771.

Presents a critical review of studies of the effects on adults of breaking conventionally defined moral rules in controlled experiments. Observes that committing immoral acts does affect the transgressor. Sense of responsibility for immoral actions and subjective definition of behavior as immoral may mediate effects.

1208.   Kohlberg, Lawrence, and Peter Scharf. "Bureaucratic Violence and Conventional Moral Thinking." Moral and Psychological Education: Theory and Research (item 1521), pp. 85-100.

Compares the moral thinking of two soldiers implicated in the slaughter of civilians at MyLai with the reasoning of a soldier who refused to participate. Attempts to show how the men's actions followed from their reasoning. This article has often erroneously been cited as having appeared in the American Journal of Orthopsychiatry.

1209.   Krebs, D.L. "Altruism: An Examination of the Concept and a Review of the Literature." Psychological Bulletin, 73 (1970): 258-302.

Provides a thorough and in-depth review of the literature relating to altruism. Independent variables associated with altruism are organized on the basis of source of experimental measurement and level of generality. Characteristics of benefactor and recipient are categorized as state variables, trait variables, social roles and demographic attributes, and characteristics influenced by norms. Dependency and interpersonal attractiveness were two of the factors found to be related to altruism. Other correlates are reported, and the normative level of analysis is criticized.

1210.   Krebs, Dennis. "A Cognitive-Developmental Approach to Altruism." Altruism, Sympathy and Helping. Edited by L. Wispe. New York: Academic Press, 1968.

Presents a cognitive-developmental interpretation of altruism that offers a solution to the perplexing phemomenon of the situationally specific nature of moral behavior. Argues that understanding the structure of social reasoning as it perceives social situations provides a more adequate way of understanding altruism.

1211.   Krebs, D.L. "Empathy and Altruism." Journal of Personality and Social Psychology, 32 (1975): 1134-1146.

Finds that if one sees oneself as similar to another, one is likely to experience more intense empathy with that person. Also, the more one empathizes with a person, the likelier one is to behave altruistically toward that person.

1212. Krebs, D.L. "Infrahuman Altruism." Psychological Bulletin, 76
       (1971): 411-414.

       Suggests that although there is a good deal of descriptive
       evidence for helping behavior in animals, experimental support
       for the assumption that the helping responses were based on
       altruistic motivation is lacking.

1213. Krebs, Dennis, and Ali Rosenwald. "Moral Reasoning and Moral
       Behavior in Conventional Adults." Merrill Palmer Quarterly,
       23 (1977): 77-87.

       Found that Kohlberg's test of moral development predicted an
       everyday moral behavior--an individual's mailing in a
       questionnaire he has been paid to complete.

1214. Kuhmerker, Lisa.   "Learning to Care--The Development of
       Empathy." Journal of Moral Education, 5 (1975): 25-33.

       M.L. Hoffman's (item 1150) stage theory of the development of
       empathy is explained. The relationship of role taking to
       empathy is an important dimension of Hoffman's theory.

1215. Kupfersmid, Joel H., and Donald M. Wonderly. "Moral Maturity
       and Behavior: Failure to Find a Link." Journal of Youth and
       Adolescence, 9 (1980): 249- 261.

       Examines the available evidence on whether individuals
       operating at the postconventional level of moral reasoning
       behave significantly different from those functioning at lower
       moral maturity levels. Research is examined in five areas:
       resistance to temptation, resistance to social influence,
       student activism, prosocial behavior, and antisocial behavior.
       The evidence suggests no significant link between moral
       reasoning and behaviors in the above areas.

1216. Lane, J., and N.H. Anderson. "Integration of Intention and
       Outcome in Moral Judgment." Memory and Cognition, 4 (1976):
       1-5.

       Explores the process (rule) by which subjects integrate cues
       of intent and value to reach a judgment of how grateful the
       recipient of an action should feel. It was found that previous
       work on the cognitive algebra of human judgment may generalize
       to the moral realm.

1217. LaPierre, R.T. "Attitudes vs. Actions." Social Forces, 13
       (1934): 230-237.

Reports a fascinating study of social prejudice in which the attitudes of hotel and restaurant owners was found to bear little relationship to their actual behavior when confronted with a patron of another race.

1218.   Latane, B., and J.M. Darley. The Unresponsive Bystander: Why Doesn't He Help? New York: Appleton-Century-Crofts, 1970.

Reports a synthesis of the authors' research on bystander intervention. A theoretical framework for explaining the intervention process is presented. The authors suspect that the major variance in behavior in helping situations will be determined by the conclusions reached regarding rewards and costs. Social norms are seen as relatively unimportant.

1219.   Lazarowitz, R.; W.G. Stephan and S.T. Friedman. "Effects of Moral Justifications and Moral Reasoning on Altruism." Developmental Psychology, 12 (1976): 353-354.

Finds that exposing college subjects to justification for altruism at the next highest level will lead to an increase in altruism. More than one level above the subject, however, produces no significant impact.

1220.   Leming, James S. "Cheating Behavior, Situational Influence, and Moral Development." Journal of Educational Research, 71 (1978): 214-217.

Subjects higher in moral reasoning cheat less than other subjects, however, in a low-risk situation it was found that all subjects cheated equally, regardless of level of moral reasoning.

1221.   Leming, James S. "Cheating Behavior, Subject Variables, and Components of the Internal-External Scale under High and Low Risk Conditions." Journal of Educational Research, 74 (1980): 83-87.

Finds that cheating behavior is situationally specific. Cheating behavior was not found to be related to locus of control. Under high-risk conditions high ability students cheated significantly less than under low-risk conditions.

1222.   Leming, James S. "An Exploratory Inquiry into the Multi-factor Theory of Moral Behavior." Journal of Moral Education, 5 (1976): 179-188.

It was found, using selected dimensions of Wilson's moral components, that age and empathy were the primary predictors of moral reasoning, and biographical variables were the best predictor variables for choice on moral dilemmas.

1223. Leming, James S.   "Moral Reasoning, Sense of Control, and
       Social-Political Activism among Adolescents." Adolescence, 9
       (1974): 507-528.

       Finds that high school activists and nonactivists are similar
       in moral reasoning and sense of control.

1224. Lickona, Thomas.   "A Cognitive-Developmental Approach to
       Altruism." Paper presented at the Annual Meeting of the
       American Psychological Association, New Orleans, 1974. ED 102
       455.

       Argues that concern for others is fundamentally a matter of
       cognitive definition of one's relationship and responsibility to
       others.

1225. Lickona, Thomas.   "What Optimizes Moral Development and
       Behavior? Where the Theories Converge." Paper presented at
       the Biennial Meeting of the Society for Research in Child
       Development, Denver, 1975. ED 118 221.

       Reviews different theories of moral development and suggests
       that the development of mature moral reasoning is facilitated by
       the imposition of real responsibilities, and by an environment
       that provides strong situational supports.

1226. Liebert, R.M. "Moral Development: A Theoretical and Empirical
       Analysis." The Functions of Language and Cognition. Edited
       by G.J. Whitehurst and B.J. Zimmerman. New York: Academic
       Press, 1979, pp. 229-264.

       Reviews and critiques the cognitive-developmental perspective
       on moral development. Presents the functional perspective on
       moral development that emphasizes action, effects of culture,
       situational determinants, moral changes as a result of age-
       correlated changes in knowledge, and actual and expected
       consequences as a major determinant of moral arguments, issues,
       and actions.   Concludes that innate self-interest is the
       functional determinant of moral action and that external conse-
       quences influence reasoning and action to a remarkable extent.

1227. Linford, J.L. "Conscious and Unconscious Moral Judgment, Moral
       Character, and Conventional Conduct in Adolescence."   Ph.D.
       dissertation, California School of Professional Psychology,
       1977. 38/06-B, p. 2834.

       The capacity to consciously symbolize dream content was found
       to be related to level of moral judgment. No relationship
       between cheating and judgment was found, and a negative
       relationship was detected between resistance-to-cheating and
       socialization.

1228. Macaulay, J., and L. Berkowitz, eds. Altruism and Helping
       Behavior. New York: Academic Press, 1970.

       Contains an excellent collection of papers on social
       psychological studies of some antecedents and consequents of
       altruism and helping behavior.   Papers are grouped under the
       following headings: situational determinants of helping, social
       norms and the socialization of altruism, guilt, equity, justice
       and reciprocation, and naturalistic studies of altruism.

1229. McKinney, J.P., M. Connally and J. Clark. "Development of a
       Prescriptive Morality: An Historical Observation." Journal of
       Genetic Psychology, 122 (1973): 105-110.

       Presents data that argues that the increase in severity of
       moral judgment among college students between 1929 and 1958 was
       due to increasingly severe judgments on issues regarding what
       one ought to do rather than regarding what one ought not to do.
       These changes are discussed in terms of the increased use of
       love-oriented socialization over the years studied.

1230. McLaughlin, John A., and Beth Stephens. "Interrelationships
       among Reasoning Moral Judgment and Moral Conduct." American
       Journal of Mental Deficiency, 79 (1974): 156-161.

       Factor analysis suggests that with increasing age, reasoning
       measures tend to combine with measures of moral judgment and
       conduct in both retarded and nonretarded subjects.   A low or
       moderate relationship among these variables was observed.

1231. Macmillan, Charles J. "The Concept of Adjustment." Ph.D.
       dissertation, Cornell University, 1965. 26/11, p. 6556.

       Concludes that the term "adjustment" has little significant
       meaning.   It is a value-laden term and when it is used the
       person has already made crucial value decisions.

1232. McNamee, Sharie. "Moral Behavior, Moral Development and
       Motivation." Journal of Moral Education, 7 (1977): 27-31.

       Moral behavior was assessed in a situation where it was
       necessary to violate the experimenter's authority to help
       someone.   It was found that as level of moral reasoning rose, an
       increasing percentage of subjects helped.   Subjects' interpre-
       tation of the situation varied with their levels of moral
       reasoning.

1233. McNamee, Sharie. "Moral Behavior, Moral Development and
       Motivation." Paper presented at annual meeting of American
       Psychological Association, 1975. ED 117 007.

Finds that only at Kohlberg's stage 6 do subjects defy authority and go to the aid of a student in need of assistance. At stages 1-5 there was an increasing percentage of those willing to help. The results confirm Kohlberg's theory regarding the relationship between moral judgment and moral action.

1234. Masterson, Mark. "The Social Behavior of Students at Different Stages of Development." Moral Education: A First Generation of Research and Development (item 1513), pp. 188-215.

Observes and characterizes high school students' social behavior by developmental stage. Finds major differences in social behavior when students are categorized by stage of moral reasoning. Taken from author's dissertation (item 1194).

1235. Masterson, Mark R. "Structures of Thought and Patterns of Social Behavior: Stages of Ego and Moral Development and Their Relationship to Interpersonal Behavior." Ed.D. dissertation, Boston University, 1980. 41/05, p. 2019.

Lower stage students demonstrate hostile anticonventional and somewhat dominant behavior. Higher stage students are affectively neutral, but supportive of classroom norms. Ego stages capture better patterns of behavior than do moral stages.

1236. Medinnas, G.R. "Behavioral and Cognitive Measures of Conscience Development." Journal of Genetic Psychology, 109 (1966): 147-150.

Little relationship was found between actual behavior and expressed moral attitudes of 12- and 13-year-old children.

1237. Merelman, R.H. "Moral Development and Potential Radicalism in Adolescence." Youth and Society, 9 (1977): 29-53.

Reports and discusses the results of a study that found that advanced moral judgments (Kohlberg) and potentially radical political beliefs apparently came together in mid-adolescence. During this period potential radicals began to master the advanced cognitive skills that enabled them to begin to construct a radical ideology and connect it to moral reasoning. Youthful radicals were seen as political moralists.

1238. Milgram, Stanley. Obedience to Authority. New York: Harper Colophon Books, 1975.

An extensive report of the classic but controversial study in which subjects were asked to inflict apparently harmful shocks on others. The alarming finding was that most of those asked to do so, did. See also Journal of Abnormal and Social Psychology, 64 (1963): 371-378.

1239. Mischel, Walter, and Harriet Mischel. "Moral Behavior from a Cognitive Social Learning Viewpoint." Paper presented at the biennial meeting of the Society for Research in Child Development, 1975. ED 116 792.

Explains the concept of cognitive and behavioral construction competencies, and claims that cognitive competencies are among the best predictors of moral behavior. Moral competence includes reasoning, role taking, and empathy. Concludes that age-related changes in the style and content of moral reasoning and conduct reflect changes in the individual's cognitive and verbal capacities in interaction with social learning variables salient for him/her at different points in the life cycle.

1240. Moore, Gary, and Beth Stephens. "Two Year Gains in Moral Conduct by Retarded and Nonretarded Persons." American Journal of Mental Deficiency, 79 (1974): 147-153.

It was found that an equivalence of conduct exists for retarded and nonretarded persons of comparable MA in situations requiring honesty and truth telling. Both groups manifested increases in moral conduct in late adolescence. This paper is followed by a discussion by Aronfreed (pp. 154-155) and a reply by Stephens (p. 155).

1241. Musgrave, P.W. "Moral Decisions of Some Teenagers: A Sociological Account." Cambridge Journal of Education, 7 (Lent Term, 1977): 40-49.

From data from interviews with 16 15 year olds it appears that moral behavior depends on the unthinking and routine application of recipes that are rarely formulated explicitly. The problem is grasped and almost instantaneously the decision is made.

1242. Myrdal, Gunnar. An American Dilemma: The Negro Problem in Modern Democracy. New York: Harper and Row, 1962.

In the introduction Myrdal observes that the "American Dilemma," that is, the practice of racial discrimination, is best understood as a result of the conflict between moral valuations preserved on the general plane and the valuations on specific planes of individual and group living. The moral struggle goes on not only between people but also within them. In order to defend behavior people will twist and mutilate their beliefs about social reality (rationalization).

1243. Nardi, Peter M. "Moral Socialization: An Empirical Analysis of the Hogan Model." Journal of Moral Education, 9 (1979): 10-16.

Hogan's five character-trait dimensions model of moral development is empirically assessed. The dimensions were used to predict a measure of rule-breaking behavior. Results indicate support for the model.

1244. Nelson, E.A.; R.E. Grinder; and M.L. Mutterer. "Sources of Variance in Behavioral Measures of Honesty in Temptation Situations: Methodological Analyses." Developmental Psychology, 1 (1969): 265-279.

Explores the issue of generality versus specificity of honesty by studying the extent of intraindividual consistency of sixth-grade children across six temptation situations. It was found that only about 15% of the total behavioral variance was due to persons.

1245. Page, Monte M., ed. Nebraska Symposium on Motivation 1979: Beliefs, Attitudes and Values. Lincoln: University of Nebraska Press, 1980.

An excellent collection of papers on the psychology of attitudes. The place of attitudes in personality and their role in determining behavior receive major attention.

1246. Petronio, R.J. "The Moral Maturity of Repeater Delinquents." Youth and Society, 12 (1980): 51-59.

Finds that repeater delinquents reason at a higher level than nonrepeater delinquents. A rationalization hypothesis is prepared. As adolescents commit more than average delinquent behavior they find the normative mechanisms of control inadequate for justifying their behavior. As a result they rationalize a higher set of moral standards that minimizes their badness.

1247. Rokeach, Milton. Beliefs, Attitudes and Values: A Theory of Organization and Change. San Francisco: Jossey-Bass, 1970.

Argues that beliefs, attitudes, and values are organized together to form a functionally integrated cognitive system. A change in any part of the system will affect other parts and eventually result in behavioral change. The book consists of careful conceptual clarification of the concepts used and reports research that tests deductions of his theory.

1248. Rokeach, Milton. "Long-Range Experimental Modification of Values, Attitudes, and Behavior." American Psychologist, 26 (1971): 453-459.

Finds that relatively enduring changes in values, attitudes, and behavior can be brought about as a result of a rather brief experimental treatment involving a self-confrontation procedure. Subjects were told that they ranked freedom and equality differently from other students and that their ranking showed more of an interest in self than in others.

1249.   Rokeach, Milton. "Long-Term Value Change Initiated by Computer Feedback." Understanding Human Values (item 1520), pp. 210-225.

Through a computer program subjects are exposed to consistencies and inconsistencies between their value rankings and the value rankings of selected groups. It was found that the value rankings became more similar to the rankings of the same-sex and pro-civil rights groups presented in the initial computer interaction. Also in Journal of Personality and Social Psychology, 32 (1975): 467-476.

1250.   Rokeach, Milton. The Nature of Human Values. New York: Free Press, 1973.

From a massive analysis of data on human values it is concluded that there exist 18 terminal and 18 instrumental values held by all men. Rokeach argues that these values are culturally derived and that the individual value system of an individual represents the basis for all his future beliefs and actions.

1251.   Rokeach, Milton. The Open and Closed Mind. New York: Basic Books, 1960.

Contains a collection of papers on Rokeach's Dogmatism Scale--an attempt to develop a scale that is sensitive to both right-of-center and left- of-center dogmatism. The correlates of open and closed belief systems are assessed.

1252.   Rokeach, Milton. "Persuasion That Persists." Readings in Values Clarification (item 1504), pp. 65-74.

Rokeach explains how through the process of cognitive dissonance--exposing individuals to inconsistencies and contradictions in their value system--long-term changes in core values and personal behavior can be achieved.

1253.   Rokeach, Milton. "Some Unresolved Issues in Theories of Beliefs, Attitudes and Values." Nebraska Symposium on Motivation 1979 (item 1245), pp. 261-304.

Addresses the attitude-behavior controversy and makes observations about the weaknesses of prior research and suggests approaches to improve the methods of this area of inquiry. The solution, as seen by Rokeach, is in the necessity to study behavior from the point of view of the interrelationships between belief, attitude, and value.

1254. Rokeach, Milton, and Joel W. Grube. "Can Values Be Manipulated Arbitrarily?" Understanding Human Values (item 1520), pp. 241-256.

Reports the results of two studies in which the unidirectional nature of value change following self-confrontation is explored. The unidirectional hypothesis of value change is supported.

1255. Rosenberg, Milton J., et al. Attitude Organization and Change. New Haven, CT: Yale University Press, 1960.

Contains six papers that report on inquiries into consistency among attitude components. The papers underline the key role that striving for consistency plays in attitude-change dynamics.

1256. Rosenham, D.L. "Learning Theory and Prosocial Behavior." Journal of Social Issues, 28, 3 (1972): 151-163.

Altruism constitutes a paradox for learning theory--how is it one engages in actions without tangible rewards? It is suggested that affect, cognition, and self-reinforcement are possible explanations.

1257. Rosenham, D.L.; Bert S. Moore; and Bill Underwood. "The Social Psychology of Moral Behavior." Moral Development and Behavior (item 519), pp. 241-252.

Discusses highly significant situational factors that influence moral behavior. The following social-psychological processes likely to affect behavior across a variety of situations are discussed: diffusion of responsibility, victim derogation, evaluation apprehension, and momentary moods.

1258. Ross, M., and M. Ditecco. "An Attributional Analysis of Moral Judgment." Journal of Social Issues, 31 (1975): 91-109.

Analyzes the psychology of moral judgment from the framework of attribution theory. The relevance of perceptions of responsibility for moral evaluation is examined. Four factors are proposed to influence the sophistication of responsibility attributions: specification, motivational biases, linguistic usage, and attributional context.

1259. Rothman, Golda R. "The Relationship Between Moral Judgment and
       Moral Behavior." Moral Development and Socialization (item
       542), pp. 107-127.

       Arguing that there exists a relationship between moral
       reasoning and moral behavior, cites a wide range of studies to
       pin down the nature of the relationship. Argues that the
       evidence indicates that there is increased coordination of
       judgment and behavior with developmental stage, although the
       picture is a complex one with situational and personal factors
       confounding attempts to develop a clear and direct pattern of
       relation.

1260. Rotter, Julian C. "Beliefs, Social Attitudes and Behavior: A
       Social Learning Analysis." Cognition, Personality and
       Clinical Psychology. Edited by Richard Jessor and Seymour
       Feshbach. San Francisco: Jossey-Bass, 1967, pp. 112-140.

       Presents a formula based on social learning theory that
       attempts to account for all the variables related to the
       relationship between beliefs, social attitudes, and social
       behavior.

1261. Rubin, K.H., and F.W. Schneider. "The Relationship Between
       Moral Judgment, Egocentrism, and Altruistic Behavior." Child
       Development, 44 (1973): 661-665.

       Measures of communicative egocentrism and moral judgment were
       positively correlated with the incidence of altruistic behavior
       in 7-year-old children.

1262. Rule, Brendon G., and Andrew R. Nesdale. "Moral Judgment of
       Aggressive Behavior." Perspectives on Aggression. Edited by
       Russell G. Green and Edgar C. O'Neal. New York: Academic
       Press, 1976.

       Reviews research related to people's moral judgments of
       aggressive acts. Finds that observers' judgments are not solely
       the result of the fact that one individual has harmed another;
       rather, judgments are influenced by many personal and
       situational factors.

1263. Rushton, J.P. "Socialization and the Altruistic Behavior of
       Children." Psychological Bulletin, 83 (1976): 898-913.

       Reviews the recent research on altruistic behavior by children
       under four headings: generality, person variables, environmental
       variables, and theories of social learning and cognitive
       development.

1264. Rushton, J. Philippe, and Christine Littlefield. "The Effects
       of Age, Amount of Modeling, and a Success Experience on
       Seven-to-Eleven-Year-Old Children's Generosity." Journal of
       Moral Education, 9 (1979): 55-56.

       Finds that modeling is an effective inducer of generosity and
       that the amount of modeled behavior determines the amount of
       imitated behavior.

1265. Saltzstein, H.D.; R.M. Diamond; and M. Belenky. "Moral Judgment
       Level and Conformity Behavior." Developmental Psychology, 7
       (1972): 327-336.

       Stage 3 subjects were found to be more likely to conform than
       children at either higher or lower stages.

1266. Sanders, Keith R., and L. Erwin Atwood. "Value Change Initiated
       by the Mass Media." Understanding Human Values (item 1520),
       pp. 226-240.

       Self-confrontation of values and the resulting dissatisfaction
       with one's values resulted in value shifts regardless of the
       channel through which the self-confrontation was presented:
       interpersonal, television, and print. The title is misleading
       as this study has nothing to do with mass media.

1267. Santrock, John W. "Moral Structure: The Interrelations of Moral
       Behavior, Moral Judgment and Moral Affect." Journal of
       Genetic Psychology, 127 (1975): 202-213.

       No support was found--for a trait of morality the domains of
       moral behavior, judgment, and affect were found to be
       orthogical. There was some evidence, however, that guilt was
       predictive of altruism.

1268. Schwartz, Shalom H. "Awareness of Consequences and the
       Influence of Moral Norms on Interpersonal Behavior."
       Sociometry, 31 (1968): 355-369.

       Shows that awareness of consequences of one's potential acts
       for the welfare of others activates one's norms, thereby
       permitting them to influence behavior.

1269. Schwartz, S.H. "Normative Explanations of Helping Behavior: A
       Critique, Proposal and Empirical Test." Journal of
       Experimental and Social Psychology, 9 (1973): 349-364.

       Finds that the impact of norms on behavior is a function of
       the tendency to deny or ascribe responsibility to the self. The
       moral action studied was donating bone marrow to a stranger.

1270. Schwartz, Shalom H. "Words, Deeds, and the Perception of
       Consequences and Responsibility in Action Situations."
       Journal of Personality and Social Psychology, 10 (1968):
       232-242.

       Proposes, and cites evidence to support, that people's norms
       and their behavior can be expected to correspond only when
       pertinent norms are activated in choice situations. Activation
       is shown to depend on how consequences and responsibility are
       perceived.

1271. Schwartz, S.H., et al. "Some Personality Correlates of Conduct
       in Two Situations of Moral Conflict." Journal of Personality,
       37 (1969): 41-57.

       Finds that college freshmen high in level of moral thought
       were less likely to cheat than those low in level of moral
       thought. No significant difference on this variable was noted
       for helpfulness.

1272. Selman, Robert L. "Level of Social Perspective Taking and the
       Development of Empathy in Children: Speculations from a
       Social-Cognitive Viewpoint." Journal of Moral Education, 5
       (1975): 35-43.

       Describes a cognitive-developmental approach to empathy in
       which empathetic understanding is a function of basic
       social-cognitive processes and concepts. Discusses recent
       research which supports this viewpoint.

1273. Sheehan, T.J., et al. "Moral Judgment as a Predictor of
       Physician Performance." Moral Education Forum, 5(1980): 2-7.

       In a correlational study moral reasoning was found to be a
       clear predictor of clinical performance. The study was based on
       a sample of 244 practicing physicians.

1274. Sherif, Carolyn W. "Social Values, Attitudes and Involvement of
       the Self." Nebraska Symposium on Motivation 1979 (item 1245),
       pp. 1-64.

       Argues that the study of attitudes has become trivialized of
       late due to the separation of the concept from personality and
       self-system. In the last half the author's "Social
       Judgment-Involvement Theory," which focuses on an individuals
       selection of his/her position from a set of ordered
       alternatives, is presented. From this a person's attitude
       structure is determined according to degree of personal
       involvement.

1275. Shields, David. "Education for Moral Action." Religious
       Education, 75 (1980): 129-141.

       Presents Haan's (item 1180) alternative approach to Kohlberg's
       framework for moral development. The interpersonal morality of
       Haan holds that moral truth must be constructed; it is that upon
       which we can conscientiously agree. The research on the
       relationship between moral reasoning and moral action is
       interpreted from the interpersonal-morality perspective. The
       educational implications of interpersonal morality are seen to
       involve interdependence and negotiation.

1276. Shoben, E.J. "Moral Behavior and Moral Learning." Religious
       Education, 58 (1963): 137-145.

       Examines the evidence for the claim that the more deeply one
       is committed to religious belief the less likely one is to
       violate the moral canons of a group in which one's religion
       prevails. The correlation between virtue and religion was found
       to be weak. An interpretation is offered.

1277. Shotland, R.L., and W.G. Berger. "Behavioral Validation of
       Several Values from Rokeach Value Scale as an Index of
       Honesty." Journal of Applied Psychology, 54 (1970): 433-435.

       The values Honesty and Salvation were found to be related to
       pencil returning following taking the Rokeach value survey.

1278. Smith, M. Brewster. "Attitudes, Values and Selfhood." Nebraska
       Symposium on Motivation 1979 (item 1245), pp. 305-350.

       Points out the futility of trying to understand attitudes
       apart from their broader context as an aspect of personality and
       experiences of selfhood.

1279. Smither, Suzanne. "A Reconsideration of the Developmental Study
       of Empathy." Human Development, 20 (1977): 253-276.

       A conception of empathy based on ordinary language usage is
       presented. In this view the nature and processes of skills
       involved are shown to be dependent upon the particular
       dimensions of the situational context.

1280. Staub, Ervin. "Instigation to Goodness: The Role of Social
       Norms and Interpersonal Influence." Journal of Social Issues,
       28, 3 (1972): 131-150.

       The distinction between knowing and personally accepting a
       norm is emphasized. It is also argued that people behave not
       only according to norms but also according to the attitudes and
       expectations of other people also in the situation.

1281.   Staub, Ervin. Positive Social Behavior and Morality, Volume I:
        Social and Personal Influences. New York: Academic Press,
        1978.

        The first of two volumes that comprise an encyclopedia of
        theory and research into the phenomenon of prosocial behavior.
        In this volume Staub attempts to set forth a model of how
        situations and personality interact to determine behavior. He
        argues that strength of personal goals and potential of a given
        situation to activate those goals are the important determinants
        of behavior.

1282.   Staub, Ervin. Positive Social Behavior and Morality, Volume II:
        Socialization and Development. New York: Academic Press,
        1979.

        In this volume Staub attempts to assess how prosocial
        characteristics and processes develop. He offers a schema that
        includes classes of influences on children, varied principles of
        learning and development, and developmental outcomes. The
        bibliography for the two volumes is extensive.

1283.   Staub, Ervin. "The Use of Role Playing and Induction in
        Children's Learning of Helping and Sharing Behaviors." Child
        Development, 42 (1971): 805-816.

        In a study with kindergarten children it was found that role
        playing was more effective than induction in increasing helping
        and sharing behavior.

1284.   Stotland, Ezra, et al. Empathy, Fantasy and Helping. Beverly
        Hills, CA: Sage Publications, 1978.

        Expanding upon Stotland's earlier work in the study of
        empathy, this book reports on a new research thrust that
        explores the relationship of empathy to helping behavior.
        Reports on the development of a new empathy scale and its use in
        research.

1285.   Tate-Hackney, Janet L. "A Study of the Association Between
        Value System Hierarchy and Level of Ego Development." Ed.D.
        dissertation, University of Houston, 1978. 39/07, p. 4156.

        Value hierarchy (Rokeach) was found to be unrelated to stage
        of ego development (Loevinger).

1286. Toch, Hans. Violent Men: An Inquiry into the Psychology of
       Violence. Chicago: Aldine, 1969.

       Based on interviews with communal offenders, a typology of
       reasons for violent behavior was developed. It was found that
       anticipations shape reality in a self-confirming manner.
       Violence-prone people classify people and communications as
       either threatening or nonthreatening.

1287. Triandis, Harry C. Attitude and Attitude Change. New York:
       Wiley, 1971.

       Discusses the entire range of topics related to the study of
       attitudes. Included in the book are chapters on attitude
       measurement and methodology, attitude theory, attitude
       formation, determinants of attitudes, and attitude change.

1288. Triandis, Harry C. "Values, Attitudes and Interpersonal
       Behavior." Nebraska Symposium on Motivation 1979 (item 1245),
       pp. 195-259.

       Through a series of heuristic theoretical equations, flow
       charts, and numerous definitions and hypotheses a synthesis in
       social psychology is attempted. A major focus of this synthesis
       is the relationship of attitude and behavior. The notion of
       subjective culture is related to the concept of attitude in this
       formulation.

1289. Tsujimoto, R.N., and P.M. Nardi. "A Comparison of Kohlberg's
       and Hogan's Theories of Moral Development." Social
       Psychology, 41 (1978): 235-245. NR

1290. Turiel, E., and G.R. Rothman. "The Influence of Reasoning on
       Behavioral Choices at Different Stages of Moral Development."
       Child Development, 43 (1972): 741-756.

       Subjects were asked to change a moral choice when presented
       with reasons for such a change at reasoning above or below their
       own stage. Only at stage 4 did reasoning above lead to a shift
       in choice.

1291. VanDyke, P., and J. Pierce-Jones. "The Psychology of Religion
       of Middle and Late Adolescence: A Review of Empirical
       Research, 1950-1960." Religious Education, 58 (1963):
       529-537.

       Contains a survey of the empirical research related to the
       psychology of religion and the development of ethical attitudes
       during middle and late adolescence.

1292. Walster, Elaine, and Jane A. Piliavin. "Equity and the Innocent
       Bystander." Journal of Social Issues, 28, 3 (1972): 165-189.

       Attempts to integrate equity theory and data concerning the
       reactions of bystanders and victims caught up in emergencies.

1293. Walters, Gary C., and Joan E. Grasec. Punishment, San Francisco:
       W.H. Freeman, 1977.

       In an extensive review of available literature the effect of
       punishment on human beings is analyzed. The focus is on
       psychological literature. Child development is one of the
       central foci of the book.

1294. Weiss, Jacqueline. "Self-Actualization and Moral Maturity: The
       Relationship Between Degrees of Self-Actualization and Levels
       of Moral Maturity in Selected Undergraduate College Students."
       Ed.D. dissertation, University of Southern California, 1980.
       40/09, p. 4974.

       The significant correlations derived lend substantial support
       to the hypothesized relationship between degrees of
       self-actualization and levels of cognitive moral development.

1295. Wilson, Richard W. "A New Direction for the Study of Moral
       Behavior." Journal of Moral Education, 7 (1978): 122-131.

       An attempt is made to reconcile the points of dispute between
       a social learning and cognitive-developmental view of moral
       development. A synthesis model of moral development is offered
       based on the impact of internal capabilities and external
       influences on cognitive and affective domains.

1296. Wispe, Lauren, ed. Altruism, Sympathy and Helping: Psychological
       and Sociological Principles. New York: Academic Press, 1978.

       An excellent collection of papers representing a variety of
       viewpoints on the origins of altruism. Contains, among others,
       papers by Wilson on the genetic evaluation of altruism, Krebs on
       the cognitive-developmental interpretation of altruism, Ekstein
       on the psychoanalytic interpretation, and B.F. Skinner on the
       ethics of helping people.

1297. Wispe, Lauren G., ed. "Positive Forms of Social Behavior."
       Journal of Social Issues, 28, 3 (1972).

       A special issue featuring 12 papers on a diverse set of
       questions related to prosocial behavior.

1298. Wright, Derek. The Psychology of Moral Behavior. Baltimore: Penguin Books, 1971.

Presents a broad but thorough overview of the antecedents and correlates of moral behavior. Contains chapters on altruism, moral insight, character, delinquency, resistance to temptation, moral ideology and religion, education, and morality.

1299. Wright, Derek. "The Punishment of Children: A Review of Experimental Studies." Journal of Moral Education, 1 (1972): 221-229.

Experiments on the effects of timing intensity, vicarious punishment, relationship to the punishing agents, and explanatory talk are reviewed.

1300. Zimbardo, Philip, and Effe B. Ebbesen. Influencing Attitudes and Changing Behavior. Reading, MA: Addison-Wesley, 1969.

Written in a readable and interesting style, this book provides a useful introduction to attitude theory and attitude and behavior change.

1301. Ziv, A., and S. Shulman. "Influence of a Model's Overall Meaning on Moral Judgment and Resistance to Temptation in Children." Journal of Moral Education, 4 (1975): 121-127.

A model's behavior (on film) and the reinforcement received did not affect the children's resistance to temptation and moral judgment. The overall meaning of the model's behavior, however, did significantly influence children's behavior.

1302. Zuckerman, M., and H.T. Reis, "Comparison of Three Models for Predicting Moral Behavior." Journal of Personality and Social Psychology, 36 (1978): 498-510.

Three models for predicting altruistic behavior were compared: intention; moral norms and ascription of responsibility; and attitudes and self-monitoring. Donating blood was found to be predicted best as a function of intentions and attitudes.

Additional Topics

Sociological Perspectives on Moral Development

1303. Adler, Franz. "The Value Concept in Sociology." American Journal of Sociology, 62 (1956): 272-279.

Argues that values cannot be discovered apart from human behavior. Internal states cannot be observed apart from action. Norms have meaning only when seen as sets of verbal and nonverbal behavior.

1304. Andenaes, Johannes. "The Moral or Educative Influence of Criminal Law." Journal of Social Issues, 27, 2 (1971): 17-31.

Argues that the threat of punishment contained in criminal law not only works through fear, but may also have moral or educative effects. These effects are analyzed and the relevant research assessed.

1305. Ball-Rokeach, Sandra J., and Irving Tallman. "Social Movements as Moral Confrontations: With Special Reference to Civil Rights." Understanding Human Values (item 1520), pp. 82-94.

Attempts a theoretical analysis of the cognitive functions served by social movements. Social movements are viewed as value-exhorting consciousness-raising movements that attempt to increase individual awareness about positions taken with respect to certain values with a view to inducing dissatisfaction and, ultimately, value change. Five moral-confrontation strategies are discussed.

1306. Beardsley, Elizabeth L. "Moral Development as an Objective of Government." Moral Development and Politics (item 1531), pp. 41-50.

Provides a set of propositions that show how nonpaternalistic and nonauthoritarian governments may facilitate the moral development of citizens.

1307. Benedict, Ruth. Patterns of Culture. New York: Penguin Books,
       1946.

       A study of the ruling motivation of three cultures. May be
       read as an argument for the cultural determination of good and
       evil.

1308. Bidwell, Charles E. "Schooling and Socialization." Interchange,
       3, 4 (1972): 1-27.

       Explores the extent to which schools contribute to the general
       growth of commitment to values and moral rules. Argues that
       there are only two major formulations of moral socialization
       processes   (the   social-control   and   activity-structure
       perspectives) and that these perspectives are complementary.
       Shows how these perspectives can help us understand the moral
       dimensions of schooling.

1309. Boehm, Christopher. "The Moral System." Morality Examined
       (item 1528), pp. 25-39.

       Discusses the purpose of a moral system--to provide the
       necessary modicum of order so that a society may survive--and
       the complexity within all moral systems.

1310. Bohm, David. "On Insight and Its Significance, for Science,
       Education and Values." Education and Values (item 1525), pp.
       7-22.

       Argues that if we let our values "float freely," the likely
       result will be a complete breakdown of private morality and
       public order. Values are seen as conditioned presuppositions
       about what is important. In order to clear up our general con-
       fusion about values a general quality of insight needs to be
       developed.

1311. Cherkaoui, M. "Basil Bernstein and Emile Durkheim: Two Theories
       of Change in Educational Systems." Harvard Educational
       Review, 47 (1977): 556-64.

       Compares the viewpoints of Durkheim and Bernstein on three
       major themes: role of school, curriculum change, and social
       conflict.

1312. Devlin, Patrick. The Enforcement of Morals. New York: Oxford
       University Press, 1965.

       Discusses the limits of individual freedom within society, the
       boundaries of the public and private in the realm of morals, and
       the point at which the law may enter. Two controversial themes
       receive attention: (1) the denial that there is a private realm
       of morality into which the law cannot enter; (2) the notion that

the morality which the law enforces must be popular morality. Since immorality can harm society it is judged correct to use law to enforce morality. The argument presented originates in the analysis of the use of law to ban homosexuality.

1313. Durkheim, Emile. The Evolution of Educational Thought. Boston: Routledge and Kegan Paul, 1977.

Contains a view of moral education on the secondary level that complements his lectures to primary school teachers (Moral Education, item 1314). The emphasis now is on preparing students for social change by developing an understanding of the social order as constantly changing. There is no conflict with the earlier work since Durkheim feels that children should learn to appreciate and love their society before they develop a critical perspective on it.

1314. Durkheim, Emile. Moral Education: A Study in the Theory and Application of the Sociology of Education. Glencoe, IL: The Free Press, 1973.

Argues, from a sociological perspective, that morality is a socially accepted system of rules that predetermine conduct. The justification for these rules is in the societal stability promoted. Three elements involved in the concept of morality are presented: discipline, attachment to the group, and autonomy or self-determination. The implications of these elements for the practice of moral education is discussed. This is probably the best statement of moral education, which has the goal of bringing young people into a state of enlightened allegiance and conformity to societal norms.

1315. Geis, Gilbert, and John Monahan. "The Social Ecology of Violence." Moral Development and Behavior (item 519), pp. 342-356.

Reviews the spectrum of behaviors leading to violent consequences, and the shewed character of social and legal efforts to predict, inhibit, and control violence. A more morally acceptable approach to violence must examine more logically the entire realm of socially harmful actions.

1316. Ginsburg, Morris. On the Diversity of Morals. London: Heinemann, 1956.

A collection of Ginsburg's papers. The title essay is a refutation of ethical relativism, showing the convergence of ethical rules and principles, and the nature of their universality. Cites basic values held in common by people of different religions and cultural persuasions.

1317. Gouldner, A.   "The Norm of Reciprocity: A Preliminary
       Statement." American Sociological Review, 25 (1960): 161-178.

       Makes the case for a universal moral norm that defines certain
       actions and obligations as repayments for benefits received.
       The role that this norm plays in maintaining the cohesion and
       stability of a society is discussed.

1318. Halsey, A.H.   "The Sociology of Moral Education."   Moral
       Education in a Changing Society (item 1515), pp. 31-45.

       Discusses the relationship of moral education to the changing
       pattern of education in the United States and Great Britain.
       Discusses the sociological perspectives of Marx, Durkheim, and
       Talcott Parsons and how they view the moral and economic
       socialization process.

1319. Hart, H.L.A. Law, Liberty and Morality. New York: Vintage
       Books, 1963.

       Presents a critique of the doctrine that morality ought to be
       given the force of law. Discusses the normative, philosophical,
       and practical considerations that must be taken into account
       when law attempts to impose official sanctions against deviant
       but innocuous conduct.

1320. Ingram, D.   "Moral Education--A Sociological Study of the
       Influence of Society, Home and School." Educational Research,
       18 (1976): 237-238. NR

1321. Kaplan, John.   "A Legal Look at Prosocial Behavior: What Can
       Happen for Failing to Help or Trying to Help Someone."
       Journal of Social Issues, 28, 3 (1972): 219-229.

       Examines the relationship of law to altruistic behavior.

1322. Kluckholm, Clyde. "Values and Value-Orientations in the Theory
       of Action." Toward a General Theory of Action. Edited by
       Talcott Parsons and Edward Shills. New York: Harper and Row,
       1962, pp. 388-433.

       Argues that values are not completely relative to the cultures
       from which they derive. There are many values that are founded
       upon the fundamental biological similarities of all human
       beings: they arise also out of the circumstance that human
       existence is invariably a social existence.

1323. Lauderdale, P.   "Deviance and Moral Boundaries," _American_
      Sociological Review, 41 (1976): 660-676.

      Attempts to explain how the definition and volume of deviance
      can change in a particular social system independent of the
      actions of the deviants within that system. An external threat
      to the corporate social system is seen as highly significant in
      this regard.

1324. Lewis, C.S.   _The Abolition of Man_.   New York: Collier Books,
      1962.

      Sets forth eight objective values that all civilizations have
      held in common: laws of general and special beneficence, duties
      to parents, duties to children, the law of justice, law of good
      faith and veracity, law of good mercy, and law of magnanimity.

1325. Macbeath, A.   _Experiments in Living: Gifford Lectures 1948-1949_.
      London: Macmillan and Sons, 1952.

      A study of comparative morals and a discussion of morality in
      the light of anthropological evidence regarding primitive
      peoples. Holds that the main structure of the moral life, the
      nature of the moral ideal, and the grounds of moral obligation
      are in principle the same everywhere and for all men.

1326. Marks, Russell.   "Moral Education and the Social Order."
      Viewpoints, 51 (November 1975): 31-49.

      Argues that moral education is socially constructed and
      dialectically related to the social order. It is held that
      historically, moral education was often based on a view of
      American society that legitimized the status quo. The early
      20th-century claim that there were great intellectual
      differences between persons and that these differences closely
      correlated with morality is examined and contrasted with
      Kohlberg's views on the principle of justice. It is argued that
      both views define events in relation to the social order.
      Questions regarding the purposes of moral education are, at
      bottom, questions of competing constructs of reality.

1327. Mitchell, J.J.   "Social Custom and Psychological Health."
      Journal of Humanistic Psychology, 14 (1974): 49-55.

      Argues that anxieties and neuroses not only are the result of
      society but that many are also the direct result of the
      individual's loss of faith in society and estrangement from self
      and community.

1328. Musgrave, P.W. "Sociology and Moral Education: New Directions?"
       Journal of Moral Education, 6 (1976): 14-21.

       The field of moral education is analyzed at four levels:
       social structural, institutional, action, and the social
       psychological. A definition of morality focused on choice is
       presented, and is applied to moral education with a view to
       illuminating future directions for research.

1329. Ossowska, Maria. Social Determinants of Moral Ideals.
       Philadelphia: University of Pennsylvania Press, 1970.

       Systematically analyzes the factors that can be said to
       influence morality in a society. Using a variety of societal
       factors such as industrialization, urban versus rural,
       demographics, professional differentiation, bureaucracy, etc.,
       moral phenomena are treated as the dependent variables. This is
       one of the few books to attempt a sociology of morality.

1330. Parsons, T. "The School Class as a Social System: Some of Its
       Functions in American Society." Harvard Educational Review,
       29 (1959): 297-318.

       Sketches how schools socialize children into social norms and
       contribute to the selection of individuals for needed roles in
       society. The view that schools mold children to meet the needs
       of society is viewed as both necessary and desirable.

1331. Peterson, Howard L. "The Quest for Moral Order: Emile Durkheim
       on Education." Journal of Moral Education, 4 (1974): 39-46.

       Durkheim's theory is discussed and five main criticisms are
       advanced. The criticisms focus on the coercive and limiting
       nature of Durkheim's views.

1332. Pickering, W.S.F., ed. Durkheim: Essays on Morals and
       Education. London: Routledge and Kegan Paul, 1979.

       Consists of 14 essays and other items by Emile Durkheim that
       have not before been translated into English. The essays deal
       with the nature of morals and their relationship to the proper
       methods of education. The two sections of this volume are
       introduced by Pickering who analyzes the selected essays.
       Contains an excellent bibliography of French, English, and
       American sources.

1333. Renshaw, Peter. "Socialization: The Negation of Education?"
       Journal of Moral Education, 2 (1973): 211-220.

Explores the conceptual distinction between 'education' and 'socialization.' Both Durkheimian and interactionist models of socialization are examined. Argues that only through education can children become critically aware of reality in a manner that will lead to effective action upon it.

1334. Rescher, Nicholas. "What Is Value Change? A Framework for Research." Values and the Future. Edited by Kurt Baier and Nicholas Rescher. New York: The Free Press, 1966, pp. 68-91.

Presents a methodological examination of the problem of value change with special reference to foreseeable changes in American values induced by social and technological change. A cluster of concepts related to the explication of value change is presented. Some ways in which value change can come about are illustrated. Suggests that a cost-benefit framework is the best way to understand the impact of societal-technological influences on societal values.

1335. Sabini, John P., and Maury Silver. "Moral Reproach and Moral Action." Journal for the Theory of Social Behavior, 8 (1978): 103-123.

Explores the problem of why morally reproaching another is a frequently inhibited action. It is held that it is easy to morally reproach another only when the actor stands in a proper relationship to the wrongdoer and only when it is perceived that the action is in the proper relation to the norm invoked in the reproach. The consequences of not making a moral reproach are seen as moral drift. The relationship of gossip to moral reproach is explored.

1336. Schrag, Francis. "The Child in the Moral Order." Philosophy, 52 (1977): 167-177.

Discusses two views of the child in the moral order: a paternalistic view and an antipaternalistic view. That data, according to Schrag, supports the view that there are sharp differences between children and adults. Antipaternalism appears to be warranted by the need to keep all paternalism out of our lives.

1337. Sugarman, Barry. The School and Moral Development. London: Croom Helm, 1973.

Attempts to synthesize the whole debate on moral education by placing it within a broad sociological and social-psychological framework. The point of reference for the analysis is Wilson's conception of the morally educated person. Analyzes the social functions of the school, moral socialization, the school as social system, and the formal structure of the school as they contribute to the development of the attributes of the morally

educated person. Wide and narrow teacher-pupil relations and
open and closed learning situations are seen as especially
important in the moral education of youth.

1338. Sumner, William G. Folkways. Boston: Ginn and Co., 1906.

Presents the position that moral standards are a product of
folkways, which themselves are the' result of interactions
between men and their environment. This is probably the classic
statement of cultural relativism in morals.

1339. Tapp, June L., ed. "Socialization, the Law and Society,"
Journal of Social Issues, 27, 2 (1971).

A special edition containing excellent articles on the role of
law as socializer, legal development, and socialized values in
law and society.

1340. Tittle, Charles R. Sanctions and Social Deviance: The Question
of Deterrence. New York: Praeger, 1980.

Using a broad data base the relationship between individual
perceptions of the probability of being caught and punished for
deviant acts, and engaging in deviant acts, was examined. Finds
that fear of sanctions leads to significant curtailment of
deviance. Contains an extensive bibliography on the subject.

1341. Turnbull, Colin M. The Mountain People. New York: Simon and
Schuster, 1972.

Describes the disintegration of a people (the Ik) when moved
from their homeland to an inhospitable climate. The moral
fabric of life falls apart with frightening results. Cruelty
and insensitivity become the norms.

1342. Williams, Robin M. "Change and Stability in Values and Value
Systems: A Sociological Perspective." Understanding Human
Values (item 1520), pp. 15-46.

Values are seen as core conceptions of the desirable within
every individual and society. They serve as standards or
criteria to guide not only action but also judgment, choice,
attitude, evaluation, argument, exhortation, rationalization,
and attribution of responsibility. A central point of the paper
is that values are multifaceted cognitions and affections
representing far more than mere standards or criteria for
action. Factors in societies that are related to value change
are also discussed.

1343.   Wilson, Richard W.   "A Moral Community of Strangers."   Moral
        Development and Politics (item 1531), pp. 22-40.

        Within a sociobiological framework it is argued that social
        cooperation is a universal quality of humans.   Unfortunately,
        however, the social systems man currently lives under promote
        socio-centrism and limit full moral development.

1344.   Zimring, Franklin, and Gordon Hawkins.   "The Legal Threat as an
        Instrument of Social Change."   Journal of Social Issues, 27, 2
        (1971): 33-48.

        Discusses conditions influencing the outcome of threats that
        attempt to produce social change.   Factors considered are
        variations in the type of custom, the rationale for change, the
        social characteristics of the threatened audience, and the
        extent of law enforcement.

1345. Bower, William C. <u>Moral and Spiritual Values in Education</u>. Lexington: University of Kentucky Press, 1952.

Presents the philosophy of values that formed the basis of the Kentucky plan. The four phases of this approach in practice were discovery of values as they arise in experience; identification of the values, development; and symbolic expression giving suitable overt form to render the values communicable and capable of being reproduced. See also item 1372.

1346. Brickman, W.W. "The Teaching of Secular Moral Values from Ancient Times to 1800." <u>Paedagogica Historica</u>, 11 (1971): 337-350.

A brief historical account of Man's efforts to impart moral values and direct moral action on the basis of sanctions having human, not religious, origins.

1347. Brickman, William W. "The Teaching of Secular Moral Values in the Nineteenth Century: U.S.A., England, France." <u>Paedagogica Historica</u>, 12 (1972): 370-385.

The focus is on the struggle to establish a basis for moral education independent of religious institutions.

1348. Brickman, W.W. "The Teaching of Secular Moral Values in the Twentieth Century." <u>Paedagogica Historica</u>, 13 (1973): 5-22.

Presents a brief but broad cross-cultural perspective on the development of moral education in the 20th century.

1349. Bruneau, Willliam. "An Annotated Bibliography for Moral Education in the U.S. 1850-1939." <u>Moral Education Forum</u>, 4 (Winter 1979): 26-27.

Contains 29 references.

1350. Bruneau, William A. "A Resource Bibliography for the History of Moral Education in Western Europe." <u>Moral Education Forum</u>, 3 (Fall 1979): 8-15.

Presents an annotated list of original sources drawn from the history of moral education in France, Germany, and the United Kingdom. As Bruneau correctly notes, the history of moral education is a rich, but as yet untapped, area of resources.

1351. Bruneau, W. "Towards a History of Moral Education: Some
       Fundamental Considerations and a Case Study." Paedagocica
       Historica, 15 (1975): 356-378.

       Discusses how one can best approach--"get a handle on"--the
       historical study of moral education. Argues that it is
       necessary to limit the area of inquiry. Uses Hare and Wilson to
       define the topic and provide a starting point. Using John Locke
       as a case study, Bruneau illustrates the utility of his approach
       in the history of moral education.

1352. Cameron, W.J.   The Mind of McGuffey.   Oxford, OH: Miami
       University, 1937. NR

1353. Castle,   E.B.   Educating the Good Man: Moral Education in
       Christian Times. New York: Collier, 1962.

       A short history of moral education in the West from the times
       of Jesus and St. Paul until today. Contains a good bibliography
       on the subject. Originally published under the title Moral
       Education in Christian Times (1958).

1354. Chapman, William E. Roots of Character Education. Schenectady,
       NY: Character Research Press, 1977.

       Analyzes the 1920s, when character was a lively issue in
       American education. Provides a conceptual context for the times
       and an appreciation for the shifting positions taken by char-
       acter educators during the 1920s. Contains analyses of the
       movement from the perspectives of conception of character,
       methodology suggested, and disciplinary bases. An extensive
       list of references is provided.

1355. Charters, W.W. The Teaching of Ideals. New York: The Macmillan
       Co., 1927.

       Develops a theory of character traits and ideals that are
       considered desirable.   A program of direct and indirect
       techniques for instilling the traits is spelled out. This
       volume is representative of the rationale and methods of the
       Character Education Movement of the early 20th century.

1356. Childs,   John   L.   Education and Morals: An Experimentalist
       Philosophy of Education. New York: Appleton-Century-Crofts,
       1970.

       A discussion of the social and pragmatic basis of morality.
       This perspective provided the intellectual underpinning of moral
       training as conceived in many schools across the United States
       until 1939.

1357. Church, Robert. "Moral Education in the Schools." Morality
      Examined (item 1528), pp. 57-81.

      Presents a succinct yet thorough overview of the historical
      development of moral education in the United States. Traces the
      common schools' attempt to fill voids created by increased
      mobility and the decreasing influence of family and community as
      moral educators. Church also discusses McGuffey's Readers'
      attempts to instill morality through literacy. Dewey is
      presented as the next major influence, changing the 19th-century
      perspective by offering a flexible, individualistic alternative
      to codified morality. Finally, post-World War I influences are
      discussed.

1358. Church, Robert L., and Michael W. Sedlak. Education in the
      United States: An Interpretive History. New York: The Free
      Press, 1976.

      A readable history of U.S. education a central theme of which
      is the role of the schools in the imposition of values on youth.

1359. Commager, Henry S. "McGuffey and His Readers." Saturday Review,
      June 16, 1962, pp. 50-51, 69-70.

      Appraises the place of the Readers and their morality in U.S.
      history. Argues that although their moral influence was
      significant, the greatest impact of the Readers was intellectual
      and cosmopolitan. Concludes that on the whole their contri-
      bution was beneficent.

1360. Cope, H.F. "Selected List of Books on Moral Training and
      Instruction in the Public Schools." Religious Education, 5
      (1911): 718-732.

      Provides 350 references to books, monographs, and articles on
      moral education, mostly from the previous 50 years.

1361. Cremin, Lawrence A. American Education: The Colonial Experience.
      New York: Harper and Row, 1970.

      See chapters 1 and 9 for an analysis of religion's influence
      on moral instruction in colonial schools.

1362. Cremin, Lawrence. The Transformation of the School: Progres-
      sivism in American Education 1876-1957. New York: Vintage
      Books, 1961.

      Although Cremin does not directly discuss moral or character
      education efforts, the history of the progressive movement, with
      its interest in child-centered education and preparation for
      life, is the history of changing conceptions of the moral ends
      of education.

1363. Debroch, Guy. "Physical Science and Moral Confusion." Reflections on Values Education (item 1510), pp. 3-17.

The old physical view of the world was rooted in the concept of an absolute world order that contained an absolute moral order. When the old physical vision of the world collapsed, the moral vision was also lost and has not been replaced. Suggests a way out of this situation by using the attitude within the scientific methodology.

1364. Dunkel, H.B. Herbart and Education. New York: Random House, 1969.

Contains discussions of Herbart's views of the moral aim of education and assesses his impact on practice in the late 19th century.

1365. Elson, Ruth M. Guardians of Tradition: American Schoolbooks of the Nineteenth Century. Lincoln: University of Nebraska Press, 1964.

A detailed study of 19th-century textbooks used through grade eight, based on a study of over 1,000 books. Although there is no section specifically devoted to moral education, the theme runs through the book. As the title suggests, the school books are seen as an essentially conservative social influence.

1367. Fiering, Norman S. "Moral Philosophy in America, 1650-1750, and Its British Context." Ph.D. dissertation, Columbia University, 1969.

Traces the origins and describes the early nature of American moral philosophy.

1368. Finklestein, B. "Pedagogy as Intrusion: Teaching Values in Popular Schools in Nineteenth-Century America." History of Childhood Quarterly, 2 (1975): 349-378.

Discusses the scope and flavor of teachers as conveyors of moral tradition in 19th-century America. The reference section is rich in sources on the nature of 19th-century school life.

1368. Flattery, John J. "Case Study of Adult Value Education Program in the United States Air Force." Ed.D. dissertation, Boston University, 1975. 35/12, p. 7594.

Traces the development of the Air Force adult value education program from an authoritarian, institutionally oriented perspective to a non-authoritarian, personally oriented program designed to help individuals explore their own values.

1369. Ford, Paul L., ed. The New England Primer: A History of Its
       Origin and Development. New York: Teachers College Press,
       1962.

       Contains a reprint of the 1897 edition of Ford's book. Ford
       presents a history of the origin and development of the Primer
       and a reproduction of the earliest known edition (1727). That
       religion and education were one in the early days of this
       country becomes apparent from this study.

1370. Germane, C.E., and E.G. Germane. Character Education. New York:
       Silver, Burdett and Co., 1929.

       Presents a variety of techniques for developing character:
       assignments, school government, homeroom, etc.

1371. Goodman, Ruth. "Ideals of Life and Man and the Common School
       Theories of Moral Education for the Public Schools from Horace
       Mann to John Dewey."   Ph.D. dissertation, Washington
       University, 1969. 30/12, p. 5261.

       Traces the recommendations of leading American educators for
       teaching ethical ideals in the common school. Examined are the
       ideals of Mann, Harris, Hall, Thorndike, Fairchild, and Dewey.

1372. Hartford, Ellis F. Moral Values in Public Education. New York:
       Harper and Brothers, 1958.

       Presents the history, theoretical bases, programs, and
       evaluation of the "Kentucky Movement." This movement began in
       1949 and was an attempt to emphasize moral and spiritual values
       in public education. The approach placed emphasis on students'
       reasoning their way out of identifiable situations.   The
       teacher's role was to assist the students. The goal was to
       discover and develop the basic values in one's own experiences.
       The end result was seen as a system of values rationally derived
       from experience. The volume is a rich source of information
       about an often neglected dimension of the history of moral
       education.

1373. Herdon, Ursula S. "Herbart's Concept of Morality in Education
       and Its Role in America." Ph.D. dissertation, The University
       of Alabama, 1980. 41/08, p. 3454.

       Delineates Herbart's concept of morality in education and
       traces its impact on American education.

1374. Hilliard, F. "The Moral Instruction League, 1897-1919." Durham
       Research Review, 12 (1961): 53- 63. NR

1375. Hiner, N. Roy. "Herbartians, History and Moral Education."
       School Review, 79 (1971): 590-600.

Discusses the Herbartian movement of the 1890s and its
perspective on moral education. Herbartians felt that moral
education could be achieved by relating content from history and
literature and arranging it to correspond with the alleged
stages of development of the race. Dewey's objections and the
objections of others to this conception of moral education are
discussed.

1376. Hollins, Walter H. "A Comparative Content Analysis of a Sample
      of McGuffey and Modern Elementary School Readers." Ph.D.
      dissertation, University of Illinois, 1959. 20/08, p. 3124.

      The "Modern Reader" is found to have content identical to that
      of earlier readers. The claim that it was frivolous and lacking
      in educative value is not supported.

1377. Hughes, Raymond G. "An Analysis of the Fourth, Fifth and Sixth
      McGuffey Readers." Ph.D. dissertation, University of
      Pittsburgh, 1943. NR

1378. Hunt, Thomas C. "Moral Education and Public Schools: Evaluation
      in 19th Century Wisconsin." Paper presented at the annual
      meeting of the American Educational Research Association,
      Boston, 1980. ED 183 447.

      Describes how the influx of diverse religious groups forced
      the schools into a nonsectarian approach to moral education.

1379. Hutchison, H. "An Eighteenth Century Insight into Religious and
      Moral Education." British Journal of Educational Studies, 24
      (1976): 233-241.

      Reviews the thoughts of the 18th-century writer James Barclay
      on moral education. Similarities between his thinking and the
      assumptions of contemporary moral educators are noted.

1380. Jewett, James P. "Moral Education in American Public Schools:
      1800-1860." Ph.D. dissertation, University of Chicago, 1950.
      NR

1381. John, G. "The Moral Education of Emile." Journal of Moral
      Education, 11 (1981): 18-31.

      Examines Rousseau's advocacy of a secular approach to
      morality. The influence of Rousseau's ideas on the
      secularization of moral education is traced.

1382. Jones, Vernon. Character and Citizenship Training in the Public
      School, Chicago: University of Chicago Press, 1936.

A survey and review of efforts in the 1930s to foster moral character.

1383. Kaestle, Carl.   The Evaluation of an Urban School System, New York City, 1750-1850.   Cambridge,   MA: Harvard   University Press, 1973.

Contains a description of how moral and spiritual training were interwoven in early New York City schools. Examples from curriculum materials demonstrate the overt and direct focus on moral/spiritual training.

1384. Kandel, I.L. "Character Formation: A Historical Perspective." The Educational Forum, 7 (1961): 307-316.

Presents a historical view of character education. Points out that character education is more difficult today with the declining influence of family and church and the extensions of more media and communications.

1385. Katz, M.B.   Class, Bureaucracy and Schools.   New York: Praeger, 1971.

Contains an introduction to the underlying rationale of character training in late 19th-century America.

1386. Katz, Michael B.   The Irony of Early School Reform.   Boston: Beacon Press, 1968.

Within a description of the failure of mid-19th-century reform efforts is a description of the school's role in the moral education of youth. Moral education was inexorably tied into social needs and was seen as a means of reducing social chaos. It was essentially authoritarian in tone and practice.

1387. Kenyon, Earle W. "The Character Education Inquiry, 1924-1928: A Historical Examination of Its Use in Educational Research." Ph.D. dissertation, University of Texas at Austin, 1979. 40/07, p. 3743.

Concludes that the Character Education Inquiry has been well-regarded and contributed refined assessment technology as well as knowledge of the nature of character and its formation. It both suppressed and stimulated subsequent thought and research.

1388. Lannie, Vincent P. "The Teaching of Values in Public Secondary and Catholic Schools: A Historical Perspective." Religious Education, 70 (1975): 115-137.

Describes how the conception of teaching values in religious schools has shifted in response to historical forces.

1389. Lauderdale, William B. "Moral Intentions in the History of American Education." Theory into Practice, 14 (1975): 264-270.

Traces the major intentions in moral teaching from the colonial period to the present. Concludes that at present there is an absence of clarity, no defined program, and little interest in moral training in the school.

1390. Lazerson, Marvin. Origins of the Urban School. Cambridge, MA: Harvard University Press, 1971.

Presents a history of public education in Massachusetts between 1870 and 1915. A central theme is how the urbanization of New England society during this period created the impression that a prior rural, social harmony had been shattered. Documents how the schools were trained to preserve the social and moral characteristics that were perceived to have existed at an earlier time. Social amelioration was to be achieved through new techniques of teaching traditional moral values. The role of the kindergarten in this process receives considerable attention. Also extensively treats manual training and vocationalism in the restoration of traditional values.

1391. Lindberg, Stanley W. The Annotated McGuffey. New York: Van Nostrand Reinhold Co., 1976.

A brief but entertaining introduction covering the life and mind of McGuffey is followed by selections from McGuffey Eclectic Readers (1-6) covering the period 1836-1920. The annotations are most informative in revealing the historical background of many of the tales and the diverse authorship of the Readers.

1392. Lynn, Robert W., and Elliott Wright. The Big Little School. New York: Harper and Row, 1971.

Presents a history of the Sunday school in the United States and of historical shifts in the values it has attempted to foster.

1393. McClellan, B. Edward. "Moral Education and Public Schooling: An Historical Perspective." Viewpoints, 51 (November 1975): 1-15.

Presents a general discussion of the relationship between society and moral education in 19th- and 20th-century America. The character of life in 19th-century America allowed for fixed moral rules and the easy equation of virtue with reward. This conception became questionable with the emergence of corporate and bureaucratic society. A new emphasis on the standard of social consequence replaced more fixed notions. Since the early

20th-century the tension in moral education has been between the reformers and defenders of tradition.

1394.   McCluskey,   Neil   G.   Public Schools and Moral Education: The Influence of Horace Mann, William Torrey Harris and John Dewey Dewey. New York: Columbia University Press, 1958.

Traces the views of Mann, Harris, and Dewey on moral education and their interpretation of religion's place in the enterprise. Contains a thorough bibliography.

1395.   McKown, Harry C.   Character Education.   New York: McGraw-Hill, 1935.

A lengthy (472 pp.) and rich source on the character education movement of the early 20th century in the United States. Contrasts direct and indirect methods of character education and analyzes a wide range of vehicles for character education. The references at the end of each chapter provide a useful view of the knowledge base underpinning the character education movement.

1396.   Meyer,   D.H.   The Instructed Conscience: The   Shaping   of   the American National Ethic.   Philadelphia: University   of Pennsylvania Press, 1972.

Presents   a   general   discussion   of   19th-century   moral philosophy. Discusses the critical role that the teaching of moral philosophy in colleges played in the development of a set of national values during a time of great change.

1397.   Michaelson, Robert.   "Moral and Spiritual Values Revisited." Religious Education, 62 (1967): 344-351.

Reviews the events that led up to the Education Policies Commission and places the Commission within a historical perspective. Explores the question of whether values can be taught without teaching religion.

1398   Michaelson,   Robert.   Piety in the Public School.   London: Macmillan, 1970.

Discusses the history of the relationship between religion and the public school in U.S. history.

1399.   Minnich, Harvey   C.   Old Favorites from the McGuffey Readers. New York: American Book Company, 1936.

Contains a representative sample from the first through sixth Readers.

1400.   Minnich, Harvey C. William Holmes McGuffey and His Readers, New
        York: American Book Co., 1936.

        A history of the man, his books, and their influence on the
        national character.

1401.   Morlan, Grover C. "Moral Education in the American Public
        Elementary Schools Since 1835." Ph.D. dissertation, The
        University of Iowa, 1934. NR

1402.   Morrison, John L. "Alexander Campbell and Moral Education."
        Ph.D. dissertation, Stanford University, 1967. 27/12, p.
        4107.

        Campbell's (1788-1866) views on moral education, which
        although supernaturalist was also within the mainstream of
        American Progressive Pragmatic educational thought, are
        discussed. His impact on the educational thought of the middle
        frontier in the 1800s is traced.

1403.   Mosier, Richard D. Making the American Mind: Social and Moral
        Ideas in the McGufffey Readers. New York: Russell and
        Russell, 1947.

        The major study of the social and moral ideas in McGuffey's
        Readers. He attempts to point out those ideas and values in
        American culture that the Readers sought to conserve, defend,
        and perpetuate.

1404.   Neumann, Henry. Education for Moral Growth. New York:
        D. Appleton, 1928.

        Reviews the role of separate subjects in ethical education.
        Concludes that Dewey was right in his analysis that school
        environment is more important than individual classes.

1405.   Palmer, George H. Ethical and Moral Instruction in Schools.
        Boston: Mifflin, 1908.

        Describes a variety of approaches to character education.

1406.   Pietig, Jeanne. "John Dewey and Character Education." Journal
        of Moral Education, 6 (1977): 170-180.

        Character education programs of the first three decades are
        examined. Their trait-inspired approach to morality (virtues
        and vices), found to be too narrow, is given as the reason for
        their failure. John Dewey's broader approach, which focused on
        school reform, is then discussed.

1407.   Saunders, D.A. "Social Ideas in McGuffey Readers." Public
        Opinion Quarterly, 5 (1941): 579-589.

Presents a brief review of the major moral themes in McGuffey's Readers.

1408. Schultz, Stanley K. The Culture Factory: Boston Public Schools, 1789-1860. New York: Oxford University Press, 1973.

Contains a description of how moral and spiritual training were interwoven in early New England education. Examples are presented from the Boston Primer.

1409. Scully, James A. "A Biography of William Holmes McGuffey." Ph.D. dissertation, University of Cincinnati, 1967. 28/08, p. 2998.

A straightforward compilation of data about the life of McGuffey.

1410. Sheehan, N.M. "Textbooks and Course Guidelines: Moral Education from an Historical Point of View--the Alberta Context." Paper presented at the annual meeting of the Canadian Society for the Society of Education, Fredericton, New Brunswick, 1977. ED 150 058.

Examines the place of morals and values in the early school in the North West Territories (1885-1905). Concludes that the moral education influence present was the direct result of one man, the Superintendent of Schools in the North West Territories.

1411. Sloan, Douglas. "The Teaching of Ethics in the American Undergraduate Curriculum, 1876-1976." Education and Values (item 1525), pp. 191-254.

Discusses trends in conceptions of ethics and how it is taught in higher education. Special attention is devoted to the interplay of science and ethics. A very thorough and detailed historical analysis with a rich bibliography. Also in Ethics Teaching in Higher Education (item 1493).

1412. Smith, Wilson. Professors and Public Ethics: Studies of Northern Moral Philosophers Before the Civil War. Ithaca, NY: Cornell University Press, 1956.

Presents a general discussion of 19th-century moral philosophy.

1413. Sneath, E. Hershey, and George Hodges. Moral Training in the School and the Home. New York: Macmillan, 1913.

Presents a representative analysis of methods advocated during the character education era.

1414. Spring, Joel. _Education and the Rise of the Corporate State._ Boston: Beacon Press, 1962.

Presents the perspective that the history of schooling is in fact the history of the attempt of the corporate business structure of this country to exert social control over children in schools. The aim, as Spring sees it, was to produce workers to fuel the economic system. The goals of education therefore became cooperation and economically useful skills. Education for social control denies freedom and thereby, by influence, man's potential for moral action. Spring singles out the progressives for special attention in this volume.

1415. Strong, Bryan. "Ideas of the Early Sex-Education Movement in America, 1890-1920." _History of Education Quarterly_, 12 (1972): 129-161.

Discusses how sex education responded to the less rigid sexual morality that emerged around the turn of the century. The resulting attempts to teach sexual morality and hygiene are documented. The anxieties of the guardians of the old morality are apparent.

1416. Symonds, Percival M. _The Nature of Conduct._ New York: Macmillan, 1928.

One of the many books representative of the character education era.

1417. Tholfsen, T.R. "Moral Education in the Victorian Sunday School." _History of Education Quarterly_, 20 (1980): 77-99.

Discusses the moral ideology transmitted by the Victorian Sunday school and places the schools in a historical and social context.

1418. Troth, Dennis C., ed. _Selected Readings in Character Education._ Boston: Beacon Press, 1930.

Contains readings touching a wide range of topics related to character education.

1419. Tuttle, Harold S. _Character Education by State and Church._ New York: Abingdon Press, 1930.

One of the many books representative of the character education era.

1420. Tyack, D.B. "Onward Christian Soldiers: Religion in the American Common School." History and Education. Edited by P. Nash. New York: Random House, 1970.

Discusses the nature of the pre-Civil War relationship between religion and schooling and the congressional and judicial battles to separate the two.

1421. Ulich, Robert. A History of Religious Education. New York: New York University Press, 1968.

A history of education in the Judeo-Christian tradition. Of interest to moral educators because of the link between moral and religious education for most of our history. Contains many selections from documents relevant to the topic.

1422. Vail, Henry M. A History of the McGuffey Readers. Cleveland: Burrows Brothers Co., 1911.

Contains a brief history of the Readers by the author of one of the later editions.

1423. Vertinsky, Patricia A. "Education for Sexual Morality: Moral Reform and the Regulation of American Sexual Behavior in the Nineteenth Century." Ed.D. dissertation, University of British Columbia, 1975. 36/07, p. 4308.

Traces the evolution of conceptions of sex education throughout the 19th century.

1424. Wall, Margaret E. "Puritanism in Education: An Analysis of the Transition from Religiosity to Secular Morality as Seen in Primary Reading Materials 1620-1775." Ph.D. dissertation, Washington University, 1979. 40/07, p. 3831.

Traces the changes in Puritan religious belief from a theocracy to American secular morality as seen in the various books used to teach reading to primary school children between 1620 and 1775.

1425. Westerhoff, John H. McGuffey and His Readers. Nashville: Abington, 1978.

Based on the author's dissertation (item 1426), this short book includes a biography of McGuffey, an analysis of the world view contained in the Readers, selections from the Readers, and essays written by McGuffey outlining his views on education.

1426. Westerhoff, John H. "William Holmes McGuffey: Studies on the World-View and Value System in the First Editions of the Eclectic First, Second, Third and Fourth Readers." Ed.D. dissertation, Columbia University, 1975. 36/03, p. 1409.

Through content analysis of the readers and literary-
historical interpretation, the value system of the Readers is
presented. The world view and value systems were largely
theistic with salvation and righteousness as the most important
goals.

1427. Wishy, Bernard.   The Child and the Republic.   Philadelphia:
      University of Pennsylvania Press, 1968.

      Traces the American version of the child nurture movement
      between 1830 and 1900. The religious ideals and moral
      indoctrination associated with the movement receive extensive
      attention. Such methods of character education as the
      structuring of environment, persuasion, example, precept, and
      carefully formed habits illustrate the 19th century's approach
      to the socialization of youth.

1428. Yulish, S.M.   The Search for Civic Religion: A History of the
      Character Education Movement in America, 1890-1935.   Lanham,
      MD: University Press of America, 1980.

      Presents a historical perspective on the development of
      character education and character testing in America during the
      period 1890-1935. Traces the historical factors contributing to
      the character education movement and describes implementation of
      the programs in schools. Special attention is given to attempts
      to quantify character traits.

1429. Akinpelu, J.A. "Avenues of Moral Education in some Nigerian Secondary (Grammar) Schools: A Survey." Journal of Moral Education, 3 (1974): 259-269.

Contains the report of a survey of headmasters to ascertain what is being done about moral education.

1430. Beattie, Nicholas. "The Meaning of Secularism in Contemporary French Education." Journal of Moral Education, 8 (1979): 81-91.

After defining three broad positions regarding secularism in education it is suggested that future dialogue focus on specific curriculum rather than traditional grievances.

1431. Beattie, Nicholas. "Moral Education in the Real World: A Bavarian Case Study." Journal of Moral Education, 6 (1977): 191-197.

Discusses the way in which moral education was added to the Bavarian curriculum in 1972. The nature of the curriculum is discussed along with the importance of the teacher in interpreting it.

1432. Beddoe, I.B. "Perceptions of Teachers about Moral Education in Trinidad and Tobago." Journal of Moral Education, 10 (1981): 95-108.

Contains a summary of teacher's perceptions about the purposes and methods regarding moral education. Little is presented regarding the current status of moral education.

1433. Blackham, H.J. "Campaigning for Moral Education in England." The Humanist, 32 (November/December 1972): 23-25.

Describes the formation and rationale for the Social Morality Council in England: an organization in which Catholics, Protestants, Jews and Humanists tackle contemporary problems together.

1434. Blumenthal, Eileen P. "Models in Chinese Moral Education: Perspectives from Children's Books," Ph.D. dissertation, University of Michigan, 1976 (37/10, p. 6357).

Childrens books which are produced as a broad program of moral education were examined. The Chinese theory of model emulation was much in evidence.

1435. Bronfenbrenner, Urie. "Soviet Methods of Character Education:
       Some Implications for Research." Religious Education, 57
       (1962): 545-561.

       Discusses the peer collective and its role in character
       education in Soviet Russia.

1436. Buck-Morss, S. "Socio-economic Bias in Piaget's Theory and It's
       Implications for Cross-Cultural Study." Human Development, 18
       (1975): 35-49.

       Form and content of moral judgment can never be separated from
       the social/economic context in which it is embedded. The
       implications of this phenomena for cross-cultural research is
       discussed.

1437. Connell, William F. "Moral Education: Aims and Methods in
       China, the U.S.S.R., the U.S. and England." Moral
       Education...It Comes with the Territory (item 1519), 30-43.

       Compares and contrasts the approaches to moral education in
       four countries. Also in Phi Delta Kappan, 56 (1975): 702-706.

1438. Dunston, John. "Soviet Moral Education in Theory and Practice."
       Journal of Moral Education, 10 (1981): 192-202.

       Presents a thorough overview of Soviet efforts at moral
       education. Makarenko's concept of the collective as the context
       of upbringing receives special attention. Discusses many
       important documents which are not available in English
       translation.

1439. Edwards, Carolyn P. "The Effect of Experience on Moral
       Development: Results from Kenya." Ed.D. dissertation, Harvard
       University, 1974. 36/02, p. 776.

       It was found that students who had gone to schools with
       multicultural student bodies, lived at boarding schools, came
       from a modernized type of family background or studied Social
       Sciences or Law all had higher stages of reasoning than students
       from comparable but more traditional situations.

1440. Gopinathan, S. "Moral Education in a Plural Society: A
       Singapore Case Study." International Review of Education, 26
       (1980): 171-185.

       Takes a critical view of the Malaysian governments Report on
       Moral Education, 1979. The richness of the cultural tradition
       and the sweeping modernization demand that case values be
       identified and placed at the heart of moral education. The
       current government is too interested in depoliticizing the
       educational system.

1441. Gou-Zeh, Yi. "Moral Education in Korea." Journal of Moral
      Education, 8 (1979): 75-80.

      Describes the moral education system in Korea which attempts
      to reinforce deservable aspects of the Korean value system.

1442. Hakkarainen, Pentti. "On Moral Education in the Finnish
      Comprehensive School Curriculum." Journal of Moral Education,
      8 (1978): 23-31.

      Although the moral tenets of the Universal Declaration of
      Human Rights is the proposed basis of moral education, most
      moral content in instruction is found in textbooks where
      examples of morally acceptable behavior are presented. Appeals
      to authority predominate.

1443. Haq, Shafiqua. "Moral Education in Pakistan." Journal of Moral
      Education, 9 (1980): 156-165.

      The philosophical and ideological bases of moral education
      which are congenial to the Islamic concept of education are
      traced. The current status of moral education is presented.

1444. Hepworth, A.J. "Values Education - Some New South Wales
      Experiences." Journal of Moral Education, 8 (1979): 193-201.

      The multi-pronged approach to values education within a social
      studies framework is presented.

1445. Hiratsuka, Masunori. "Moral Education in Japan." Journal of
      Moral Education, 10 (1980): 53-60.

      Traces the historical development of the Japanese nation with
      respect to the education, character and spirit of the Japanese
      people. The active interest in and current provision for moral
      education in Japan's schools is discussed.

1446. Horn, Kristian. "Secular Life Philosophy as a Subject in
      Schools in Norway." Journal of Moral Education, 10 (1981):
      109-116.

      It is described how changes in legislation in recent years has
      loosened the firm hold of the philosophy of the Christian Church
      in the schools and given room for alternative secular philosophy
      in elementary schools and in teachers' colleges.

1448. Institute of the Theory and History of Education (RSFSR).
      "Draft Program for Character Building Work in School." Soviet
      Education, 1 (1958): 53-92.

Presents a detailed curriculum proposal for character development in grades 1-10. A good illustration of the process of translating moral values into a curriculum.

1449. Jian-Sheng, Lian. "Moral Education in New China." International Review of Education, 26 (1980): 198-201.

Describes in general terms the approach to moral education in the People's Republic of China. Central to this approach is the document entitled "Rules and Regulations for Pupils of Primary and Secondary Schools." This document, promulgated by the Ministry of Education, closely defines the demands made by party and state on pupils as regards ideology and morality. It serves as the pupils code of conduct to be followed in everyday study and life.

1449. Kao, Ming-Huey. "An Analysis of Moral Education in Japanese Public Schools." Ph.D. dissertation, Southern Illinois University, 1964. (26/10, p. 5917).

Traces and analyzes the development of three movements (the pragmatic, the conservative and the socialistic) in postwar Japan's moral education. The trend appears to be toward reflective morality over customary morality.

1450. Karrby, Gunni. "Moral Education in Sweden." Journal of Moral Education, 8 (1978): 14-22.

The current status of moral education in Sweden is reviewed. Objectivity and impartiality are major objectives in the presentation of moral education.

1451. Kreusler, Abraham A. Contemporary Education and Moral Upbringing in the Soviet Union. Ann Arbor, MI: University Microforms, 1976.

An analysis of the role of the schools and society in the moral upbringing of Soviet youth.

1452. Kuhmerker, Lisa. "An Aesthetic Approach to Moral Education." The Humanist, 32 (November/December 1972): 22-23.

Reports on the Italian organization Centro Coscienza's aesthetic approach to moral education. The approach involves the immersion of the child into the rich cultural tradition of the people with an emphasis on aesthetics and experiential learning.

1453. Lilge, F. Anton Semyonovitch Makarenko: An Analysis of his Educational Ideas in the Context of Soviet Society. Berkeley, California: University of California Press, 1958.

A discussion of Makarenko's ideals which form the basis for Soviet collective education. The emphasis in his thought is the submission of the individual to collective goals and morality.

1454. McCormick, R. "Political Education as Moral Education in Tanzania." Journal of Moral Education, 9 (1980): 166-177.

Since education is seen as a tool for social change, political education can be viewed as moral education in the Tanzanian Context. The nature of political education is outlined.

1455. McGeorge, Colin. "Some Old Wine and Some New Battles: Religious and Moral Education in New Zealand." Journal of Moral Education, 4 (1975): 215-223.

Describes and accounts for the present resurgence of moral education in New Zealand. The uncomfortable merger of moral and religious education in New Zealand is discussed.

1456. Madubom, Boniface N. "Nigerian Elementary Teachers' Preceptions of the Emphasis of the Current Social Studies Curriculum upon Selected Values." Ph.D. dissertation, University of Missouri, 1980. 41/11, p. 4594.

Finds that Nigerian teachers believe that selected social values ought to be emphasized by the Nigerian social studies syllabus.

1457. Magdamo, Patricia L. "An Approach to Moral Education in Phillipine Secondary Schools." Ed.D. dissertation, Columbia University, 1975. 35/12, p. 7737.

Evaluates the current state of moral education in Philippine public high schools. The current and historical roots of the norms and values of the majority lowland Filipinos are described. How traditional values are threatened by modernization is discussed as well as the current "bag of virtues" approach to moral instruction.

1458. Malkova, Zaya. "Moral Education in Soviet Schools." Phi Delta Kappan, 46 (1964): 134-138.

Describes how the moral characteristics of specific age groups form the basis for the moral education program in schools. The collective emphasis in schooling and the close home/school ties are described.

1459. Nduka, Otonti. "Moral Education in the Changing Traditional Societies of Sub-Saharan Africa." International Review of Education, 26 (1980): 153-170.

Argues that since the European partition of Africa moral education in traditional African societies has been taking place in the shadow of the conflict between the indigenous and the exotic (Western) values and institutions. The success of moral education, usually Christian, has been hampered by the difficulty in integrating western and indigenous values.

1460. Nishimato, Yoichi. "Improving Moral Education in the Upper Elementary Grades in Japan." Ed.D. dissertation, Columbia University, 1962. 23/05, p. 1628.

Analyzes the conflict between traditional Japanese culture and newer ideals of democracy and explores ways of conducting moral education within such a cultural setting.

1461. Noah, H.J. and B.B. Szekely, eds. "The Moral Education of Soviet Schoolchildren." Soviet Education, 17 (November 1974).

This special issue consists of seven articles by Russian authors. The articles reveal an interest in developing an understanding of moral norms in addition to behavioral conformity.

1462. Ogorodnikov, I.T., et al. "The Moral Education of Pupils in School." Soviet Education, 22 (July/August 1980): 142-178.

This article consists of a chapter from School Pedagogy written by a collective of authors at the Lenin Pedagogical Institute, the leading Soviet teacher training institution. It is used in most pedagogical institutes where teachers are trained. The social learning approach predominates with the emphasis on modeling, reinforcement, exhortation and collective social action.

1463. Potgieter, Pieter C. "Moral Education in South Africa." Journal of Moral Education, 9 (1980): 130-133.

The basis for moral education has been a Christian approach to life. Presents standard apartheid fare: "it helps everyone."

1464. Seshadri, C. "Moral Education in India." Journal of Moral Education, 8 (1978): 7-13.

Presents an account of the different aspects of moral education in India. The emphasis is on inculcation with strong religious emphasis.

1465. Shaw, Robert K. "New Zealand's Recent Concern with Moral Education." Journal of Moral Education, 9 (1979): 23-35.

References to moral education in New Zealand over the last fifteen years are traced through official and semi-official government reports, teacher's publications and other sources.

1466. Srivastava, H.S. "Towards the Development of a Curriculum for Moral Education." International Review of Education, 26 (1980): 193-198.

Discusses the curriculum efforts of the All India Association of Catholic Schools to improve moral education. Principal values of the world religions were made operational and integrated into a grade 1-12 sequence.

1467. Stern, Barry E. "The Relationship between Participation in Sports and the Moral and Political Socialization of High School Youth in Chile." Ph.D. dissertation, Stanford University, 1971. 32/12, p. 6799.

Participation in sports seemed to be associated with a general acceptance of society's authority structure.

1468. Taichenov, M.B. and Kh. Kh. Ianbulatou. "The Role of Words in the Moral Education of School Pupils." Soviet Education, 17 (November 1974): 66-81.

Explores the role of words in the formation of moral consciousness and behavior.

1469. van Praag, Joap. "Moral Education in the Netherlands." Journal of Moral Education, 8 (1979): 202-205.

Relates how moral education in basic schools is the counterpart of religion in denominational schools. The Dutch Humanist League is responsible for teacher training and methodology.

1470. Vidal, Giaume. "Fundamentals of Moral Education in Chile." Journal of Moral Education, 10 (1980): 49-52.

Although moral education is not a part of the school curriculum in Chile the influence of European society and the Catholic church on the goals of schooling is discussed.

1471 Weeren, D. J. "Moral Education in Today's Schools: Conclusions of a Survey of Five Educational Systems," Journal of Moral Education, 2 1972): 35-43.

A detailed comparison is made of conceptions of moral education in the United States, the USSR, the province of Quebec, Japan and France. It is concluded that there is general agreement over the importance of moral education and over the values to be inculcated.

1472. Wilson, John. "Comparative Aims in Moral Education: Problems in
       Methodology." Comparative Education, 4 (1968): 117-123.

       Presents examples of responses to a questionnaire sent to
       various countries regarding the aims of moral education. Wilson
       finds the responses maddening and uses them to illustrate the
       problems inherent in the study of comparative educational
       systems.

1473. Wilson, John. "Moral Education: Finding Common Ground."
       Comparative Education, 9 (1973): 61-65.

       Discusses the difficulty of interpreting questionnaires from
       various countries responding to the issue of the aims of moral
       education. Finds there is a common ground, but it is not
       anything that could be called moral education prevent Wilson
       finds the whole business pretty depressing. Continues item
       2819.

1474. Yesipou, B.P. and N.K. Goncharov. "I Want to be Like Stalin."
       Translated by George S. Counts and Nucia P. Lodge. New York:
       The John Day Co., 1947.

       Contains the chapters of the book dealing with moral education
       taken from the book Pedagogy. The uses of history, heros,
       literature and art to impact on childrens' morals is emphasized
       throughout. Contains a thirty page introduction by George
       Counts.

1475. Yogeshananda, Sivami. "Moral Education: A Hindu View." Journal
       of Moral Education, 3 (1974): 135-136.

       Discusses the difficulty of teaching a nonsectarian morality
       in a multi-cultural school. Suggests right motivation,
       meditation and aspiration as a focus.

1476. Zajda, Joseph I. Education in the USSR. Oxford, England:
       Pergamon Press, 1980.

       Chapter 3 "Moral Education and Political Socialization of
       Soviet Schoolchildren" contains a thorough analysis of the
       Soviet emphasis on character development in school.

1477. Broudy, Harry S. "Moral/Citizenship Education: Potentials and Limitations. Occasional Paper No. 3." Philadelphia: Research for Better Schools, 1977. ED 160 480.

Discusses the problems with implementing a moral/ citizenship education program in a pluralistic society and suggests conditions which would make such programs acceptable to communities.

1478. Durlo, H.F. "A Taxonomy of Democratic Development." Human Development, 19 (1976): 197-219.

Points out the necessity to view democratic socialization from a cognitive-developmental perspective.

1479. Eyler, Janet. "Citizenship Education for Conflict: An Empirical Assessment of the Relationship between Principled Thinking and Tolerance for Conflict and Diversity." Theory and Research in Social Education, 8 (Summer 1980): 11-26.

Finds that principled moral thinkers surpass non-principled thinkers in applying democratic principles in concrete controversial situations.

1480. Harmon, Carolyn P. "The Development of Moral and Political Reasoning Among 10, 13 and 16 Year Olds." Ph.D. dissertation, Yale University, 1973. 34/05, p. 2718.

Uses the cognitive-developmental theory to challenge traditional conceptions of political socialization.

1481. Kutnick, Peter. "The Myth of the Democratic Leader: An Insight into Political Socialization of the Primary School." Journal of Moral Education, 10 (1981): 173-185.

Presents a discussion of the political socialization literature and findings fom two studies on the child's developing conception of leadership. The author's research indicates that children's knowledge of leadership is generated through actual life and school experiences. It is argued that the more the child is involved in shared authority the better his/ her moral development.

1482. Lockwood, Alan. "Moral Reasoning and Public Policy Debate." Moral Development and Behavior (item 519), pp. 317-325.

Explores the relationship between normative moral philosophy and public policy controversy. Examines ways that moral reasoning is applicable to public policy debate, psychological research on the relatiouship between moral views and policy positions and actions, and the adequacy of certain moral points of view for resolving public policy disputes.

1483. Mancuso, James C., and Theodore R. Sarbin. "A Paradigmatic Analysis of Psychological Issues at the Interface of Jurisprudence and Moral Conduct." Moral Development and Behavior (item 519), pp. 326-341.

Reviews the literature on the relationship between psychological development and law-related behavior. They point out the great difficulty involved over the use of the terms "disease of the mind," "know" and "wrong." They urge a contextualist view of legal culpability--consideration of the total ecology of rule-following conduct.

1484. Merelman, Richard M. "A Critique of Moral Education in the Social Studies." Journal of Moral Education, 8 (1979): 182-192.

Argues that the moral education approach to social studies is pedagogically and politically unsound. Political decision making is shown to be a quite different process than moral decision making.

1485. Nelson, Jack L. "The Uncomfortable Relationship between Moral Education and Citizenship Instruction." Moral Development and Politics (item 1531), pp. 256-285.

Examines the uneasy relationship between moral education and citizenship education. Contains an account of historical relationships between moral and citizenship education. Possible relationships between moral and citizenship education are discussed. It is concluded that traditional means of citizenship instruction have acted to impede rather than enhance the capacity for the development of mature moral individuals.

1486. Oldenquist, Andrew. "On the Nature of Citizenship." Educational Leadership, 38 (1980): 30-34.

Citizenship education should foster group loyalty and white, middle-class values, especially in black and poor white neighborhoods. Discusses the simularity and differences between moral and citizenship education. Moral and citizenship education must be based on a foundation of a sense of belonging to local and national communities and a loyalty to their norms.

1487. Scheffler, Israel. "The Moral Content of American Public
       Education." Moral Education ... It Comes with the Territory
       (item 1519), pp. 20-29.

       Moral education in a democracy does not shape, it liberates.
       An anology is drawn with the scientific method--moral education
       should develop a critical moral point of view.

1488. Tapp, June L., ed. "Socialization, the Law and Society."
       Journal of Social Issues, 27,2 (1971).

       A special edition containing excellent articles on role of law
       ·as socializer, legal development, and socialized values in law
       and society.

1489. Tapp, June L., and Lawrence Kohlberg. "Developing Senses of Law
       and Legal Justice." Journal of Social Issues, 27,2 (1971):
       65-92.

       A theory of developing conceptions of law and legal justice is
       presented.   The theory is based on Kohlberg's cognitive-
       developmental approach to moral reasoning. Research is cited to
       support the arguments presented.

1490. White, Pat. "Political Education and Moral Education or Bringing
       Up Children to be Decent Members of Society." Journal of
       Moral Education, 9 (1980): 147-155.

       Argues that political education is an essential part of moral
       education and supplies the context and content of moral
       education. Rational morality commits one very concretely to a
       democratic form of society. The concepts, forms of argument and
       dispositions necessary for democratic society are the focus of
       moral/political education.

Collections of Readings

1491. Barclay, John G., ed. <u>Values Concepts and Techniques</u>. Washington, D.C.: National Education Association, 1976.

A collection of papers, mostly reprinted elsewhere, dealing with issues in values education and techniques for implementing values education in a variety of settings.

1492. Beck, Clive M., Brian S. Crittenden, and Edmund V. Sullivan, eds. <u>Moral Education: Interdisciplinary Approaches</u>. Toronto: University of Toronto Press, 1971.

Presents papers delivered at a 1968 conference on Moral Education at the Ontario Institute for Studies in Education. Contains sections on the search for norms in a pluralistic society, moral action, psychological processes in moral development and moral behavior and problems of methodology and practice.

*   Berofsky, Bernard, ed. <u>Free Will and Determinism</u>. New York: Harper and Row, 1966. Item 161.

*   Brandt, Richard B., ed. <u>Value and Obligation: Systematic Readings in Ethics</u>. New York: Harcourt Brace World, 1961. Item 167.

1493. Callahan, Daniel and Sissela Bok, eds. <u>Ethics Teaching in Higher Education</u>. New York: Plenum Press, 1980.

Presents the series of papers which provided the background for Hastings Center's study of the status of the teaching of ethics in American higher education. Contains sections on general issues in the teaching of ethics, the teaching of ethics in the undergraduate curriculum, and recommendations on the teaching of ethics.

1494. Carr, William G., ed. <u>Values and the Curriculum: A Report of the Fourth International Curriculum Conference</u>. Washington, DC: National Education Association, 1970.

Reports the results of a conference sponsored by the National Education Association's Center for the Study of Instruction. The focus of the conference was the central place that values should play in education. The topic is construed in very general terms by the participants and the distinction between moral and nonmoral issues is frequently blurred.

*   Castaneda, N.H. and G. Nakhnikan, eds. Morality and the Language of Conduct. Detroit: Wayne State University Press, 1963. Item 169.

*   Chazan, Barry I. and Jonas F. Soltis, eds. Moral Education. New York: Teachers College Press, 1973. Item 171.

*   Clausen, John A., ed. Socialization and Society. Boston: Little Brown, 1968. Item 492.

1495. Cochrane, Donald B. and Michael Manley-Casimer, eds. Development of Moral Reasóning: Practical Approaches. New York: Praeger Publishers, 1980.

*   Cochrane, Donald B., Cornel M. Hamm and Anastasios C. Kazepides, eds. The Domain of Moral Education. New York: The Paulist Press, 1979. Item 30.

1496. Collier, Gerald, John Wilson and Peter Tomlinson, eds. Values and Moral Development in Higher Education. London: Croom Helm Ltd, 1974.

A collection of papers on moral education as a function of higher education. Topics covered are the understanding of moral development from the perspective of different disciplines and the potential contributions of specific subject areas and institutional contexts on moral development. The volume features an introduction and postscript by John Wilson.

1497. Damon, William, ed. New Directions for Child Development, No. 2: Moral Development. San Francisco: Jossey-Bass, Inc., 1978.

A collection of non-traditional and controversial papers on moral development. Especially noteworthy is the paper by Kohlberg in which he drops stage 6 from his typology and comes out for indoctrination as an appropriate methodology for moral education.

*   Daniels, N., ed. Reading Rawls: Critical Studies on Rawl's "A Theory of Justice." New York: Basic Books, 1974. Item 176.

*   DePalma, David J. and Jeanne M. Foley, eds. Moral Development: Current Theory and Research. Hillsdale, NJ: Lawrence Erlbaum Associates, 1975. Item 494.

*   Dworkin, Gerald, ed. Determinism, Free Will and Moral
        Responsibility. Englewood Cliffs, NJ: Prentice Hall, 1970.
        Item 182.

1498.   Erickson, V. Lois and John M. Whiteley, eds. Developmental
        Counseling and Teaching. Monterey, CA: Brooks/Cole, 1980.

        Contains thirty-two papers dealing with recent theoretical
        research and intervention issues involved with attempting to
        deliberately promote psychological growth through counseling and
        teaching programs. Only five of the papers have not been
        published elsewhere. Twenty of the articles represent the
        complete issue of Conseling Psychologist, 6, 4 (1977).

1499.   Fenstermacher, Gary D., ed. Philosophy of Education 1978:
        Proceedings of the Thirty-Fourth Annual Meeting of the
        Philosophy of Education Society. Champaign, IL: Philosophy of
        Education Society, University of Illinois, 1979.

*   Foot, Philippa, ed. Theories of Ethics. London: Oxford
        University Press, 1967. Item 186.

*   Fowler, J. and A. Vergote, eds. Toward Moral and Religious
        Maturity: The First International Conference on Moral and
        Religious Development. Morristown, NJ: Silver Burdette, 1980.
        Item 403.

        Contains a collection of papers which constitute the best
        single source of information on recent thought on the interplay
        between religious and moral development.

1500.   Hennessy, Thomas C., ed. Values/Moral Education: The Schools
        and the Teachers. New York: Paulist Press, 1979.

        A collection of articles on effective methods of moral and
        value education during different levels of schooling.

1501.   Hennessy, Thomas C., ed. Values and Moral Development. New
        York: Paulist Press, 1976.

        The papers in this book are revisions of lectures given at the
        Institute in Moral and Ethical Issues in Education held at
        Fordham University in the Spring of 1975. The book contains
        three sections. Part I introduces the philosophical groundwork
        for the analysis of moral and ethical growth. Part II is
        devoted primarily to papers that emphasize programs directed to
        fostering growth among students in moral-related areas. Part
        III is devoted to papers that describe and report research in
        moral education and related areas.

*   Hollins, T.H.B., ed. <u>Aims in Education: The Philosophic Approach</u>. Manchester, England: Manchester University Press, 1964. Item 69.

1502.   Holtzman, Wayne H., ed. <u>Moral Development: Proceedings of the 1974 ETS Invitational Conference</u>. Princeton, N.J.: Educational Testing Service, 1975.

*   Hook, Sidney. <u>Determinism and Freedom</u>. New York: Collier Books, 1970. Item 206.

*   Hudson, W.D., ed. <u>The Is/Ought Question</u>. Longon: Macmillan, 1969. Item 208.

1503.   Kazepides, A.C., ed. <u>The Teaching of Values in Canadian Education</u>, Yearbook of the Canadian Society for the Study of Education. Edmonton, Alberta: University of Alberta, 1975.

        Contains a diverse and interesting set of seven papers on issues seldom addressed in moral education.

1504.   Kirschenbaum, Howard and Sidney B. Simon, eds. <u>Readings in Values Clarification</u>. Minneapolis, MN: Winston Press, 1973.

        Contains 37 articles on values clarification and related topics. Includes sections on values clarification and school subjects, values in religious education, values in the family, and other approaches to valuing.

*   Kohlberg, Lawrence. <u>Collected Papers on Moral Development and Moral Education</u>. Cambridge, MA: Center for Moral Education, Harvard University, 1973. Item 618.

*   Kohlberg, Lawrence. <u>Essays on Moral Development</u>. Volume 1: The <u>Philosophy of Moral Development</u>. New York: Harper and Row, 1981. Item 624.

*   Kohlberg, Lawrence. <u>Essays on Moral Development</u>. Volume 2: The <u>Psychology of Moral Development</u>. New York: Harper and Row, forthcoming. Item 625.

1505.   Kohlberg, Lawrence. <u>Essays on Moral Development</u>. Volume 3: <u>Education and Moral Development</u>. New York: Harper and Row, forthcoming.

        A collection of papers that focus on the implications of stage theory for the understanding and practice of moral education.

1506.   Kuhmerker, Lisa, Marcia Mentkowski, and V. Lois Erickson, eds. <u>Evaluating Moral Development and Evaluating Educational Programs That Have a Value Dimension</u>. Schenectady, NY: Character Research Press, 1980.

Presents a collection of papers delivered at a 1979 conference on the "state of the art" in the evaluation of moral education programs. The papers range from reports of the evaluation specific curriculum projects to more broad considerations regarding the future of evaluation in moral education.

*   Kuhn, Deanna, ed. Stage Theories of Cognitive and Moral Development: Criticisms and Application. Cambridge, MA: Harvard Educational Review, 1978. Item 655.

*   Langford, Glen and D.J. O'Connor, eds. New Essays in the Philosophy of Education. London: Routledge and Kegan Paul, 1973. Item 219.

*   Lickona, Thomas, ed. Moral Development and Behavior: Theory, Research and Social Issues. New York: Holt, Rinehart and Winston, 1976. Item 519.

A collection of high-quality papers dealing with such issues as how morality is learned, research into the psychological bases of moral thought and behavior, and morality and social issues. Contains papers by Kohlberg, Aronfreed, Bronfenbrenner, Mischel, Eysenck, Hoffman, Selman, Rest, et al.

1507.   Lipman, Matthew and Ann M. Sharp, eds. Growing Up with Philosophy. Philadelphia, PA: Temple University Press, 1978.

A collection of papers, many of which, explore dimensions of teaching moral philosophy to children.

*   Macaulay, J. and L. Berkowitz, eds. Altruism and Helping Behavior. New York: Academic Press, 1970. Item 1228.

1508.   McBee, Mary L., ed. New Directions for Higher Education, Rethinking College Responsibilities for Values, No. 31. San Francisco: Jossey-Bass, 1980.

Contains a diverse and interesting collection of papers assessing the role and responsibilities of colleges in the development of student values.

1509.   Macmillan, C.J.B., ed. Philosophy of Education 1980: Proceedings of the Thirty-Sixth Annual Meeting of the Philosophy of Education Society. Normal, IL: Philosophy of Education Society, Illinois State University, 1981.

*   Macy, Christopher, ed. Let's Teach Them Right. London, Pemberton Publishing, 1969. Item 424.

1510.   Meyer, John R., ed. Reflections on Values Education. Waterloo, Ontario: Wilfred Laurier University Press, 1976.

Contains a series of essays on values education dealing with theoretical problems, the learning environment and the helping facilitator. Contains essays on the development of the theory and a method of assessment of moral judgment (Kohlberg).

1511. Meyer, J.R., B. Burnham and J. Cholvat, eds. Values Education: Theory/Practice/Problems/Prospects. Waterloo, Ontario: Wilfred Laurier University Press, 1975.

1512. Mosher, Ralph, ed. Adolescents' Development and Education. New York: McCutchan, 1979.

Contains a collection of papers on developmental and moral education about half of which were published elsewhere. Witty and sometimes illuminating comments by Mosher preceed the various sections.

1513. Mosher, Ralph, ed. Moral Education: A First Generation of Research and Development. New York: Praeger, 1980.

Contains a series of papers describing the framework for and practices of the Danforth project in moral education. This project has as its foci Kohlbergian moral development and the guidance work of Mosher and Sprithall. This volume is not an impartial appraisal of the field as a whole. All of the authors were involved in the project, and therefore there is little detached critical analysis of it.

1514. Munsey, Brenda, ed. Moral Development, Moral Education and Kohlberg. Birmingham, AL: Religious Education Press, 1980.

A collection of 16 papers dealing with basic issues in philosophy, psychology, religion, and education as they relate to the Kohlbergian perspective on moral development and moral education.

1515. Niblett, W.R., ed. Moral Education in a Changing Society. London: Faber and Faber Limited, 1963.

Contains a series of addresses presented in London in 1962.

1516. Overly, Norman L., ed. The Unstudied Curriculum: Its Impact on Children. Washington, D.C.: Association for Supervision and Curriculum Development, 1970.

Contains a collection of papers on the nature of the hidden curriculum and its impact on children.

*   Page, Monte M., ed. Nebraska Symposium on Motivation 1979: Beliefs, Attitudes and Values. Lincoln, NB: University of Nebraska Press, 1980. Item 1245.

1517. Peters, R.S., ed. Psychology and Ethical Development. London:
       George Allen and Unwin, 1974.

       Contains a collection of papers, all published elsewhere.
       Part II consists of seven papers on ethical development.

1518. Piediscolzi,   Nicholas   and   Barbara   Ann   Swyhart,   eds.
       Distinguishing Moral Education, Values Clarification and
       Religion-Studies.   Proceedings   of   American   Academy   of
       Religion, 1976, Section 18. Missoula, MT: Scholars Press,
       1976. ED 146 063.

1519. Purpel, David and Kevin Ryan, eds. Moral Education ... It Comes
       With the Territory. Berkeley, CA: McCutchan Publishing Corp.,
       1976.

       A collection of papers focusing on the topics of the hidden
       curriculum, values clarification, the cognitive-developmental
       approach, and the cognitive approach to moral education.

1520. Rokeach, Milton, ed. Understanding Human Values: Individual and
       Societal. New York: The Free Press, 1979.

       Contains a collection of eighteen research reports on the
       conceptualization   and   measurement   of   individual   and
       supraindividual values, the major determinants and consequences
       of value organization and change that are naturally occuring,
       the effects of inducing awareness about one's own and others'
       values, and the role that values and value education should play
       within   the   context   of   the   educational   institution.   The
       reference section of the volume is comprehensive with respect to
       Rokeach's definition of the value concept and value change.

1521. Scharf, Peter, ed. Moral and Psychological Education: Theory
       and Research. No location: R F Publishing, 1978.

       A collection of readings, all originally published elsewhere,
       on the cognitive-developmental approach to moral education.

1522. Scharf, Peter, ed. Readings in Moral Education. Minneapolis:
       Winston Press, 1978.

       A   collection   of   readings   dealing   primarily   with   the
       developmental approach to moral education. Contains a section
       on criticism of Kohlbergian programs.

*   Sellars, W.S. and John Hospers, eds. Readings in Ethical Theory,
       2nd ed. New York: Appleton-Century-Crofts, 1970. Item 252.

1523. Sizer, Theodore, ed. Religion and the Public Schools. Boston:
       Houghton Mifflin, 1967.

       A collection of readings featuring 17 articles on such topics
       as teaching about religion; the challenge of religion to our
       educational   system;   the   relationships   among   secularism,
       pluralism, and religion; and theological perspectives on public
       education.

1524. Sizer, Theodore R. and Nancy F. Sizer, eds. Moral Education:
       Five Lectures. Cambridge, MA: Harvard University Press, 1973.

       Contains five lectures presented at Harvard University on
       moral education by Gustafson, Peters, Kohlberg, Bettelheim and
       Keniston.

1525. Sloan, Douglas, ed. Education and Values. New York: Teachers
       College Press, 1980.

       A collection of papers dealing with the relationship between
       values and education. The papers are largely theoretical. The
       authors   are   scientists,   philosophers,   theologians   and
       historians. A version of this volume first appeared as a
       special issue of Teachers College Record (February 1979).

*   Snook, I.A., ed. Concepts of Indoctrination: Philosophical
       Essays. London: Routledge and Kegan Paul, 1972. Item 367.

1526. Sprinthall, Norman A. and Ralph L. Mosher, eds. Value
       Development ... As the Aim of Education. Schenectady, NY:
       Character Research Press, 1978.

       A collection of papers with the focus on psychological and
       moral development as a goal for education.

1527. Steinberg, Ira S., ed. Philosophy of Education 1977: Proceedings
       of the Thirty-Third Annual Meeting of the Philosophy of
       Education Society. Urbana, IL: Philosophy of Education
       Society, University of Illinois, 1977.

1528. Stiles, Lindley J. and Bruce D. Johnson, eds. Morality Examined:
       Guidelines for Teachers. Princeton, New Jersey: Princeton
       Book Company, 1977.

       This book of readings is designed to provide teachers with a
       background for understanding the complexity of ethical issues as
       well as to offer specific help for teaching moral values. The
       papers in this volume grew out of Northwestern University
       Faculty-Student Seminar. The essays tend to deal with the
       topics in a somewhat superficial manner.

1529. Strike, Kenneth A., ed. Philosophy of Education 1976: Proceedings of the Thirty-Second Annual Meeting of the Philosophy of Education Society. Urbana, IL: Philosophy of Education Society, University of Illinois, 1976.

1530. Taylor, Monica J., ed. Progress and Problems in Moral Education. Slough, Berks, England: NFER Publishing Company Ltd, 1975.

A collection of readings by British authors centering around the issues of the place of moral education in the curriculum, difficulties in communication about moral education, neutrality, and discipline. The authors react to each others positions.

1531. Wilson, Richard W. and Gordon J. Schochet, eds. Moral Development and Politics. New York: Praeger, 1980.

A fascinating collection of papers exploring the relationship of moral development to political life. The book contains fifteen papers grouped under four general headings: Theory and Context; Moral Development as Liberal Ideology; Institutions, Moral Behavior, and the Polity; and Learning to be a Virtuous Citizen.

*   Wallace, G. and A.D.M. Walker, eds. The Definition of Morality. London: Methuen, 1970. Item 268.

*   Windmiller, Myra, Nadine Lambert and Elliot Turiel, eds. Moral Development and Socialization. Boston: Allyn and Bacon, 1980. Item 542.

1532. Wynne, Edward, Character Policy: An Emerging Issue. Washington, DC: University Press of America, 1982.

A collection of papers from the now defunct interdisciplinary monthly Character. The articles reflect the point of view that values education should be concerned with the transmission of substantive values.

Author Index

The references below are to entry numbers, not page numbers.

Subject Index

The references below are to entry numbers, not page numbers.

ABOUT THE COMPILER

JAMES S. LEMING is Assoicate Professor of Education at Southern Illinois University. Leming's other works include *Contemporary Approaches to Moral Education: An Annotated Bibliography* and *Guide to Research* and many contributions to journals such as the *Journal of Moral Education, Social Education, Theory and Research in Social Education,* and the *Journal of Educational Research.*